The Absent Prince
In search of missing men

a family memoir

Una Suseli O'Connell

The Absent Prince

Published by The Conrad Press in the United Kingdom 2020

Tel: +44(0)1227 472 874
www.theconradpress.com
info@theconradpress.com

ISBN 978-1-913567-10-1

Typesetting and Cover Design by: Charlotte Mouncey, www.bookstyle.co.uk
Cover image created with author's own images

The Conrad Press logo was designed by Maria Priestley.

Printed and bound in Great Britain by Clays Ltd, Elcograf S.p.A.

Absent thee from felicity awhile
And in this harsh world draw thy breath in pain
To tell my story

Hamlet Act 5, Scene 2
William Shakespeare

To Lea and Peter, to whom I owe my life.
To Polly and Lucy, in gratitude for theirs.

Contents

Introduction

When my parents died in the late 1990s, I inherited a great many papers and documents. What I discovered about my family shocked me and yet, I realised that by choosing not to throw away their letters and journals, Peter and Lea had made a courageous and far-reaching decision: they had bequeathed me a gift. As their only child, I understood that if I wished to tell their story fully and honestly, I needed to consider their lives and the lives of my grandparents and great grandparents, in a wider context and, above all, without judgement or reproach.

Peter and Lea met at a tuberculosis sanatorium in Davos in 1946. Peter was studying at St. John's College, Cambridge. Lea, who had left school at fifteen, was a dental assistant. In 1951, my father went to the United States where he spent four years at Groton School in Massachusetts. He taught the sons of the gilded elite, worked as a yardsman in the Chicago Stockyards and travelled across the Atlantic in the heyday of the great ocean liners. Peter and Lea married in 1955 when they were in their late thirties. Due to her history of TB, Lea was denied a visa to join her husband in the United States; reluctantly, Peter returned to the UK. In 1959, they founded The School of English Studies, Folkestone where Peter became a pioneer in the development of the teaching of English as a Foreign Language.

Lea, homesick for her native Switzerland and still struggling with the side effects of tuberculosis, returned home for long periods of time. Peter, ever in pursuit of new and cutting edge teaching methods, travelled extensively. He taught in China shortly after the death of Mao Tse-tung and in Bulgaria during the Cold War. Whenever my parents were separated, they wrote each other long letters: my father's are passionate and eloquent; my mother's, heartfelt and sad.

The Absent Prince follows the chronology of diaries and personal letters across several generations. I have endeavoured not to judge actions, only to reflect on choices and decisions. In writing, I introduce my own story when it is relevant and when I recognise the unconscious repetition of family dynamics.

Some names have been changed to protect anonymity.

Family Trees

O'Connell
(Peter - Paternal)

Arnold
(Peter - Maternal)

Kummer
(Lea - Paternal)

Gilomen
(Lea - Maternal)

O'Connell (Peter - Paternal)

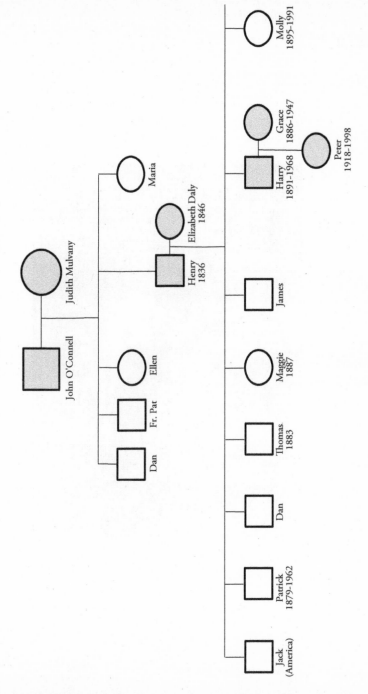

Arnold (Peter - Maternal)

Kummer (Lea - Paternal)

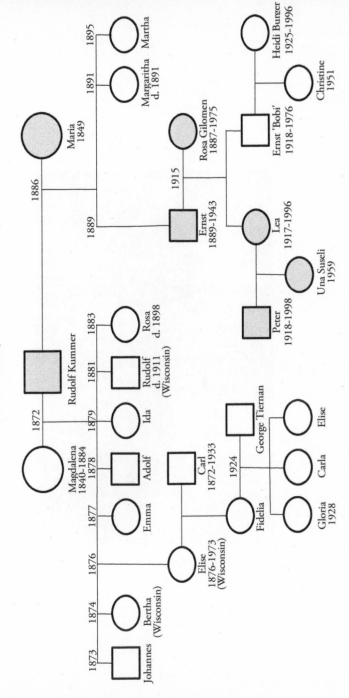

Gilomen (Lea - Maternal)

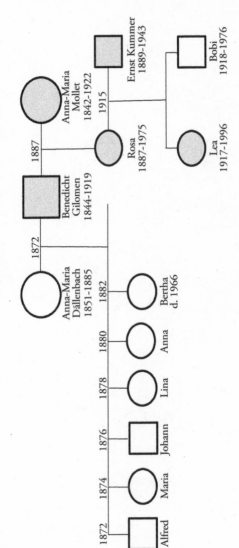

Chapter One

The Faithful and the Faithless

I'm very fond of newspaper vending machines because they are so delightfully un-twenty-first century. They are entirely mechanical, have no moving parts and only accept coins. But their days are numbered. Before too long, the only remaining example will be on display at the National Museum of American History in Washington.

When I drive long distances in America I like to pull up in small towns, park my car on Main Street, offer up my seventy-five cents for a local newspaper and settle down in an unchained coffee shop. I give myself over to understanding the lives people lead in communities such as Monroe, Wisconsin or Beaufort, North Carolina and the section of the paper that allows me to do this most fully is the obituary page. From an obituary I get a sense of what was important to a person; the tone of writing tells me how the deceased was seen by others; I learn about family and personal tragedies, the opportunities offered during a lifetime and the consequences of accepting or declining those opportunities.

In 1978 my father, Peter O'Connell, was living in Bulgaria where he heard tell of an old woman in the mountains near Sofia who could accurately predict the day of your death. Dad told me of his intention to visit her: he thought it would be useful to know how many years he had left, so he could prioritise his interests and plan his time better. I never had the courage to ask him about his visit, but I often wondered whether he lived his life differently with an anticipated date of death forever in mind. It's not something you can easily forget; unless you develop Alzheimer's, which my father did, so perhaps that fact got swallowed up with so many of the others. I wonder too whether the date the oracle predicted turned out to be the correct one: September 5th, 1998.

I was on a sailing boat in Narragansett Bay, off the coast of Rhode Island, when I heard the news that my father was dying. I was a hostage to circumstance, unable to return to land until the following day and I went below deck in search of solitude. On the wall of the cabin I read these lines from the poem *Merlin and the Gleam* by Alfred, Lord Tennyson:

> *And so to the land's*
> *Last limit I came--*
> *And can no longer,*
> *But die rejoicing,*
> *For thro' the Magic*
> *Of Him the Mighty,*
> *Who taught me in childhood,*
> *There on the border*
> *Of boundless Ocean,*
> *And all but in Heaven*
> *Hovers The Gleam.*

I found the words soothing and oddly appropriate. My father had a profound need to believe in something beyond the limitations of time and space and he spent a lifetime seeking to make a spiritual commitment, to offer his devotion to a god who would protect him from the turbulence and uncertainty of life. Shortly before he died, he wrote in a letter to his aunt: *I wish most heartily that I could find it possible in my heart and in my mind to accept the gospel of Christ. I have prayed often and fervently for faith but there is only silence.*

In a talk I gave at a memorial dinner in 1999 to celebrate the life of my father, I said that the religion with which Peter most identified was Buddhism: 'It's the only one which makes any real sense,' he used to say. Twenty years later, having read his letters and diaries, I recognise that sense had little to do with it. He settled on Buddhism rather like a butterfly alights on a bluebell. It was a feeding station, a brief opportunity to rest awhile before resuming his lifelong search for meaning and connection. Peter pursued many different traditions, from Christian Science to Indian mysticism, but like a homing pigeon, he invariably circled back to his Catholic roots. Throughout his life he remained both repelled and captivated by Christianity.

Our lives are conditioned by our collective inheritance, our genetic formula, the conditions of the present and our biographical choices. If the first three are especially damaged, the ability to productively manage the last can be significantly affected. I am interested in the threads that weave family tapestries: the warp threads on the loom that are set up under tension, the ones created by war and exile, by death, loss and grief. The weft threads pass back and forth across the warps, creating the story and shaping the lives of individual family members. Eventually the warps are obscured by the relentless movement of the wefts, but they remain, holding the picture in place, unconscious sources of the difficulties we continue to weave today.

You have to do your own growing, no matter how tall your grandfather was
Abraham Lincoln

My grandfather, Harry O'Connell, lived with us until he died in 1968 when I was nine years old. Grandpa spent a lot of time in his room. As a small child, I was curious to know what he did in there every day. One afternoon, I crept along the corridor and looked through the keyhole. He was resting in bed, and I was shocked to see a huge hole in his leg. I felt a combination of horror and betrayal. Why hadn't my grandfather told me about this? We were a team, he and I. I would climb onto his lap and lay my head on his chest, listening to the thump, thump, thump of his beating heart, inhaling the smell of whisky and pipe tobacco and feeling the scratch of his tweed jacket against my cheek. He called me NGF – 'The Nicest Girl in Folkestone' or the 'Naughtiest', and we had an unspoken understanding that the first version belonged to him. When my parents went out for the evening and left him in charge, he allowed me absolute freedom to do what I wanted; this included watching hours of television, often until I decided for myself to switch off and go to bed. My father had a very strict policy about television. Every morning he and I would sit down with the TV section of the newspaper in order to allocate my daily allowance, both in terms of time and suitability.

So, Grandpa had a secret and it was clearly a big one; one that he couldn't share with me. I wondered who he talked to about his leg with the hole you could poke a stick through and how it came to be there.

Harry was born in Ireland in 1891, the seventh of eight children. When he was nine years old, his eldest brother, Jack, was banished from the family home for dating a Protestant girl. My great-grandfather, Henry, left money on the kitchen table with a note, instructing his son to buy a one way ticket to America. No-one knows for sure what happened to Uncle Jack, but it's thought that his outspoken political opinions led to his early death in a street fight.

Harry was sent to St Patrick's College, Cavan on a clerical scholarship and then to the National Seminary. He became increasingly disillusioned with the hypocrisy of the clergy. Having witnessed an intoxicated priest lose his balance in the choir loft and fall to an ignominious death on the altar, Harry renounced the Catholic church. He enrolled in medical school but was repulsed by the blood and gore of the dissecting room. Eventually, with all his options exhausted, Harry left Ireland for England. At the outbreak of war in 1914, he applied, unsuccessfully, to join His Majesty's Navy, eventually signing up as a private with the Royal Fusiliers. He spent the next two years on the Western Front.

Unlike Jack's misdemeanour, a *spoiled priest* could not so easily be concealed, and when Harry left Ireland to fight for the Protestants, he became the second son to be ostracised by the family.

A young woman leaves Ireland and moves to England. A year later she returns, wearing elegant clothes and expensive jewellery. Her mother asks her where she got the money to buy these fine things: 'While I was in England, I became a prostitute,' she answers. The mother is horrified: 'You became a what?' The daughter repeats that she became a prostitute, to which her mother replies: 'Oh, thank goodness. I thought you said you became a Protestant'.

I laughed out loud when my cousin Dominic told me this joke, but in the same moment, I understood the profound sense of betrayal my great-grandfather would have experienced as a result of the choices made by his two sons. Oliver Cromwell's armies arrived in Ireland in 1649 and began killing Catholics and confiscating their land. He outlawed their religion, denied them the right to vote or receive an education and banned all Irish literature and music. Being Catholic was central to Irish pride and identity and aligning yourself, in any way, with a Protestant was seen as a betrayal of the worst kind.

Greater love hath no man than this, that a man lay down his life for his friends.
The Gospel of John 15:13

My grandfather fought at the Battle of the Somme and was wounded at High Wood in July 1916. The Royal Fusiliers suffered particularly high losses, including all their officers. Harry had been given his stripes back in England, but had turned them in upon being told that, as an officer, he could no longer go out drinking with his mates.

Much has been written about the bloody and pointless slaughter at the Battle of the Somme and the horrific conditions the soldiers experienced: the relentless exploding of shells and machine gunfire; the liquid mud in the trenches; the icy duckboards from which a man could slip and drown in water only a few feet deep; the smell of latrines and rotting corpses, the rats, the lice, the trench foot and the sickly-sweet smell of gangrene. There was no comfort at the end of a day, no hot bath and clean pyjamas, no loving warmth. At daybreak, each soldier was issued with a daily ration of alcohol in the hope that doping him with whisky would stop him from going mad with fright. Every man carried a field dressing and this was the first line of treatment for the wounded – one soldier caring for another. They fought on, maintaining a bravado beneath which lay extraordinary tenderness and an often unbroken bond of loyalty.

The war poet, Robert Graves, who fought at High Wood, observed that religious devotion during World War One was rare. He describes a Catholic priest, offering his blessing to a group of soldiers as they prepared for battle, rallying them with the cry that if they died fighting for the good cause, they would go straight to Heaven. One can only imagine that the German Catholic priests inspired their troops with the same sentiment.

The following is taken from a letter written by my father in 1990:

Harry and his section were on a break in their trench, rifles resting against the back wall. A German sniper had positioned himself in clear view of every 'Tommy' in the trench. Suddenly there was a shot and a bullet went through the barrel of the first rifle. A pause and then another. The British soldiers got the message and began signalling bulls or near misses. The German sniper shot through every rifle and avoided every man in the British trench. I've always been grateful to that

*German and realise that I owe my life to a good sport (but
a bad soldier, I suppose).*

I once rescued a sharpnose shark in North Carolina. It had
got caught between two rocks and was lying in shallow water,
languidly slapping its tail fin. Its eye was a pale iridescent green
circle and the unearthly beauty of it made me gasp. When
I looked into that shark's eye, I saw nothing that made me
afraid, only the splendour and vulnerability of another living
creature. I flipped the shark over with the help of a branch and,
having recovered, it returned to deep water. I felt oddly elated
afterwards, like I'd done a really good thing. I'd saved a life,
even if that life would have been lost, sooner or later, to a Core
Sound fisherman or to another sea creature: that sharpnose
was alive because of me. What I felt was a drop in the ocean
compared to what the German sniper must have experienced.
Perhaps some of those resting Royal Fusiliers went on to die
in battle; maybe some like Harry O'Connell survived the war,
fathered children and lived a long life. My life, as it came to
me through my father and my grandfather, owes a debt of the
utmost gratitude to a German whose name I do not know,
whose face I would be unable to recognise in a photograph,
but whose memory is anchored and honoured in our family.

In July 1916, two British cameramen were sent to the
Western Front to compose a pictorial record of World War 1.
In one frame, the camera pans a company of Royal Fusiliers.
The men stare unflinchingly into the lens, some smile and wave
their caps and rifles; one man is wearing a German *Pickelhaube*.
Did he find the helmet lying on the field of battle or did he have
to kill the *Boche* by running his bayonet into the soldier's soft

flesh, cracking ribs as he twisted it and withdrew the blade? Did my grandfather kill Germans with his bayonet too? I suppose he must have done. I pause the film and scan the faces, hoping to recognise Grandpa, but I don't see him. I wonder whether some of those soldiers knew Harry and how many of them were to die in the battle for High Wood?

On his 25th birthday, my grandfather was shot in the right leg, and a piece of shrapnel from an exploding shell pierced his lung. When Private O'Connell arrived at the military hospital in Southsea, he was told that his leg would have to be removed as gangrene had begun to spread. Fortunately, his cousin, who was a well-known doctor in the area, examined the leg and insisted that it was not to be amputated. Thus began a period of care and convalescence and, for Harry, the promise of a gentler and kinder life.

Harry's ward sister, Grace Arnold, was much loved by the soldiers in her section. She was known for her kindness, her raven black hair and lavender blue eyes. In spite of stiff competition, Harry's Irish charm captivated beautiful Nurse Arnold and on January 5th, 1918, Harry and Grace married in a Protestant ceremony in South London. In December 1918, a month after the war ended, their son Peter was born.

Harry and Grace on their wedding day, 1918

When I go from hence, let this be my parting word, that what I have seen is unsurpassable
Rabindranath Tagore

According to Peter, his father rarely spoke about the war and, when pressed for details, would simply say: 'It was the greatest experience of my life'. How does a man find words to speak about such things? How does he integrate his battle memories into a post-war life and his subsequent roles as a husband and father? Harry O'Connell and many thousands like him fought, not for God and Country, but for each other. They went into battle out of love and loyalty to their brothers in arms. There is a fellowship of fate during war that has a quality and depth that seems to take precedence over everything that follows, even family. At the core of extreme physical pain, aching loss and lifelong grief, lies love.

In his autobiography, published in 2007, Harry Patch, the last surviving soldier of WWI, revealed that Armistice Day was not the day he remembered the fallen. His Remembrance Day was September 22nd,1917, the day his pals died in battle. He was, he explained, always very quiet on that day, and didn't want anybody talking to him.

Every year, my grandfather resisted celebrating his birthday, insisting that he didn't want to see a show in London or go to The Tavernetta in Folkestone for dinner. How can a man continue to celebrate the day of his birth when it coincides with the day he almost lost his life, with the day so many of his friends lost theirs? July 16th was Grandpa's Remembrance Day, the day he lost his pals and, like Harry Patch, he didn't want anybody talking to him.

On July 21st, 1969, my father woke me in the early hours of the morning and told me that something very important was about to happen. He carried me into the sitting room where I was astonished to see my mother and the au pair sitting in front of the television. I had already had my daily quota of 'the idiot's lantern' as Dad called it, so I knew that this must be something very important indeed. I am grateful to my father for not leaving his ten-year-old asleep in bed that night, for recognising the significance of Neil Armstrong's: 'One small step for man, one giant leap for mankind'. Thirty years later I had a brief encounter with the astronaut Eugene Cernan at a watch fair in Switzerland: The last man on the moon was advertising the first watch on the moon. He had recently published his autobiography and as I was curious to see a moonwalker close up, I stood in line for the book signing. His inscription reads: *For Una – Dream the Impossible – Gene Cernan.* In the final chapter Cernan is in the garden with his five-year-old granddaughter and she points up into the sky at her grandfather's moon. Cernan, trying to use words and ideas that a small child will understand, explains that it's far, far away in the sky, out where God lives. The little girl looks at him in amazement and says she hadn't realised that 'Poppie' had gone to Heaven when he went to the moon.

Like the Twelve Apostles, the Twelve Moonwalkers were missionaries for mankind, but they were not men of God; they were test pilots, men who could exercise self-control whilst facing the ever present possibility of death. If the computer system failed or if they sprung a leak in their suits, they would die. Pete Conrad, when asked what it felt like to stand on the moon, replied: 'Super...really enjoyed it.' The more thoughtful answers seem to come much later, when the astronauts are old men. They speak of the moon's majestic beauty, of the blacker than black sky and the beautifully illuminated blue marble that we call Earth. Astronauts and soldiers face death with an immediacy that is rare, and this offers them an opportunity to recognise the vulnerability as well as the tender beauty of life on our planet.

The tendency to regard one's opponent as a fool or a knave, or both, is a deplorable feature of life. We should always be ready to acknowledge that the other man has motives as pure and ideals as lofty as those that we claim for ourselves.
Peter O'Connell, diary entry, July 1945

In 1934, Harry and Grace arranged for their fifteen-year-old son to correspond with a German boy. In the summer of 1935, Karl-Friedrich was invited to Wallington to stay with the O'Connells, and the following year Peter visited the Flinsbachs in Hamburg. The friendship between the boys continued after they left school.

In 1937, Karl-Friedrich writes:

Dear Peter, I am now in the Arbeitsdienst (working camp). At 5 o'clock we get up. After breakfast there is a flag display. At first it is very hard to work like a farmer but we have much fun and we are all so happy. In the afternoon we have drill but without weapons. Sometimes we hear dance music in the evening (but no jazz).

The letter is stamped with a swastika.

A year later, Karl-Friedrich writes from Hannover, where he is at university, studying to be an engineer:

It is already two years since I was in England. Oh Peter, I have a little homesickness to you and your parents. I spent there the best time of my live. Don't forget me, Peter. Your friend, Karl.

On December 31st 1938, Karl writes:

This Christmas we had a marvellous tree. My mother spread boiled starch over the branches and then shed salt on them. It looked like a tree covered with snow.

This was the last letter Peter received from his friend. He continued to write to him throughout the war, but he never heard back. In 1948, a letter arrived from Louise Flinsbach, Karl-Friedrich's mother:

> *My dear Peter,*
> *May I still call you so? In our thoughts you will always be Peter, the old friend of our Karl-Friedrich. We were so very glad hearing from you after such a long time. Alas, my Peter, our boy is missing since Stalingrad. Our hope for seeing him again diminishes more and more.*
> *Peter, you may be assured that you were never forgotten by Karl-Friedrich and us. We have often spoken about you. Karl-Friedrich always mentioned your parents with great regard and affection.*

My grandparents could have chosen a French or Spanish penfriend for their son but they specifically picked a German boy. I wonder what went through my grandfather's mind as he made ready to welcome the son of a man who, just a few years earlier, might have put a bullet through his head? Or, then again, might not?

Harry was twenty-six years old when he married Grace, who was five years his senior. In view of the 700,000 British men who died during World War One, Grace would have felt fortunate to have found a returning soldier who was not only gentle and charming but still had all his limbs. The British Army had granted Harry a full disablement pension and he supplemented this with his inventions. He was initially quite successful, but, during the Depression, his business ventures began to fail with increasing regularity.

Grace Arnold came from a family of successful entrepreneurs. Her maternal grandfather, George Leonard Turney, was a factory owner, the Mayor of Camberwell and a governor of Dulwich College. A street was named after him in South London and he died a wealthy man. Grace's paternal ancestors were less distinguished. Her father, Charles Arnold came from a long line of commercial travellers, and it was a tremendous shock to GL Turney when his daughter Jessie eloped with the flour salesman. He broke off all contact with her and they were not reconciled until shortly before the birth of her tenth child, Dorrie, Grace's youngest sister.

Grace's brothers were adventurers and pioneers. Arthur fought in the Second Boer War. Bert and Edgar founded the town of Black Diamond in Canada, and Edgar later travelled to Western Australia where he became a gold miner. Leonard set up wireless stations in Egypt before founding MK Electric in 1919. It was into this trail-blazing, overtly masculine family that my grandfather married. Harry O'Connell grew up in more modest circumstances. The son of an Irish farmer, he had no experience of homesteading or gold-digging in far-flung corners of the British Empire. He was a man in exile and, unlike the Arnold brothers, Harry did not feel the steady hand of his male ancestors guiding him from behind. He was viewed with suspicion by his swashbuckling brothers-in-law, who questioned whether the young Irishman would be a good husband to their sister Grace.

When Grace was sixteen years old, her mother died of pneumonia, and she was left to care for her father and raise her three younger siblings. My great-grandfather suffered from cerebral thrombosis and his increasing paralysis gradually altered his once kindly personality. It was not until he died when Grace was twenty-five that she found herself free to live her own life. Her choices, as an unmarried woman in Edwardian England, would have been limited. She became a nurse and, when war broke out, she was assigned to the Portsmouth military hospital to care for wounded soldiers returning from the Western Front.

Peter often spoke about his mother's kindness and her ability to create a container for men whose minds and hearts were as broken as their bodies. Grace had spent nine years caring for her father, a man who had won regimental prizes for swordsmanship in the Yeomanry Cavalry and who must have felt deeply frustrated by his advancing paralysis. I imagine my grandmother secretly welcomed the flirtations of the soldiers at Southsea hospital. She had made great sacrifices in her young life and the gentle, yet persistent attentions of Private Harry O'Connell must have soothed her sad heart. After years of caring for others, Grace yearned for solid ground, for someone dependable and kind who would take care of her. Harry had a hole in his leg, but otherwise his wounds would have seemed minor.

Maybe Harry nurtured the same dream. At last, he had found someone who would love and care for him. Finally, he could belong somewhere and to someone. Grace was beautiful and compassionate, but she also understood the ugliness and the grief of war. She and Harry knew what it meant to watch men die, men with whom they had created a bond of friendship. Harry and Grace were soul mates; they were two peas in a pod.

Harry never took Grace home to meet his family in Ireland and not simply because his new wife was an English Protestant.

Following the Easter Rising and the Irish war of Independence, men like my grandfather were no longer welcome in Ireland. As a Catholic Irishman who had voluntarily served in the British Army, he belonged neither to the unionists of the north nor to the republicans of the south. In March 1918, when conscription was introduced in Ireland, many Irishmen declared that they would take to the hills or die fighting in their homes rather than join the British Army.

Harry and Grace's marriage, according to my father, was not a happy one. Peter's perspective, I came to realise, was coloured by his own experiences and the challenges he faced as an only child of separated parents. His family narrative was reduced to good and bad, believer and non-believer, the faithful woman and the faithless man.

I have very few photographs of my father's childhood and no letters, diaries, papers or books. The family home was bombed during The Blitz and nothing survived; nothing but my grandmother's bible. The black leather is worn to a crumbling brown and on the inside cover is a dedication:

'Be ye kind one to another'
To Gracie with love from Harry, Sept. 1926

The full verse, taken from Ephesians, 4:32 is:
Be ye kind one to another, tender hearted, forgiving one
another, even as God for Christ's sake hath forgiven you.

Below Harry's words, Grace has written in a firm hand: *Christ the solid Rock I stand, All other ground is sinking sand.* I feel sad that Harry's ground was so unsteady; sad that Grace was unable to lean into him in her search for affection and protection.

Harry O'Connell was a man untethered, afloat in a vast ocean without islands. He had ceased to belong to his family, his country, his religion and, for the rest of his life, he struggled to recover a sense of solid ground. I never knew my grandfather to get angry or sad, and he was rarely joyful. I imagine that by the time I was born, his grief had withdrawn to a place so deep that no-one could hear the weeping. He signed his birthday cards to me with a simple, one-word 'Grandpa'; no good wishes, jokes or reflections. He had no hobbies, no male friends; he never went for walks or out to dinner. He rarely left Folkestone except once, in 1961, when he joined my parents on a holiday to Switzerland. In spite of his reclusive tendencies, Harry was extremely popular. Perhaps, due to his own unspeakable experiences, he acquired the reputation of being a good and gentle listener, especially with young people. My cousin, Nigel Metcalfe, remembers Grandpa as a quiet man who offered very little of himself. *When he did speak though, you listened carefully because what he said was invariably thoughtful and well considered.* Every evening at six o'clock, Harry would enjoy a large malt whisky, and when asked if he took water with his whisky, he replied: *Water rots your boots, imagine what it does to your stomach. The only thing to take in whisky is more whisky.* I suppose he had a drinking problem, although I never saw him drunk. He was mellow and charming and no-one could have imagined the aching grief caused by his wartime experiences, and the huge hole it blew through his heart.

In 1974, a Frenchman, Philippe Petit, walked across a wire fastened between the Twin Towers of the World Trade Centre in New York. He had no safety harness and over a period of forty-five minutes, Petit made eight crossings. The walk was unauthorised, but no-one was willing to risk either a rescue attempt or an arrest mission for fear that the young man might fall the quarter-mile to his death. It strikes me that my grandfather's life, after the age of 25, was a kind of internalised version of Petit's journey along the tightrope; it required tiny steps, a Zen-like focus and a very small world. Harry survived by a process of concentrated withholding, both of his joy and his rage. He rarely judged or advised, he never enthused or shared; he simply listened. For those who knew him, his priest-like ability to pay attention was a great gift. For those who loved him, for those, like his son, who needed his guidance and approval, his warmth and engagement, it was a profound loss.

One of my favourite obituaries is for Beulah Mae Whitehead of New Bern in North Carolina, who died in 2015 at the age of 90. She had eight great-grandchildren, thirteen great-great-grandchildren and was a lifetime member of the Missionary Baptist church. In my imagination, Beulah Mae cradles her great-great-grandbabies, speaking softly and welcoming each one into her large and faithful family.

All I know about my own great-great-grandmother in Ireland is the name of one of her daughters, born during the early years of the Irish Potato Famine. Eliza Daly, my great-grandmother, married and gave birth to eight children, the seventh of whom was my grandfather. I don't know anything about Eliza's experiences during The Great Hunger, when a million died and a million emigrated. I don't know whether her memories as a small child affected her ability to be a kind and loving mother towards her many children, or whether terrible hardship formed a brittle shell around her good heart. My great-grandfather, Henry, was ten years older than Eliza and would have experienced the Famine as a young boy. I have never known raging hunger; I have never had to witness those close to me starve and die simply because English Protestants hated me for who I was – an Irish Catholic. Harry had hoped to escape what he considered to be his father's narrow political and religious views, but an unconscious loyalty guided him to Northern France, where he witnessed his friends die on the battlefields simply because the 'Boches' had been taught to hate him and his comrades for who they were –'Tommies'.

Harry's nemesis was his brother-in-law, Jack Metcalfe, who had been raised Anglican but converted to evangelical Christianity after the war. In 1917 he married Grace's sister, Dorrie. Together, Dorrie and Jack founded The Wallington Bible Institute. Jack was a charismatic preacher, and all but three of the ten Arnold siblings joined his church.

My father's religious upbringing was complex and conflicted. My grandfather had lost his faith in the Catholic seminary and my grandmother, who had been raised as a Baptist, found a natural fit with the doctrinal certainty of The Wallington Bible Institute. Peter remembers his mother sitting for long hours at the table, reading and annotating her bible with a pencil. Judging from some of her references, Harry was already struggling with debt and drinking regularly in the public houses of Wallington.

Publicans and debtors are the scum of the earth and are synonymous with wickedness. They have no religious status, writes Grace in her Bible.

She considers too the sin of adultery:

Adultery is like stealing. According to Hebrew law, restitution can be made for stolen goods. The Adulterer, however, can never make restitution for his sin.

Harry's Catholic family would have agreed with Grace's views on adultery; equally, the O'Connells would have considered the status of their Protestant daughter-in-law to have been beneath that of a prostitute. Jack Metcalfe told his sons that he would rather they married prostitutes than Roman Catholics, and his youngest son, following in the footsteps of his Aunt Grace, duly married a Catholic. Harry must have struggled to understand how a political battlefield in France could so swiftly have been replaced by a religious war zone in Surrey. Harry's denial of religion and Grace's salvation through religion created a perfect storm, and Peter stood on the fault line, struggling with a small boy's inability to choose between two people, both of whom he loved and depended on for his physical and emotional survival. This early religious conflict resulted in powerful feelings of guilt and alienation that my father struggled with throughout his life.

The three youngest Arnold daughters, Grace, Ruby and Dorrie, gave birth to three sons within three months of each other, and the boys were christened together in April 1919. The cousins, Peter O'Connell, Toby Fleming and David Metcalfe, grew up together and remained very close throughout their lives. All three followed in the footsteps of their great-grandfather Turney, and became successful and respected men in their chosen fields.

Harry O'Connell had no visible ancestors, no religion and no palpable pride in where he came from. Peter's internal landscape, therefore, resembled a tree with roots and leaf cover on one side, shallow earth and bare branches on the other. It would have made it hard for him to feel anchored and balanced in life. My father was raised as an Arnold, surrounded by a clan of aunts, uncles and cousins. The O'Connells belonged to the past, and my grandfather's family was as good as forgotten.

Peter and his cousin Toby attended Dulwich College, a prestigious private school where my father proved to be a natural scholar and a conscientious student. In 1937, shortly before he was due to sit his final examinations, the Headmaster called Peter into his study and explained that his father had not paid his fees and regrettably, therefore, he could no longer remain as a pupil at the school. Unable to take his exams, he lost his place at Cambridge to read Medicine, and the shame of this experience, together with the unspoken rage he felt towards his father, was something Peter carried with him for the rest of his life. Shortly before he died, at a time when Alzheimer's had claimed most of his mind, my father called me, sounding distressed and apologetic. He told me that he was in the debtors' prison in Dover for non-payment of taxes, and he hoped I would forgive him for the terrible shame he had brought on the family. I thought of all the times Her Majesty's Revenue and Customs had returned his cheques, explaining that they had already received his income tax payment for the year, and I felt helpless in the face of his desperation. I realised too that the shame belonged to his father, and that Peter had dutifully carried it for almost sixty years.

Peter left Dulwich College in 1937 and found a job as a clerk at Guthrie and Co East India Merchants. He referred to this period in his life as *deeply humiliating, bleak and shameful.* The threat of war offered an opportunity for liberation, and Peter tried repeatedly to join Her Majesty's Navy. Eventually he wrote a letter to the First Sea Lord:

My Lord,
I am extremely anxious to serve in His Majesty's Navy in time of war, and as all my efforts to enter any of the Reserves have failed, I am presumptuously writing to you as Head of the Navy. It was my ambition to be a naval surgeon, but, owing to financial difficulties, I had to give up medicine. One volunteer is worth ten pressed men and the only obstacle to a logical transfer from the Territorial Army is red tape or the good King's regulations. I feel sure that a few words spoken in official quarters would be sufficient to extricate me from this difficulty and enable me to join the RNSR. I should be extremely grateful to your Lordship for any assistance in this matter.
I have, Sir, the honour to be, Your obedient servant, Peter O'Connell.

Peter never did fulfil his ambition to become a naval officer. Instead, he joined the Royal Signals and, in 1941, he was posted to Northern Ireland: *I went into the army, very happy to be away from the troubles at home,* he writes.

In February 1942, after just eight months as a serving soldier, Peter was invalided out of the war with suspected tuberculosis. He spent four months at a hospital in Belfast, and was subsequently transferred to a sanatorium in Bournemouth. I always had the impression that my father felt rather inadequate, even humiliated by his lack of military distinction during World War II, especially in comparison to his two cousins: Toby served on a minesweeper in the Red Sea and David was decorated for his bravery at Dunkirk.

During his year of enforced rest, Peter read a great many books and kept a literature journal, in which he wrote detailed summaries and reflections. It was an attempt to use his time fruitfully, and also perhaps a way of regaining the momentum of his lost schooldays at Dulwich. He critiqued his own work, and in the margins, offered himself suggestions for improvement. The books, which he borrowed from the Belfast Public Library, ranged in subject matter from economics, divorce reform and politics, to African missionaries, American history and Arctic exploration. His favourite subject, however, was Irish history and the Catholic Church.

For more than two decades, Ireland and the O'Connells had existed beneath the radar, and it was during his time in Belfast that Peter first made contact with his family across the border: *I spent my days serving the King Emperor and my evenings mixing with the rebels,* he writes. In Virginia, County Cavan, he was fed and loved by his aunts and he drank whisky with his cousins, developing a particularly close bond with his father's namesake, Harry O'Connell.

My grandfather's sister, to whom he was closest both in age and affection, was Molly. When Harry was invalided out of the war in 1916, his medals were sent to Aunty Molly. My cousin Ralph told me that as children, he and his siblings had been warned by their mother never to touch the suitcase on top of the wardrobe because it contained their Uncle Harry's war medals. 'One day,' she told her children, 'he'll be back to collect them, and we must keep them safe'. In the West of Ireland, it is still common to say to a child: 'To whom do you belong?' rather than: 'What's your name?'After my father died in 1998, I began researching my Irish family history. I telephoned every O'Connell I could find in the Virginia phone book, believing, correctly, that once I told them 'to whom I belonged', they would point me in the right direction. At a family reunion a few months later, my cousin Ita approached me and said in a quiet voice: 'We've been waiting for you. We knew that one day you'd come'.

There is a generational amnesia that, to a greater or lesser degree, appears to be present in all families, and my father's interest in Ireland was something he found distinctly confounding: *It's strange how strong the pull of Ireland is to 'exiles'. I observe with some amazement the same force in myself. Born and raised entirely in England with an English mother and dozens of English relations, I still find myself cheering for Ireland at Twickenham and I have a very warm feeling for the country and its people. God bless Ireland.* I can relate to this pull. I have three passports, and for the past twenty years I have chosen to travel exclusively as a citizen of the Republic of Ireland.

One of the books my father read during his time in Belfast was *The Irish Republic* by Dorothy Macardle. It documents the years between 1916 and 1926, the period known as 'The Crossness'. My father writes with rage and indignation about the unconscious colonising of Ireland by the English. Peter, at twenty-four years old, would have known all about the insoluble nature of divided loyalties, of England against Ireland,

Protestant against Catholic and the confusion he felt about the ways of his mother and those of his father.

In 1966, my grandfather decided to have the walls of his bedroom painted in repeating bands of green, white and orange. My mother, who had a flair for interior design, was appalled by this display of bad taste. The colours, I realised many years later, are those of the Irish flag. In 1969, the year after my grandfather died, my father took us to Ireland where he made a big to-do about explaining the flag's historical significance: green symbolises Irish republicanism and the Roman Catholics; orange represents William of Orange and the Protestants, and the white band in the centre is the hope for eventual peace between the two.

In July 1942, my father was discharged from the Bournemouth Sanatorium and relieved of his wartime duties with the Royal Signals. Peter describes this period in his life as *the homeless years* when he cared for his mother, who was suffering with pulmonary tuberculosis, and drifted ever further away from his father. Through no fault of his own, he had seen very little warfare. Perhaps, if he had experienced more frontline action, he and Harry might have been able to share an understanding of what it meant to defend your country, kill your enemy and lose your friend to a foreign bullet. They may not have spoken about the things they had seen and done during two world wars, but the bond of shared experience, of physical and emotional trauma, might have provided Peter with an opportunity to reflect on the origins of Harry's silence, and the depths of his father's broken heart.

In the Spring of 1944, Peter and Grace were living at The Graham Hotel in Brighton, and it was from this address that Peter applied to and was accepted by St John's College, Cambridge to read History. The war raged on, but for Peter life became gentler and kinder. He played cricket for Magdalene College, ate roast chicken and waffles with his friends, Lethbridge and Symons, punted to Grantchester for *Rupert Brooke worship* and swam in the Cam. In his diary of July 21ˢᵗ, he writes:

Midnight – the moon is shining between white lacy clouds and the gable heads and turrets of Second Court stand out dark against the pearly sky. It is at such times as this that the spirit of Cambridge speaks to those who have any ears at all. The beauty of the evening and a disturbed mind drew me away from Barkers' 'Greek Political Thought' as dusk fell and I wandered along the Backs, listening to the wind whispering in the long tresses of the willows and watching the moon glittering on the still waters of the Cam. Lethbridge and Symons appeared in the magic gloaming, swimming like a couple of nyads from Trinity Bridge up to the Bridge of Sighs. Puffing and dropping silver beads of moonlit water they climbed out onto the bank and we went back to Symons rooms in Third Court for coffee and a yarn. Coming back through Second Court the mystery and loveliness of this old Tudor building held me in a spell; the oriel window of the combination room gleamed in the moonlight and I could see the ghost of unhappy Charles proposing to the woman who became his devoted wife and evil genius, the ill starred Henrietta Maria. Ghosts thronged the shadowy court for John's has had close bonds with English history for the past 400 years and if all who have resided in Second Court and who have become famous in their country's annals were to return, we could dispense with text books and learn our history orally. It would not be the most dispassionate and objective history, but it would certainly be vivid.

In order to supplement his grant, Peter followed in the footsteps of his maternal grandfather and worked as a travelling salesman during the long summer holidays. By day he peddled toilet seats in the East End of London and at night he returned to his rooms at the Cambridge Club on Montague St where he dined with the Principal of Gordon's College in Khartoum and the former Chief Justice in Singapore. It was a curiously conflicted life.

How pleasant and gracious life is in Cambridge! I'm longing for next year now I'm truly re-established in mind and body or at least within measurable distance of it. Thank God for Christian Science.
August 1945

During his first year at Cambridge, Peter abandoned his mother's evangelical Christianity and joined the Christian Scientist student group. Mary Baker Eddy, the founder of the movement, believed that prayer and bible study, combined with an understanding of science and medicine, could restore individual health and transform character.

Grace remained in Brighton, and in spite of the good sea air her tuberculosis did not improve. Her younger brother, Leonard, who had made his fortune with the invention of the three-pin plug, chose to gift his sisters, Grace and Ruby, the sum of one thousand pounds each. Peter suggested his mother use the money to seek a cure in Switzerland and eventually, she agreed. In the late summer of 1946, therefore, Peter travelled to Davos in search of a sanatorium for his mother.

Chapter Two

So much suffering in Nirvana castles

Zen Master Seung Sahn

Rosa, Ernst, Bobi and Lea Kummer, 1919

My mother, Lea Kummer-Gilomen, and all her ancestors, dating back to the sixteenth century, were born in Switzerland. They grew their roots, their culture and their identity in the canton of Bern, raising their families and burying their dead on Swiss soil for twelve generations.

Lea was born in Biel/Bienne on July 18th, 1917. The town is entirely bilingual and local law declares that people are permitted to communicate in either French or German; it is not uncommon for both languages to be used interchangeably within a single conversation. Biel is home to Rolex, Omega and Swatch and the town proudly lays claim to the French philosopher Jean-Jacques Rousseau who, in 1765, lived for a short time on the lake's Ile St Pierre. He described his stay on the island as: *le temps le plus heureux de ma vie*. My mother would certainly have agreed with Rousseau. She loved her hometown and often spoke about the happiness and sense of joy that defined her early life in Biel.

After she died in 1996, I discovered, amongst her possessions, a padlocked calfskin journal. I knew my mother as a very private person and she rarely left drawers or doors unlocked. She walked a fine line between a neurotic fear and an intuitive sense that her privacy was being invaded. The inner sanctum of her life was wrapped in keys and codes, in phonetic Swiss script and German shorthand.

The first entry in my mother's diary is dated May 11th, 1933. She is fifteen years old and at finishing school in Yverdon-les-Bains, on the shores of Lake Neuchatel. The journal spans eighteen years and her last words are: *Suffering... it exists everywhere*. Today the Pensionnat Saint-George is a residential centre for adults with psycho-social difficulties. In 1933 it was a boarding school for young women, whose parents wished to refine their daughters' linguistic, social and cultural skills: On May 22nd Lea writes: *This afternoon I lay behind the tennis courts in the sunshine. I wanted to be alone to enjoy the beautiful book I am reading. I always seek solitude when I have something special to read, to write or to think about.*

Seeking solitude was not something I ever associated with my mother. Dad was often away and she disliked being alone in our big Edwardian house in Folkestone. I realise now that what Lea feared was not being alone, but being abandoned and feeling lonely. By the time I was born, she had lost so much that was beautiful and precious in her life and solitude was something she avoided rather than coveted.

The Saint-George girls visited museums and theatres; they enjoyed afternoon tea in elegant hotels, played tennis and attended dances at The Gentleman's Institute of Boudry. In February, they spent a week skiing in the mountain resort of Villars. In her journal, Lea writes: *The view to Mont Blanc was simply breathtaking and I felt quite overwhelmed by the natural beauty of the landscape. I realise how lucky I am to be Swiss.* The year ended with a grand ball and, inspired by tsars, emperors and the Viennese opera, the girls designed and sewed their own gowns before dancing into the early hours with the Boudry Boys.

My mother often spoke about the magical year she spent at the pensionnat in Yverdon and promised me that, one day, I too would have my own finishing school experience. In Switzerland young men are legally obliged to complete seventeen weeks of military service and, until the early 1970s, young women were required to attend a five week housekeeping course. In 1971, Swiss women were given the right to vote and they promptly took the decision to phase out the so-called 'Roesti-kurs'. The only schools that survived the transition were the exclusive ones, intended for the daughters of diplomats, foreign princes and maharajas. Eventually, my mother found the Sonnhalde School of Housekeeping in the small town of Worb, near Bern. She was disappointed that it was only a three month course, but thrilled in her anticipation of what lay ahead for me in her beloved Switzerland. In January 1978, therefore, having passed my A Levels and completed a twelve week secretarial course, I left for Switzerland to be finished.

I was miserable in Worb and begged my mother to let me come home. Some of the girls were already engaged to farmers whom they planned to marry just as soon as they had learnt how to look after them properly. We darned socks, repaired men's shirt collars and once a week, the local farmers would deliver duffel bags of dirty clothes to the laundry so we could practice our washing and ironing skills on the real thing. Visiting speakers taught us how to operate household appliances, bathe a baby and manage our housekeeping budgets. There was certainly no time for tennis tournaments or dancing. I soon gained a reputation for being strident, informing Fraulein Indermuehle that I had no need for any of the skills she was teaching me because I was off to university and, if my husband ever had a frayed collar, he would buy himself a new shirt because that was what we did in England. My mother felt badly for me and she was also ashamed of my behaviour.

In the Spring of 1934 Ernst and Rosa enrolled their daughter at the Benedict School in Biel where Lea took courses in shorthand, typing, English and French. She maintained a busy social life, attending garden parties, private soirees and dances at the Bern Casino: *When you are young,* she writes, *the world is your oyster.*

My mother was known for her beautiful shoes and the secret, she once told me, was to buy them a size too small which served to accentuate their elegance. I was never allowed to wear pretty shoes and Mum used to take me to Clarks in Folkestone where

I was fitted with sturdy, leather lace-ups. At university I owned a pair of much-coveted red, suede, winklepicker ankle boots and, with my first pay cheque, I bought a very expensive pair of shoes in London's South Molton Street. I never showed my shoes to my mother and hid them in my flatmate's bedroom when my parents visited me in Clapham.

In the 1970s Lea underwent several failed operations on her broken feet and subsequently had to wear bulky, custom-made shoes. They didn't help much. She was in constant pain and couldn't walk any great distance. She warned me not to follow in her footsteps but I remained captivated by the image of my elegant young mother dancing, if a little painfully, with so many handsome uniformed officers. I imagined her girlfriends, seated in rows along the walls of the Casino, following the movements of Lea's dainty feet with their eyes, feeling just a little envious of her effortless style and grace.

1935 has been a year of tremendous joy and happiness but there was pain and disappointment too. For the year ahead, I wish myself the very best of luck, together with the hope that my deepest longing will be fulfilled. Suffering is an inevitable part of life - it offers important lessons and it helps develop inner strength.

I wonder about my mother's *deepest longing* and am curious too about her experience of suffering; it seems to be at odds with the fun-loving eighteen-year-old who has the world at her fingertips. After three months in London studying English and Commerce, an experience she describes as: *one of the happiest times of my life,* she was sent to Yugoslavia for six weeks.

Europe in 1936 was in a state of turmoil. In Germany,

Hitler's Nuremberg Laws had stripped Jews of their citizenship, and the rise of the Metaxas dictatorship in Greece added to the far-right régimes of Salazar in Portugal and Mussolini in Italy. It was against this political landscape that Lea began her solo journey across Europe, travelling to Gakowo via Vienna. This area, now part of Serbia, had a long history of German settlement, and many unmarried women came down the Danube in search of husbands. In her journal, Lea writes: *To the obvious disappointment of the Schwarz Family, I am leaving without an engagement ring on my finger. I quite like Tibor but when I choose to get married, it certainly won't be to a man like him.* This decision may well have saved her life. After WWII, President Tito carried out a genocide of ethnic Germans in retaliation for killings perpetrated by the Nazis. During the four years of Communist occupation in the small town of Gakowo, eight and a half thousand people died in internment camps of starvation, typhus and malaria. It is possible that Tibor was among them.

On July 18th, 1937 Lea writes in her journal: *Life is so beautiful. At times, it feels as though there aren't enough hours in the day to do it justice and I fear that I am not fully appreciating all the joy and happiness in my life. There is one thing, however, that continues to worry me: What does the future hold for me?*

I am surprised by her question. It has a sense of foreboding, as if my mother realised that time was limited and she needed to stockpile her gifts. As the years roll by, her sense of anxiety and vulnerability gain momentum. Her life is relentlessly exciting, but it lacks adult supervision. There appear to be few, if any, engaged elders stewarding her in the ways of the world, offering her wisdom, support and their full attention.

Gradually, the solitude she had found so nourishing in Yverdon slips into loneliness and an overall feeling of unease. Maybe my grandparents were unaware of the physical and moral risks to which they were exposing their young daughter.

I was thirteen when we went to Yugoslavia on holiday. At the pool one afternoon, the waiter brought me a drink and explained that it was a gift from the gentleman sitting at the bar. The man, who was in his early thirties, walked over to me and, in broken English explained that he was a photographer on a film shoot, and would like to take pictures of me. My parents were charmed by him and agreed that he could take me into the old town of Dubrovnik. I was flattered by the attention, but it also unsettled me and I was relieved when we returned to England. Peter and Lea, however, had given Klaus our phone number and he began to call regularly, even visiting us in Folkestone. I was scolded for my rudeness in avoiding him, but I stood firm and said I thought he was creepy. It wasn't until he sent me red roses on my eighteenth birthday and announced he was leaving his wife that Mum and Dad intervened. I don't believe that my parents were being wilfully irresponsible; good manners had simply taken precedence over good sense. Perhaps this was also true of my grandparents with regard to my mother . Their good intentions had clouded their sense of responsibility.

A man is head of the family, but his wife is the neck
Old Swiss saying

My grandfather, Ernst, had a respectable job as a police officer. He was by no means a wealthy man, and I have often wondered how he was able to finance my mother's expensive education and trips abroad. My Aunt Heidi once told me that it was very important to my grandmother that her daughter move in the right circles and marry well. Lea's skills and accomplishments would have ensured that she was a cut above her contemporaries; in a better position, therefore, to attract a professional husband with a good income.

My grandmother Rosa was born in 1887, the only child of her father's second marriage. She grew up with her half-sister Bertha, whose mother had died when she was three years old. Bertha never married and in 1902, she moved to France where she worked as a laundress at the Grand Hotel du Louvre in Marseilles. When she returned to Switzerland she became a housekeeper at Chateau Brillantmont, an exclusive boarding school in Lausanne. Bertha recommended her younger sister Rosa for a secretarial position at the school, and it was probably in the affluent environment of the Brillantmont that the first seeds were sown for my mother's own finishing school experience at the Pensionnat Saint-George. In 1913 Bertha left Lausanne for Davos where she worked for eight years in hotels and sanatoria. Her final position was at the Savoy in Zurich from where she retired shortly before the outbreak of World War II.

My mother and I often visited Aunt Bertha before boarding the midnight sleeper from Basel to Calais. Her apartment was crowded with sofas and ottomans, upholstered in shades of olive and tobacco velvet and everything was steeped in a warm, butter-yellow light. One of my earliest memories is of lying in the soft embrace of one of Aunt Bertha's sofas, listening to the two women talking against the tick-tock of my great grandfather's longcase clock.

Bertha Gilomen died in 1966 and Lea and my Uncle Bobi were named as the sole heirs in her handwritten will. The lawyer's will, however, lists twenty-three family members, all of whom were making a claim on my great-aunt's estate. In a letter to Lea, Bobi writes: *I had no idea that any of these people existed*. I was astonished by this remark. How is it possible for so many people from one family to vanish from living memory? I returned to the Gilomen family tree in search of clues. Bertha and Rosa's father, Benedicht Gilomen, was married for thirteen years to his first wife and she gave birth to six children before she died in 1885. What became of Bertha's five siblings?

It is extremely difficult to conduct genealogical research in Switzerland. There is no equivalent to www.ancestry.com and the Bernese State Department carefully monitors and controls all documented information. Swiss passport holders may visit the archives three times a year, although there are no copying facilities available and photography is forbidden. In 1997 I telephoned the parish of Hoechstetten in Bern and requested a copy of my grandfather's death certificate. There was a moment of silence, followed by an audible intake of breath, and I was informed that such information was not available. Death, the woman told me in a tone of undisguised indignation, is a strictly personal matter. Unless, I reflected, you travel to an assisted suicide clinic in Switzerland, where it quickly becomes a very public matter. I don't like arguing with Swiss government officials, mainly because my ability to be articulate in the language suddenly fails me and I hear myself grow shrill and a little hysterical.

There is a fine line between privacy and secrecy in Switzerland. Sixty percent of the country is mountainous, and this in many ways has defined the sociology of its people. Communities are often isolated from one another and survival, especially in winter, requires a resilient and resourceful nature. People work hard and are wary of outsiders.

The village of Adelboden in the Bernese Oberland is where my mother went skiing when she was a young girl; it is where my future father-in-law carried Lea's skis up the mountain and it is where, on Boxing Day in 1959, I was christened in the village church. During my childhood we spent every Christmas holiday in Adelboden, together with Uncle Bobi, Aunty Heidi and my cousin, Christine. The Chalet Marlis is still offered as a holiday let and in 2015, I decided to spend a week there while I investigated the mystery of Aunt Bertha's lost siblings.

The flat, with its pine furniture and red and white checked curtains, was just as I remembered it, and on Sunday morning the thunderous sound of bells rang through the village and echoed off the mountainside. On Monday, I went to Stauffacher's bookshop in Bern where I struggled to find any literature on early twentieth-century Swiss social history. I was about to give up when a sales assistant brought me a book with the title *Versorgt und Vergessen/ Filed away and Forgotten.*

Hail, holy Queen, Mother of Mercy,
Hail, our life, our sweetness and our hope.
To thee do we cry
Poor banished children of Eve;

To thee do we send up our sighs,
Mourning and weeping in this valley of tears

Salve Regina

Over a one hundred year period a practice known as *verdingen* (indentured servitude) operated in Switzerland. Children were removed from their families and sent to work on farms. It is estimated that between 1860 and 1960, one hundred thousand children were *verdingt* in this way, a quarter of them in the Canton of Bern. Local parishes paid farmers a monthly allowance to provide disadvantaged children with board and lodging. Although some treated their charges well, countless children suffered terrible hardship over many years. A systematic vow of silence fell across entire communities as clergy, social workers and villagers chose to ignore the widespread abuse. Teachers who reported that children were being ill-treated often found that their contracts were not renewed at the end of the school year.

In 2000 I read an article in The Guardian about Swiss Verdingkinder. I mentioned it to my Swiss father -in-law who told me that two half-brothers from his father's first marriage had been *verding*t when their mother died. The youngest child, a girl, was not given away, and grew up with him and his brother in the second marriage. I thought of Aunt Bertha whose situation had been very similar. In 2008 Marco Leuenberger and Loretta Seglias, two Swiss historians, published *Versorgt und Vergessen,* an oral history, documenting the experiences of forty former Verdingkinder.

Today Switzerland has one of the highest per capita incomes in the world. Eighty years ago, however, the country was extremely poor. The worldwide economic crisis of the 1930s affected much of Swiss society and created a cycle of real poverty, or a constant fear of it. Sudden illness, an accident or the death of a parent could quickly disturb the fragile balance of a family already living in constrained financial circumstances. The authorities were swift to intervene, sending very young children to homes and orphanages and the older ones into servitude. I wonder whether this is what happened to Alfred, Maria, Johann, Lina and Anna, the five lost Gilomen siblings?

Communities, especially the poorer ones, were keen to pay as little as possible for the upkeep of Verdingkinder. Slaves in the Southern states of America were sold to the highest bidder, but indentured children in Switzerland were given to those famers who tendered the lowest offers. Although this practice was outlawed in 1847, in some communities these old-style auctions were still taking place well into the 1920s. The Swiss government, meanwhile, promoted the idea that hard work, self-discipline and fresh air were a natural corrective for these potentially wayward children and would provide them with the means to support themselves as adults.

Farmers worked their investments hard: former Verdingkinder describe getting up at four in the morning to help in the barn and carry milk pails to the dairy before school; girls as young as six were expected to cook, clean and knit. These children and thousands like them were taken from their families without warning. They didn't know where they were going, nor for how long. Often they were moved to farms in different cantons, and lost touch with their parents and siblings.

My friend Brigitte lost her mother to cancer in 1978 and within days, the authorities came to take her fourteen-year-old sister into care. A kindly neighbour insisted she would help with cooking and caring for the girls, and this generous intervention saved Marianne from being removed from the family home. Another friend, who grew up in the Emmental, remembers a verdingboy who lived on a neighbouring farm. He had a speech impediment and the local children would tease him. Years later children's bones were found buried on the farmer's land.

Many former Verdingkinder say they could have endured the back-breaking work, the starvation, even the violence, but they were never able to reconcile themselves to the absence of kindness and affection. As children they were not precious to the adults around them. Moments of tenderness were rare, and many sought warmth and comfort from the animals on the farm. Without good role models or mothers to explain the changes of adolescence, girls married young or gave birth to illegitimate children, perpetuating the legacy of social exclusion. Sexual abuse was not uncommon, and pregnant girls would vanish in the night to another farm in another canton, where the baby would be given up to a children's home. The need to survive their physical and emotional circumstances suffocated a natural ability for intimacy and the divorce rate amongst former Verdingkinder is high.

The fathers have eaten bitter grapes,
And the children's teeth are set on edge

Jeremiah, 31:29

In our early years in Adelboden, I stayed with my Aunt Heidi and Uncle Bobi, and my parents had a room at the Hotel Schoenegg. As a teenager, Christine began to resent sharing a room with her much younger cousin and so, when I was eight years old, I was sent to the local children's home. The Kinderheim Helios was a dark and gloomy chalet and I wasn't at all convinced by my parents' assurances that it would be huge fun living with lots of other children. Every day we would load our skis onto a sledge pulled by a donkey and walk through the village. If I saw Mum and Dad, I could wave but I wasn't allowed to speak to them. I knew nothing about the other children's backgrounds, but it was clear that I didn't belong, and my occasional supper trips to the Schoenegg only served to highlight my feelings of exclusion.

We were expected to do chores, but we had enough to eat and the adults, although strict, were not unkind. There is no comparison with my brief experience in a children's home and the ugly and painful lives led by many Heim and Verdingkinder. I can, however, identify, if only on a very small scale, with what all of them describe as feelings of abandonment, despair and a sense of powerlessness. The Helios, I subsequently discovered, had at one time been owned by Herr Bruendler, a card-carrying member of the Swiss Nazi Party.

In 2016 I came across 'Netzwerk-Verdingt', an organisation founded by a group of former Heim and Verdingkinder. They meet once a month at the 'Kaefigturm' in the Old City of Bern and Walter, the spokesman for the group, invited me to one of their meetings. The people I met that day have come to terms with their painful childhoods, but there are thousands in Switzerland who have been completely broken by their experiences; some are literally speechless; others have taken their own lives. The stigma was so great that many never told their partners and children that they had been verdingt. Those who have been given access to their records often discover that important information has been omitted or falsified. In some cases, the files have been destroyed altogether, which many experience as a double betrayal.

As adults, many Verdingkinder chose careers that provided them with freedom and independence. Young men became long-distance lorry drivers which enabled them to travel, all expenses paid, across Europe and the Middle East. At the Kaefigturm in Bern, I spoke to Charles, known as 'Scharli', who told me of his experiences in Iran in the 1980s, delivering aircraft hangers for Iranian fighter jets. Soon after he arrived, the Iran-Iraq War broke out and he spent fifty days stranded in the desert with a colony of foreign lorry drivers. I was struck both by Scharli's resourcefulness and by his modesty. He was, I subsequently discovered, not just a truck driver but the owner of a successful transport company.

Scharli later told me that his two younger brothers had been sent to the Kinderheim Helios on the recommendation of the village doctor in Adelboden and Bern social services. Their mother, herself a Verdingkind, was working as a maid when she fell pregnant. She was immediately dismissed, even though the baby's father was the farmer's son. Scharli grew up on a farm near Bern and when, at the age of ten, he discovered that the people he lived with were not his biological family, he tried to take his own life. He put the barrel of a rifle into his mouth but as he reached down, the bullet fired, grazed his finger and went through the roof of the barn. I also spoke to Beatrice who grew up in a children's home and later became a furrier, tailoring mink coats for the rich and famous. 'I was never cold again', she reflected.

I was sorting boxes in the attic recently and re-discovered a pair of my mother's sheepskin gloves onto which she had sewn scraps of ocelot fur. Mum was both creative and determined in her aspirations towards luxury and there were two things she wanted above all else – a Mercedes and a mink. As her fiftieth birthday approached, my father finally buckled under the strain and agreed to buy her a fur coat. In the Spring of 1967, therefore, my mother and I went to Switzerland for a series of visits to Tiersbier Furrier in Biel. My mother's coat was to be custom made and, to avoid possible taxation at the border, she requested that an old label be sewn into the lining. My father, who was a stickler for rules, was horrified when he discovered what my mother had done, and I recall an ongoing argument between them as we drove home to England. By the time we reached Dover, the coat had been carefully folded so that the label was clearly visible, and I was lying across it, pretending to be asleep. This extra twist was my mother's idea; the discussion between my parents had made me hysterical and she was concerned that my nervousness might arouse suspicion. I was convinced that the deception would be instantly discovered, that my parents would go to jail and I would be sent back to the children's home. In her charming Swiss accent, Mum gaily told the customs official about our holiday and how exhausted her eight-year-old was by the long journey home. He listened, smiling politely as she chattered on, and then waved us through.

I still have an uncomfortable relationship with that mink, but like the ugly Meissen china my mother left me, I have never felt able to part with it. Each time I come across the sleek, wet-black fur hanging in the cupboard, I hear Mum's voice in my head reminding me that: 'it cost a lot of money and you must never give it away'. In the 1980s when human rights protesters were throwing buckets of red paint over women in fur coats, my mother remained undeterred, loving and wearing her mink with pride, not necessarily for the warmth it offered her, but for the way it made her feel. Her fur coat was a shield against poverty, a tangible and immediately recognisable sign that she was a person of prosperity, someone who had financial control over her life. The day before she died, Mum asked me to help her out of bed and onto the balcony, where she wrapped herself in her mink and, for one last hour, she looked happy. When I showed my husband Dan the ocelot gloves, he observed that they were a perfect match for my acrylic leopard-print coat and suggested I wear them. 'In these days of fake fur', he added, 'no-one will ever guess that they're real'.

I wonder whether my grandmother knew, as she was growing up, that she had not one, but six half-siblings. Did her father ever talk about his missing children and why they'd gone away? Perhaps Rosa made an early promise to herself to keep her own children safe from the vice-like grip of indentured service. Maybe she vowed to do everything possible to ensure that her son and daughter acquired positions of financial security on rungs high up the social ladder where the air was thinner and life was cushioned by abundance and privilege.

In Switzerland every cow is tagged and accounted for, but to this day, no one knows for sure how many children were removed from their families. If my grandmother's siblings were verdingt, then it seems likely that the same fate befell members of my grandfather's family. Rudolf, my great-grandfather, married Magdalena when he was twenty-four-years old and she was thirty-two. She brought six small children to the marriage and, five months later, she gave birth to Maria. What became of Magdalena's first husband and which of the two men was Maria's father? The story hangs like unripe fruit from the branches of the Kummer family tree.

My great-grandfather and his second wife were married for twelve years and had eight more children. In 1884, she died and at the age of thirty-six, Rudolf found himself with fourteen children to support. Shortly afterwards, he married the widowed, childless Marianne Knuchel. Second wives recognised their value, and often chose to negotiate the number of stepchildren they were prepared to accept in the marriage. The rest were verdingt. Three years later, at the age of forty, Marianne gave birth to my grandfather. Ernst was her first child, Rudolf's ninth and the fifteenth child overall.

Rudolf died in 1900 and Marianne married for the third time. I don't know if Otto Zingg was a kind and loving stepfather to the thirteen-year-old Ernst and whether it was he who saved my grandfather from the jaws of penal servitude on a Bernese farm. Ernst's two half-sisters, Elise and Bertha, had emigrated to the Mid West in 1895 and, when their father died, Elise wrote suggesting that Ernst join them in America. Marianne felt that the boy was too young to make such a long journey alone and it seems likely that she didn't want to lose her only son to the New World so soon after losing her husband. Mum always claimed that the departure of her father's two favourite half-sisters and his mother's refusal to allow him to join them in America were losses from which he never fully recovered. She even went so far as to say that they contributed to his untimely death.

My grandfather, Ernst, like his father before him, was a police-man. In Switzerland police officers are held in high regard. A bank manager in Biel once told me that his brother-in-law was a policeman: 'My mother invariably defers to him on matters of importance. A policeman always trumps a bank manager,' he explained rather sorrowfully.

In December 2008 the Biel Police Department closed and to mark the occasion, a photograph of my grandfather and his colleagues appeared in *The Bieler Tagblatt*, the local paper of the town Ernst served for more than thirty years. The headline reads: *Guardian, Servant, Friend and Helper.* I recognised my grandfather in the picture, because he is the dead spit of my mother. The photograph was taken in 1909, when a moustache was as much part of a policeman's uniform as the sheathed sabre which hung from his leather belt. The first policewomen, or Politessen as they are known, did not join the force until 1972. In spite of the kindly faces of my grandfather's colleagues, I imagine that the long absence of women in the Swiss police force would have created a rather muscular *modus operandi*. The Swiss authorities considered that poverty was socially inherited, and believed that removing children from their impecunious circumstances would guarantee greater social and economic productivity in ensuing generations. This policy came at a terri-ble price for thousands of children and their families as well as for the soul of the country.

In 2013, the government offered an official apology to all former Heim and Verdingkinder. At the same time, an initiative was launched seeking financial reparation for the surviving victims, together with a comprehensive investigation into the history of Switzerland's indentured children.

In the spring of 2016, Dan and I visited the 'Stolen Childhood – Verdingkinder Speak' exhibition at The Ballenberg museum near Bern where Gottlieb Brunner had offered to be our guide. 'Godi' has a freckled face and warm, sad eyes and, like many former Verdingkinder, he is strong but suffers from spinal fractures incurred during childhood when he was made to carry heavy weights up and down mountainsides. Godi was verdingt when he was eleven years old and at fifteen was committed to the Waldau Psychiatric Clinic where he spent a year undergoing electric shock treatment for enuresis. In his early twenties, Godi began dating Gertrud, a young widow with two small children; within three months, he was summoned to an interview with social services, where a panel of four administrators informed him that, unless he married this young woman, both she and her children would be sent to institutions. Reluctantly, he agreed.

In spite of the appalling abuse Godi experienced, both as a child and later as an adult, his determination enabled him to gain professional qualifications and sufficient savings to start his own painting and decorating firm. He is an accomplished artist, poet and wood-carver and a man of great sweetness and integrity. As we said goodbye at the bus stop in Brienz, we heard the unmistakeable moan of an alphorn calling from across the valley and by nightfall Godi had sent us a new poem with reflections of our day on the Ballenberg.

Later that year I travelled to Bern to see Scharli and to visit an exhibition at the Kaefigturm entitled: 'Verdingkinder – Portraits by Peter Klaunzer'. The idea behind the project was to pay homage not only to the twenty-five men and women whose photographs shaped the exhibition, but also to dignify the hundreds and thousands of former Heim and Verdingkinder who had died in recent years. The sentence that accompanied Charles Probst's picture was: *I wanted to kill myself* and I asked Scharli what, as an adult, had kept him from making another attempt on his life. He replied that having been told he was worthless and would never amount to anything, he was determined to prove people wrong. He had always relied on himself, trusted only himself and never depended on others to provide him with anything, least of all a sense of his own worth.

Scharli explained that what is important to him is not the compensation money. His hope is that the stories of the Verdingkinder will be recorded in the history books to be read by future generations of Swiss schoolchildren. That is the legacy he and others wish to leave behind because, as he pointed out, the money will soon be gone, as will the school groups passing through the Ballenberg and the Kaefigturm.

Both my grandfathers, Ernst and Harry, were foot soldiers; one was fighting a war against poverty, the other a war against the Kaiser. Policy-makers debate strategy in ivory towers far removed from the fields of battle and deliver imperfect visions, seen through a glass darkly. It is men like Harry and Ernst, physically present on the front line, taking lives and taking children, who are left with the wounds and scars, indelibly engraved on their bodies and in their hearts. For the Verdingkinder the day they were forcibly removed from their homes is a defining memory. Many remain mistrustful of policemen, of the men who took them away from their families, their identities, their childhoods and, above all, their mothers.

Ernst worked as a policeman during a thirty-year period that spanned the First World War, the Depression of the 1930s and the early years of WWII. He would have been both witness and player in this field of human heartbreak, contractually obliged to remove children from their families for the greater social good. In 1933 when my mother was sewing ball gowns and reciting French poetry at her finishing school in Yverdon, hundreds of thousands of people in Switzerland were living lives of utter wretchedness and desolation.

Ernst was gentle and loving and my mother described him as 'the truest, kindest man in all the world'. I wonder how he made the transition every morning, climbing into his policeman's uniform and going out to meet the world with a rattling sabre and a flexing muscle. A change of career would have been difficult in such economically challenged times, and it was too late by then for a move to America.

My grandmother, Rosa Gilomen, was descended from Huguenots, French Protestants who, like my Irish Catholic ancestors, suffered torture and persecution in their homeland. Following the revocation of the Edict of Nantes by the Catholic King, Louis XIV in 1685, Huguenots, like my ancestor Pierre Guillaume who later adopted the more Germanic sounding Gilomen, were forbidden either to practise their faith or leave the country. Twenty-two thousand Huguenots defied him, and left France for Switzerland, risking imprisonment and execution. Men were sent as galley slaves to the French fleet, women were confined to convents and children were forcibly removed from their parents and baptised into the Catholic faith. Reformed Protestants believed that salvation lay not in the hands of priests but in people's individual rights to interpret scripture for themselves. Like Irish Catholics, French Protestant Huguenots were prepared to sacrifice their lives for their passionately held beliefs and convictions.

My grandmother had the build of a matron but the aura of a baroness. Her manner was gracious and confident and even with her limited grasp of English, she charmed the birds out of the trees when she visited Lea and Peter in England. Rosa had a razor-sharp mind and she was highly ambitious. Lea was her project and Rosa's mission was to raise her daughter to the sky-scraping heights of her own imagination. She was in absolute service to the idea of making Lea happy and, like King Midas, she believed that money offered the best guarantee for happiness.

In 1939, at the age of twenty-two, Lea met Hans Balmer at a dance in Bern. Two weeks later, World War II broke out and all able-bodied men were mobilised to the borders in order to defend the country from a possible German invasion.

Switzerland, with its long history of neutrality, did not send its soldiers into active service, but its geographical position at the heart of Europe meant that for six years the Swiss were sitting ducks, at risk of invasion from all directions. Daily life in the Swiss Army was, for the most part, rather dull but the seemingly futile manoeuvres had to be carefully balanced against the very real possibility of a German invasion. As Hitler marched onward, many feared that Switzerland, like its neighbour Austria, would be annexed into the federal state of Germany.

Lea's relationship with Hans developed against a backdrop of instability and urgency. Their love grew, as did their sense of belonging to something higher and deeper than the circumstances that separated them. One day, they promised each other, when the war was over, they would marry, raise a family and live a happy life. They gave each other a sense of purpose and even though, for many years, Hans only came home on leave, Lea waited patiently and she loved wholeheartedly. I know very little about Hans Balmer; my mother rarely mentioned him, but when she did she sounded wistful rather than bitter. My father, however, was venomous in his diaries, referring to Balmer as: *a coward and a bastard; a man who deserves a whipping.*

In 1985, I moved to Switzerland to live with Stephan. He and I had first met when he was a student at my parents' English Language school. I applied for a position as Head of English at the College of Commerce and Industry in Biel, where the Principal was a man named Hans Baumer. At the time I was unaware of the difference in spelling of the two surnames and I sat through the interview wondering whether, in some alternative universe, he and I might have been siblings rather than total strangers. I even considered the possibility that the interview might be a pretext and that at some point during our conversation he would mention his father and ask me if I was Lea Kummer's daughter. He didn't, but he did offer me the job.

During the week I was in Adelboden, I spent a day in Biel at the offices of *The Tagblatt*, looking through old newspapers in the hope of finding something relevant to Lea's early life. My journey through the decades brought me to 1967 and Hans Balmer's obituary. In the photograph he is wearing aviator sunglasses and smoking a pipe. He looks rather dashing, but it is hard to get the sense of a man whose eyes you cannot see. I learnt that Hans spent four years as a teacher before being called up for military duty in 1939. After the war he went into business where he was extremely successful. He had *an impeccable character and a gracious personality*, was a member of the Lions Club and enjoyed spending time with his wife and children.

So, Hans was a teacher? Just like my Dad. Just like me.

In my experience, teaching in Switzerland, rather like policing, is a worthy profession. At the college in Biel, my university degree offered me a high level of pay and I was allocated my own office. Whenever I wrote test papers or invigilated examinations, I was paid overtime. Once a year I taught intensive courses, run by the Bernese Teachers Association, offering advanced language skill training to Swiss teachers of English. All this provided me with a certain gravitas. As a teacher, I was respected, even admired but I was not envied. I will never, for example, be invited to join the Lions Club, nor will my obituary notice describe me as a successful business-woman.

My grandfather, Ernst, died of a heart attack in 1943, or so my mother told me. When I was nineteen, however, Dad accidentally let slip that Ernst had committed suicide. He'd been accused of stealing money and had wished to avoid a scandal:

'He shot himself or maybe he was hit by a train?' my father offered rather vaguely. The subject wasn't mentioned again and ten years went by before I found the courage to ask Mum about her father's death.

The fact that I was incapable of addressing this issue with my mother accentuated our already troubled relationship. I felt betrayed and angry as I fought the elephant in the room, ignoring my mother's sadness as I thrashed a path through my own. I spoke to my aunt, who told me that Ernst had had to keep up with Rosa's grand ambitions, which would have been impossible on a policeman's salary, so yes, she thought he had taken the money.

I remember the day I finally asked Mum about her father's suicide. She was sitting in a Lloyd loom chair, darning socks and, almost without warning, we found ourselves at the lip of the precipice: 'Why did you never tell me the truth about your father?' I asked her. It was as if she'd known the question was coming: 'I was ashamed,' she replied quietly. Then I asked my really difficult question, hoping I could catch the truth as it escaped through the look on her face: 'Did he steal the money, Mum?'

Without flinching, she looked me straight in the eye and said: 'Absolutely not.'

I accepted my mother's version of the truth and from that day forward our relationship became gentler and more loving. A few months later we were having tea together at a cafe in Adelboden. I was working as a regression therapist at the time and Mum said to me: 'I don't know what exactly it is you do, darling, but I can see that it makes you happy and so I'm happy too'. I felt touched, mindful of how many such moments she and I had lost as a result of the anger that had crowded my heart and the grief that had choked hers.

Suicide in Switzerland is a major public health concern. Until 2007, the Swiss Army allowed men to store their firearms and bullets at home. The law has now changed and ammunition must be returned to the arsenal following each military service rotation. I once wrote down the names of all the people I knew who had committed suicide; I reached a total of nineteen, sixteen of whom were Swiss. The shadow of suicide and the impulse to follow a loved one into death can travel great distances in a family. Occasionally, when my mother's immediate circumstances and her past memories collided with particular force, she would threaten to take her own life. The words were spoken to my father, but I heard them too and I would worry. When I was twelve, I spent three months at school in Switzerland and our teacher, Frau Ruprecht, would end each day with a story, often intended as a parable. One afternoon, she told us about a little girl who, cross with her mother one morning, left for school without saying goodbye. During the day her mother died, although how and why was not made clear. The moral of the story was that we should always hug our mothers before we left for school, so we wouldn't feel worse than was absolutely necessary should she die while we were gone. As I couldn't hug my mother, I decided to write to her every day. She kept all my letters, poems and drawings in an old leather valise that had belonged to Aunt Bertha, so perhaps they served their purpose after all.

I wonder what the policemen who came to my grandmother's house that August night told her – that Ernst had been struck by a train or fatally wounded by a bullet? Rosa kept her head as the scandal of a senior policeman's suicide spread across town. The obituary she wrote for the newspaper was dignified and gave the impression that her husband had simply slipped away in the night. After the funeral she published a note of thanks for the flowers and kind words offered by Ernst's colleagues at the Police Department and the town council.

I wonder whether my grandfather left a note, strategically placed, so that his colleagues would be sure to find it when they arrived at the scene? What do you do with a suicide note once you've read it? Do you throw it away or do you keep it so you can read the words over and over again, and wonder what on earth you missed and what you could have done differently? When a loved one dies after a long illness, in an accident or of old age, there is sadness and heartbreak, but the feelings are less contaminated. Suicide leaves those left behind nursing complex emotions, including guilt, longing, confusion, regret and anger.

In January of 2017 Dan and I attended the funeral service of Aloka, a former Buddhist monk who took his own life. I first met Aloka in 2007. A group of us were on a woodland walk that day and Aloka told me about his life in Zimbabwe, growing up in a family of evangelical Christians who considered his conversion to Buddhism to be a monumental betrayal. In the final week of his life, those close to him recognised that he was struggling. They did everything they could to support him, but in the end, however much Aloka was loved, his heart was broken. As one friend poignantly said in his eulogy: 'Aloka is to be commended for his courage in managing to stay alive for sixty years and three days'.

The suicide of a loved one, especially a parent, is a defining moment. Before August 6th 1943, life was in easy reach of my mother's fingertips and the world was her oyster. That night, a visible line was drawn in the sand and the promises life had made her began to drift, slowly but inexorably, to some distant horizon.

During WWII my grandfather was stationed at the border, protecting Switzerland from a German invasion. His duty, it turned out, was not only to keep the Nazis at bay, but also to prevent Jewish refugees from entering the country. In October 1938, Switzerland, in conjunction with the German government in Berlin, took the decision to stamp Jewish passports with a red 'J', thereby enabling the border guards to quickly identify and deny entry to Jewish refugees. In 1942 the Swiss border was closed to all but political refugees. In a confidential letter circulated to the Police Department, it was stressed that refugees, defined purely in terms of race or religion, for example, Jews, were not to be considered as political refugees.

On August 20th an article published in a Basel newspaper described harrowing scenes that were taking place on the Swiss border. Desperate men, women and children, suffering from exhaustion and starvation after long journeys on foot across occupied territory were reported to be clinging to the legs of Swiss policemen, begging to be granted asylum. Some refugees were physically dragged back across the border and handed over to German guards. The Police Department's response was to issue a press statement, declaring that the majority of these people were not refugees in the legal sense and it was entirely untrue that they were being severely punished on their return to Germany.

There was, however, a resistance movement in Switzerland

that chose to ignore government policy. Paul Grueninger, Head of the St Gallen Police Department, pre-dated refugee applications, which enabled those who had already arrived in the country to avoid being deported back to the German Reich. He wrote letters to the director of Dachau, then a labour camp, inviting Jewish people to Switzerland and he continued to allow refugees into the country even after a total ban had been imposed.

In May 1939, Grueninger was dismissed from his post, accused of falsifying documents and using Police Department money to buy railway tickets for Jewish refugees. Grueninger's pension was declared invalid; he and his family were evicted from their apartment and government ministers called for him to be committed to a psychiatric clinic. In the bars of Switzerland the gossip and speculation around the Grueninger case continued for decades, as many insisted that he had benefited financially from those he helped. In 1995, more than two decades after his death, Captain Grueninger was finally exonerated. 'The Jewish Foundation for the Righteous', subsequently reported that he had saved the lives of more than three thousand Jewish refugees.

I will probably never know for sure whether my grandfather was a thief or not. Perhaps he appropriated Police Department funds in order to buy a railway ticket for a Jewish family or maybe he accepted money from a grateful refugee. Ernst would have followed the case against Paul Grueninger and understood the certain fate that awaited him: dismissal, the loss of his pension and a life of shame and poverty. After many difficult years on the frontline of the Biel police force, where he followed government directives to remove children from their families,

Ernst was sent to the border where he witnessed unspeakable human horror and brutality. By 1942, policemen at the Swiss border were indistinguishable, in the eyes of Jewish refugees, from the Schutzstaffel officers of the Third Reich. Both heralded certain death.

In terms of the Verdingkinder, there might have been a glimmer of hope that these children would learn, over time, to bury the grief of their early separation from home and family and grow up to become hard-working citizens who could provide a better life for their own children. For the Jewish refugees, however, there was no hope of salvation, no better life in sight. One Basel newspaper made the observation that each rejection was tantamount to murder.

I would give anything to hear a Swiss cowbell or to see my mother's face again
Unnamed Swiss immigrant to Wisconsin

Elise and Bertha Kummer, my grandfather's half-sisters, were eight and ten years old when their mother died and it seems likely that they were 'verdingt'. In 1895, the two young women sailed from Rotterdam to New York where they boarded a train to Chicago and on to Wisconsin. For most emigrants, leaving their homeland was not a choice but a necessity, driven by hunger and poverty.

Four years after arriving in the Midwest, Elise married the German-born Carl Fritz and they moved to Madison. Carl was a carpenter and in 1901 he founded the Fritz Construction Company which went on to build some of the city's best known public buildings. In 1932 President Hoover invited Mr Fritz to the White House where he was honoured for his work. Elise and Carl later moved to Shorewood Hills, where they lived in a fine house overlooking the Blackhawk Country Club. Elise christened their first born Fidelia Helvetia (Faithful Switzerland) and spoke Swiss German to her as she was growing up. Fidelia attended the University of Wisconsin and later married George Tiernan, a successful Irish Catholic entrepreneur. Elise and Carl did not approve of their Roman Catholic son-in-law and chose not to attend the wedding.

Perhaps Elise, aware that her little brother Ernst was at risk of being 'verdingt', wished to provide him with a home and a future. She could offer him a good life in America, growing up alongside his little niece, Fidelia and learning a trade at the Fritz Construction Company. He would also have been a link to all that she had left behind and someone to whom she could speak in her native language. In spite of her great wealth, Elise never returned to her homeland. Aunt Bertha moved to New Glarus, Wisconsin, a town of chalets and umlauts, yodel music and pork products.

If I believe, as I do, that Ernst did not steal money to finance his wife's grand plans for their daughter, then perhaps I should question where the money might have come from. Even after my grandfather died, Rosa somehow managed to keep the ball in the air and I reflect on the possibility that I might have done her an injustice. As a family, we have always been savers rather than spenders. Like my mother, I experience excessive anxiety around the possibility of falling into poverty. I have no clear sense of how much money I might need in order to dispel this fear because I am very adept at imagining increasingly extreme financial catastrophes for myself. My solution, therefore, is to keep saving. It may be that my grandmother was a saver too.

In my twenties, I first had the idea of buying property in Arizona, and I began saving every two franc coin that came my way in change. I was in no hurry, as I realised that I had half a life to live before I could turn my dream into reality. Perhaps this planning for a good cause, this unshakeable belief in something that can be achieved with steady intention is a quality I inherited from my grandmother ?

The Other Side of the Mountain is a film which tells the true story of Jill Kinmont, a downhill skier and favourite to represent the United States at the 1956 Winter Olympics. She suffered a bad fall during a race and damaged her spinal cord, leaving her paralysed from the neck down. In a scene at the beginning of the film, Jill remarks to her friend Audra Jo that she wonders whether she was born lucky, or whether she is using up all her luck at once. My mother once asked a similar question. Perhaps, like Jill Kinmont, she had a premonition that one day her lucky life would come to an abrupt end, through no fault of her own. In the summer of 1975, I sat in the Fox Bay cinema in Whitefish Bay, Wisconsin, the tears rolling down my face, as I watched Jill's handsome skier boyfriend, unable to come to terms with her injuries, walk out of the rehabilitation clinic, never to return. I couldn't understand why the story affected me so deeply. Eventually I concluded that, as a skier myself, I feared that I too could be horribly damaged in a skiing accident. Jill Kinmont died in 2012 and according to her obituary in the New York Times she graduated with a BA in German and became a teacher.

In the weeks and months following her father's suicide, Hans was Lea's still point in a world that made no sense. My grandmother, managing disgrace and financial instability, would have felt relieved to know that her daughter had landed such a good catch; Hans was an officer and a gentleman. He would take care of Lea. He would take care of them both.

Hans Balmer, however, was also ambitious and, like many young men of his generation, his early twenties had been restricted by circumstance and wasted by war. In 1944 Hans was offered an opportunity he couldn't refuse. The owner of Kellenberg AG, a building firm in Biel, anticipating a period of significant growth in the post-war years, invited Hans to become the company's managing director. The only blot on Balmer's copybook was his relationship with the young woman whose father had tragically taken his own life. So, just like in the fairy tales, Mr Kellenberg requested one small favour in return for his generous offer. In 1944 Hans Balmer left teaching for business and he left my mother to marry Mr Kellenberg's nineteen-year-old daughter, Kathy.

My own heart was first broken in 1979. My relationship with Jack lasted a matter of weeks, and I always knew that he was still in love with his ex-girlfriend, but I was utterly captivated by this alpha male who rode a motorbike across campus, was on the university rowing team and had ambitions to join the British Army's Special Forces. When he went back to the girl who later became his wife, ironically also called Kathy, my heart went into a tailspin. I was completely undone, although I worked hard to appear composed and unaffected by the split.

When I heard that I had acquired a reputation as someone who 'eats men for breakfast', I was secretly pleased. I was seen as tough, not like some jilted girls I knew, distraught and showing a vulnerability I found contemptible. I went home for the weekend and talked to Mum about my broken heart. She was unsympathetic: I must have known that he would return to Kathy and I should have been more careful and less trusting. She was right, of course, and today I realise that she was speaking to her own twenty-something self, a young woman who had also loved injudiciously. At the time, however, I felt slapped rather than soothed. I wanted my mother to hold my broken heart in the palm of her hand and to speak gently and lovingly to it. I wanted her to hug me and tell me that I was worthy of love and that I would find a good man someday. Six months later, I repeated the experience with a boy who also left me to marry his ex-girlfriend. This time, I made sure I didn't like him quite as much, which meant I didn't mind quite as much either.

I never saw Jack again after he graduated at the end of that academic year. My heart grew back together again, leaving just a small scar as a reminder to exercise more caution in the future. My mother, however, lived with the daily possibility of bumping into Hans or his young wife every time she stepped out of the house.

When my grandfather committed suicide in 1943, Lea was working as a dental assistant in Biel. She had been at Dr Guebeli's practice for three years and he was a source of great comfort and stability in her life. She was still working for him when, in 1944, Hans ended their five-year relationship.

In 1968, I fell down a flight of steps at my aunt and uncle's house and cracked my two front teeth. Dr Guebeli had already retired but, as a favour to my mother, he agreed to see me. It didn't look good, he said. The teeth would need to be pulled. I remember the heated discussion that subsequently took place between my mother and her brother. Uncle Bobi said I should be seen by a practising dentist, not by one who no longer had a license or a full set of dental equipment. My mother insisted he was the best dentist there was and she trusted him completely. I found Dr Guebeli a little unnerving. He was certainly very old and, unlike our dentist in Folkestone, he had no books or toys or kindly assistant to hand him his instruments. Having pulled my two front teeth, Dr Guebeli sent me to Dr Beguin because, he explained to my mother, the technicalities of manufacturing a dental plate were beyond his scope as a dentist in retirement. Dr Beguin spoke only French, but I understood enough to realise that he didn't agree with Dr Guebeli's assessment and in his view my teeth should never have been pulled. 'Too late now,' he told my mother. For the next twelve years I lived with a dental plate that I could click like castanets against the roof of my mouth, and take out at night like an old lady's dentures.

In 1975 I was in Milwaukee, staying with our Kummer relations, when one of the supporting clips on the plate snapped. This was a serious disaster for a sixteen-year-old with a big date coming up the following night. Aunt Gloria made an emergency appointment with the dentist who declared he could make me a very handsome set of new teeth but, they didn't come cheap. I put in a long-distance call to my mother and was surprised by how quickly she agreed: even consulting my father didn't appear to be necessary. I had to wait a week for my new teeth and in the meantime, Dr Froehlich suggested I buy some dental adhesive. At the lake barbeque the following night, I had to keep slipping off into the beach grass to powder my plate with denture grip. The boy turned out to be rather a disappointment; not so my American teeth, which served me well until I was fitted with a bridge at the age of twenty-two.

In August of 1967 Dr Guebeli's son committed suicide. He was twenty-two years old and his obituary in the *Bieler Tagblatt* makes no attempt to hide the fact that he took his own life. Lea had a tremendous feeling of loyalty to her former employer and when Hansjuerg died, my mother was able to offer Dr Guebeli empathy and compassion. She of all people understood what it felt like when someone you love with all your heart chooses death over life, chooses death over you. Three days after Hansjuerg Guebeli's death, Hans Balmer died of a heart attack. My mother's commitment to Dr Guebeli and his to my mother suddenly took on an even greater magnitude. A few months later, in the Spring of 1968, when Lea was faced with the trauma of her little girl's smashed teeth, it would have made complete sense to call her old friend Dr Guebeli who was, after all, a dentist and a man who knew all about trauma. Perhaps even more importantly, Mum trusted him.

In 1946 Lea was diagnosed with pulmonary tuberculosis and Rosa arranged for her to go to a sanatorium in Davos.

For more than a century, Davos was considered to be the most exclusive health resort in Europe. Popular with artists and aristocrats, it was immortalised by Thomas Mann in his novel *The Magic Mountain*. Before the Revolution of 1917, the Russians hosted lavish concerts with gypsy choirs and bala-laika orchestras. They served their guests caviar and vodka, and butterflies imported from Africa were released into the ball-room where they flew among the palm trees. The last Romanov spent the final three years of his life at the Schatzalp sanato-rium, dying in 1942 at the age of 50.

A stay at a sanatorium could last for months, even years, so those who came to the alpine town needed deep pockets and plenty of time on their hands. So where did the money come from to finance my mother's year long period of recovery? Aunt Bertha probably made a contribution and, according to Aunty Heidi, Bobi donated a percentage of his monthly salary to his sister's sanatorium fund.

In photographs of that period, Lea smiles at the camera against a backdrop of bone-white architecture and towering, snow-capped mountains. I had always associated my mother's experiences in Davos with my father's life and times aboard the QEII, as he travelled back and forth across the Atlantic during his five years in America. I imagined glamorous friends, clandestine liaisons and dancing until daybreak. If you felt like a rest from all the excitement, you could lie on deck or on your honeycomb balcony and gaze at the icebergs or the mountains. It all seemed impossibly carefree.

The Alpina sanatorium was converted to a hotel after the war and in 2017 I decided to spend a few days there. I made a special point of requesting a room with a balcony and mountain views. When I arrived, however, the manager explained that the hotel was full of delegates, in town to attend the European Conference on Antennas and Propagation and he couldn't, therefore, give me a room with a honeycomb balcony. 'But,

I asked for one. It's there under Special Requests,' I pleaded, hoping for a miracle. A tall man with an Eastern European accent came into the lobby as we were discussing my difficulty and, for a moment, I considered throwing myself at his mercy, in the hope that he might agree to swap rooms: 'You'll be gone all day, listening to plenary speeches on electromagnetic wave theory. I'm here following in the footsteps of my poor, sick, broken-hearted mother who was unutterably miserable, but… at least she had a south-facing room with a balcony'.

And then, it dawned on me. I had come to Davos in pursuit of some romantic notion of beauty in tragedy. I had imagined sitting on my balcony with its frosted glass partitions, drinking a glass of Vetliner and watching the full moon rise over the Parsenn. When Lea arrived in Davos in 1946, she was seriously ill and had suffered terrible loss. She was thirty years old, financially dependent on her family and it was not known whether her illness was curable. Doctors often warned their female patients that they should expect to remain unmarried and childless as a result of tuberculosis. Lea's photographs show a smiling young woman, linking arms with cheerful young men, but her writings testify to a much bleaker and more desolate state of mind.

My father read a great many books during his convalescence in Belfast and my mother kept a poetry journal during her year in Davos. One untitled poem of an unknown author in her collection describes a broken heart buried in a subterranean vault. The poet expresses his hope that one day an enchanted figure will pass by and release his heart from its stone prison. As a child, I loved to visit Madame Tussaud's where Sleeping Beauty was my favourite exhibit. I knew there was an air pump in her chest which made it look as though she was breathing, but I was always on the alert, just in case she suddenly woke up, rubbed her lovely blue eyes and turned them towards me. I wanted to be there when her hundred years of solitude finally ended and her prince in shining armour carried her out of the waxwork museum and into a land of happily ever after.

Davos is the cradle of renewed hope, the valley of death and of rebirth
Wiktorowa, a Russian patient writing in the Davoser Boten, 1910

In 1887 there were three thousand consumptives convalescing in the sanatoria of Davos. The dry, thin air in this high altitude, south-facing, wind-sheltered resort was considered to be the equivalent of breathing champagne. Robert Koch's discovery in 1882 that tuberculosis was a virus, rather than a hereditary illness, put paid to the myths that TB, like insanity, was caused by nerves and a weak will. The theory then developed that it was a disease of the urban poor, synonymous with a lack of hygiene and immoral behaviour, until this too was discredited. TB, however, because it was highly contagious, remained a disease that caused intense social discomfort and many sufferers left home in shame and secret to convalesce.

Over a prolonged period air had been leaking out of my mother's right lung and eventually it collapsed. It is notoriously difficult to diagnose TB because its symptoms, which include listlessness and a lack of appetite, are similar to many other conditions. My mother's tuberculosis was misdiagnosed as depression, believed to have been induced by the tragic events that had recently occurred in her life.

Before the arrival of streptomycin in the late 1940s, being cured of TB depended on developing personal qualities associated with self-sacrifice. The strict regimes imposed by the sanatoria were, in part, designed to encourage willpower. In a letter written to Peter in July 1947, Lea says: *I am feeling well. I lie obediently on my balcony and do 'almost' everything the doctor tells me to.* Every hour of the day was managed by the ringing of bells, alerting patients to move to their next treatment. Those who were not bed-ridden followed a carefully mapped-out walking schedule, combined with long rest periods on sheltered balconies and frequent, high-calorie meals. This tightly-organised routine was also a way of diffusing boredom. Many considered themselves to be prisoners rather than patients, albeit ones incarcerated for no crime they had committed and forced to endure sentences of unspecified duration.

Tuberculosis saved my mother's life. It enabled her to escape the open prison of her hometown where she had been shamed by scandals not of her own making. The 'Zauberberg' offered her a new beginning away from the muted whisperings and pitying glances of the Biel gossips. Rosa's hope was that Davos would also offer up a suitable husband for her dear 'Leneli'.

As I lay in bed that first night under a snowdrift of feathers, I imagined my mother, spitting into her 'Blauer Heinrich', feeling lonely and fearful in her tubercular cell.

By 8.30 the following morning, the delegates had left for the convention centre, and I was able to explore the Alpina undisturbed. The lobby was charmingly old-fashioned with floral curtains, copper kettles, soft armchairs and a wooden telephone cubicle containing a rack of directories. The upper corridors were lined with wide panelled doors and fitted with large locks. The wallpaper was the colour of whipped mustard and scattered along the walls, like unsightly pimples, were bells – little cracked wooden discs with ivory centres. We had bells just like them at home in Flowergate. When I wanted Mum to come and wash the soap out of my hair, instead of shouting to her, a Swiss habit which my father deplored, I would press the little ivory button on the wall of the bathroom and, like Aladdin's djinn, Mum would appear from the other side of nowhere.

Later that morning I made my way to Cafe Schneider on The Promenade for a slice of my mother's favourite 'Nusstorte', walnuts dripping in liquid caramel and folded into a short-bread crust. Davos today is a curious blend of architectural styles. Some of the larger sanatoria have been converted into Wellness palaces and many of the glass-bunker, cruise ship-style residences are owned by Russians and Germans, often descendants of former sanatoria patients. The apartments are in huge demand, sold off-plan, for sums way beyond the financial reach of local people. They are then left unoccupied for ten months of the year, jilted for other, more seasonally suitable homes. The Alpina, I subsequently discovered, had recently been sold to a property developer, who had plans to convert the old hotel into luxury flats.

I paid a visit to the Davos Documentation Library where Dr Nelson, the Museum curator, and Dr Flury, Head of the Davos Medical Museum, were busy on a project archiving life in Davos in the 1940s. I offered them my own small selection of pictures and stories, and discovered that the young man in military uniform in one of my mother's photographs was a US soldier, one of many sent to Davos to convalesce in the aftermath of WWII. I learnt too that Execution Way, where the Alpina is situated, was the location for public hangings in the late 1800s. The Etania, a large A-framed building immediately behind the hotel is the former Jewish sanatorium. In 1946 a group of Buchenwald survivors arrived in Davos with a box containing the ashes and bones of concentration camp victims. These were later interred in the Jewish cemetery on the outskirts of the town.

I walked back to the hotel along Thomas-Mann-Weg. Davos was initially delighted by all the attention it received following the publication of *The Magic Mountain* in 1924, but this turned to dissociation from what was subsequently seen as criticism and ridicule. I passed the Villa am Stein where Robert Louis Stevenson completed *Treasure Island* and where Arthur Conan Doyle and Thomas Mann had lived during their winters in Davos. The building had a mournful, neglected feel to it and I noticed a flag with a clenched fist punching a swastika hanging in one of the windows.

After dinner I sat in the lounge of the hotel amongst the palms and the lace runners and began reading Yvonne Schmid's book: *Davos –eine Geschichte fuer sich.*

The end of Russian imperial rule and a worldwide economic downturn marked the beginning of troubled times for Davos and it was the Germans who rescued the town from financial ruin. Wilhelm Gustloff, head of the National Socialist Party in Switzerland, lived in Davos and began screening German TB patients, not for the weakness of their lungs but for the strength of their allegiance to the Fuehrer. The 'Hakenkreuz' flew over the four German-owned sanatoria and Gustloff ordered a boycott of all shops and cafes that were anti-Hitler, including the Cafe Schneider. The town became known as 'Hitlerbad', and a call to the Swiss government to expel Gustloff was denied. Aunt Bertha was living in Davos at this time.

In January 1936 David Frankfurter, a young man from Bern, travelled to Davos and shot Gustloff dead in retaliation for the persecution of Jews in Germany. Hitler used his death as a vehicle for a massive propaganda drive and streets, squares, bridges and even an ocean liner were named after Gustloff. Ironically, 'The Wilhelm Gustloff' was sunk in 1945 by a Russian submarine and nine thousand people lost their lives. It was the worst disaster at sea in recorded history. As a point of comparison, one thousand five hundred people died on the Titanic.

In August 1940 in spite of closing the borders to Jewish refugees, the Swiss government continued to allow German TB patients to convalesce in Davos. In 1945 it was said that the town was full of healthy Nazis, feigning tuberculosis in order to avoid being repatriated. A further topic of controversy was the arrival in 1946 of Jewish refugee children whose parents had been killed in the concentration camps. The shopkeepers and hotel managers were keen to resume making money as quickly as possible and vetoed the arrival of orphaned Jewish children. Finally, a group of young people destined for Palestine were admitted to Davos. They weren't given the opportunity to relax after their nightmare experiences, but were put to work cutting grass and milking cows, in preparation, it was declared, for becoming good farmers in their new homeland.

My mother arrived in Davos just a few months before the

Jewish refugees. She and the survivors of the Buchenwald concentration camp lived next door to each other on Execution Way. Perhaps she got to know some of them as she took her daily walk along the footpath that runs past the Etania sanatorium? Perhaps, as she sat enjoying a slice of Nusstorte at the no-longer-boycotted Cafe Schneider, she unwittingly made friends with some friendly Germans – Nazis in sheep's clothing? Rosa's indefatigable vision and unfailing sense of purpose were finally to bear fruit as Lea did indeed find herself a husband in Davos. He was not a Jewish refugee, an undercover Nazi or even a US airman. He was an Anglo-Irish History student at St John's College, Cambridge who had come to Davos in the hope of saving his mother's life.

Chapter Three

'He loves me. He loves me not.'

The Daisy Oracle

Peter O'Connell and his mother Grace arrived at The Alpina in September of 1946 and following Peter's return to Cambridge, Grace and Lea became friends and confidantes. The two women had a lot in common: they were both homesick, the illness they shared was socially isolating and potentially incurable, and their first loves were living with new partners. It was a powerful blend of shared circumstances.

Grace was already very sick when she arrived in Davos and by March of the following year, she had returned to England. In a letter dated May 3rd, 1947, Lea writes to Peter in German:

My poor, dear Peter,
The news of your dear mother's death affected me deeply.
I know how much she yearned to be back in her beloved
England. Twice I started a letter to tell you about her home-
sickness and beg you to come and fetch her, but I didn't
want to alarm you. I was extremely fond of your mother and
yesterday, I put a letter in the post to her. When it arrives,
it might be better if you didn't open it. I was so hopeful and
so happy when I wrote it; reading it could only cause you
pain. I wish I were beside you. I wouldn't speak, I would
just be present to you and your breaking heart. Oh Peter, I
understand what you are going through, what it means to say

goodbye forever. Only four years ago, and without warning, my dear father died and then someone else was taken from me; not into death but into life. I tell you this so you will know that I understand your grief in its infinite space and its boundless depth. I have been through it too. Everything seems so black. You feel amazed, even offended by those around you who are able to express their joy. I encourage you, dear Peter, not to despair. You have lost a lot, but you did so much to make your mother happy. She was devoted to you and I feel sure that her last thoughts were of you. Remember this, dear Peter, when your longing for the dead threatens to tear you apart. And you still have your father. I am convinced that God and Life still have gifts and great blessings to offer you (translated from German)

On June 20th Lea writes again to congratulate Peter on his degree and to suggest that he leave London and seek a position in Switzerland: *Oh Peter, I forgot to tell you that Mother offered me, as a birthday present, a holiday in England next Spring, if I am fit enough, which I hope I shall be. It would be lovely to see you and dear old England again. But I shall miss dear Mrs O'Connell very much. She wanted to show me the countryside and all the pretty spots.* In the margin, Peter has written the word *Marriage!*

In December of 1983, Lea conceived of an equally transparent match-making scheme for me and Stephan. He had spent six months at The School of English Studies, Folkestone, and in spite of her best efforts, my mother had failed to persuade me down from London to meet him. With only twenty-four hours before Stephan returned to Switzerland, she invited him to my father's birthday party. He arrived at the appointed time, only to discover that it was not, as he had been led to believe, a large and casual drinks party but an intimate supper for close friends. Mum had already orchestrated a day in the Bernese Alps on my behalf, having told Stephan how much I liked skiing. Not wishing to be ungrateful to Mrs O'Connell, the woman whose skis his own father had carried when she was a young girl, Stephan obliged. In an attempt to lure him back to Folkestone, Mum subsequently offered him a two-week English course, all expenses paid. At this point, everything went a bit pear-shaped for my mother as, unbeknown to her, Stephan had an Italian girlfriend at SES and I had a boyfriend in London.

Apollo astronauts have spoken about the difference between darkness and blackness when looking into space from the surface of the moon. The word dark describes a lack of light, as in 'It's too dark to read', whereas the word black is defined by a complete absence of light. Eugene Cernan described it as an infinity of space and time. During Lea's convalescence in Davos, she gradually began to move out of blackness and into darkness. In this dark, rather than black place, she was able to distinguish shapes in the shadows, memories of a life lived in love and plenty. In this part of herself, she could imagine the possibility of a happier and healthier future. Lea's life had reached a turning point and her newfound hope lay in the hands of a handsome, scholarly, and slightly troubled Englishman.

My father told me that Grace died alone in a Brighton boarding house and I grew up with the image of my grandmother lying on sweat-soaked sheets in a squalid attic room, a waterfall of blood cascading from her mouth and nostrils as she suffocated to death. She was Verdi's Violetta, without the loving presence of Alfredo. In 2017, I ordered a copy of Grace's death certificate, and was surprised to discover that Harry had been at his estranged wife's bedside when she died. Loving my grandfather as much as I did, I developed an unconscious resentment towards my saintly grandmother. The picture I have of her is indistinct, like a religious icon in a dimly lit chapel. Those who knew Grace, including my mother, described her great beauty and her steady and gentle character. She had a powerful sense of duty and little interest in anything casual or superficial. She married a man who proved to be irreligious and immoral and only her faith in Jesus Christ remained, together with the love she had for her son. Grace took Peter to daily prayer meetings at the Wallington Bible Institute and later enrolled him with the Wallington Crusaders. Harry would have provided no opposition and no alternative point of view.

In 1920, Aunty Dorrie, my grandmother's sister, published a book with the impenetrable title: *Reality, Profession or Possession – Which?*. She speaks to the *cold, indifferent, pleasure-seeking fools who have been inoculated with the devil's deadly poison*. Aunty Dorrie uses the word foolish a lot in her book; it's a word I dislike, because it suggests ignorance and stupidity, traits my father despised. What surprises me about my fundamentalist Christian ancestors is that they considered qualities such as honesty and kindness to be diversions, serving only to encourage a sense of entitlement. In their eyes, those who relied on such lightweight virtues cared more about religion than they did about God.

My father was named after the disciple, Simon Peter, the fisherman from Galilee, who became the Rock of the Church. In her book, Dorrie asks what might have happened had Peter told Jesus that he was a married man with responsibilities, and couldn't simply drop everything for the promise of heavenly riches? He would have been left in the dark is the answer, just like the man who felt unable to give away his earthly wealth and was therefore *destined for a Christless grave, wretched and miserable for he had chosen the shadow and lost the substance.* Just such a man was Harry, Peter's own earthly father who was clearly in pursuit of all the wrong things, chasing stability in the guise of wealth and possessions. Perhaps, little Peter concluded, this was the reason for his father's silence: he had lost his way in the shadows and could no longer retrieve the substance of his life.

In the final chapter of Dorrie's book, she offers a parable of her own invention, entitled 'The Three Ships'.

The first ship is called: *The Fool hath said in his heart, There is no God.* The owner is a man named Beelzebub and his crew are Blasphemy, Lawlessness and Adultery. The second ship is called: *Peace, Peace when there is no Peace*; the captain is Lucifer and the crew are Love-of-Money, Respectability and Seducer. This second vessel is a floating palace, filled with wealthy people, busily recording their good works. When questioned about the need to be 'born again', the passengers reply that there is no need to take the Bible literally. The third ship is called: *The Lord, my Righteousness.* Her captain is Salvation and her crew are Repentance, Faith and Humility. The three ships set sail: the first sinks in a hurricane, the second hits a rock and only *The Lord* reaches its final destination. The soul of a single prosperous businessman is saved, however. He runs up the gangway of the correct ship and is met by his wife who, long ago, had chosen the riches of Christ over the treasures of Egypt.

I wonder whether Dorrie had Grace and her brother-in-law in mind when she included this happy scene? It seems unlikely that my grandfather would have read Dorrie's book and it probably just made Grace sad to be reminded that she and Harry would not be re-united in Heaven.

It is somewhat ironic that Dorrie and Grace were descended from great wealth. Their Turney grandfather owned more than forty properties in East Dulwich and it was the ten Arnold siblings who subsequently inherited his fortune. Perhaps Dorrie stood firm, refusing to be associated with the works of Lucifer, or maybe she accepted the money and invested it in The Wallington Bible Institute?

Peter is a serious and original scholar. He is a person who thinks and feels deeply and has a reflective and sympathetic mind. He is a representative of all that is best in character and intellectual ability.
Frank Thistlewaite, Fellow, St John's College, Cambridge University.

Peter was expected to graduate from Cambridge with a First-Class degree, but his mother's death, a month before his Finals, devastated him. He lost momentum, flunked some of his papers and was awarded an Upper Second. He was a bright young man who had found his way to Cambridge against all odds and he was extremely disappointed in himself. In September of 1947 he began studying for a Teaching Diploma but withdrew from the course due to ill health. In September of 1948 he accepted a teaching position at Highfield, a small élite boys' boarding school in Hampshire, where he was to teach, coach football and run the drama and debating societies. His ultimate goal was to work in a secondary school or in adult education, but first he needed a safe haven and a relatively undemanding job.

I am conscious of deep repressed antagonism towards Dad. Mother's agony is very closely associated with my own distress, and it is not remarkable that I should feel bitter towards the man who caused much of her sorrow. Yet, this resentment towards Dad conflicts with love, and the resultant feeling is one of guilt. I believe this is at the root of my trouble.

In July 1949 Peter sought psychological treatment on the National Health, but discovered that this was only possible if he agreed to be hospitalised. He decided, therefore, to see a psychiatrist and approached his GP for a recommendation: *Dr Bell was rather stupid, saying he could not think why I wanted such treatment. Just because I don't yammer like an idiot, he thinks I am imagining it all.*

After Mum died in 1996, I arranged for Dad to see a psychotherapist, but he stopped attending appointments and told me that he was helping Dr Wilson more than she was helping him. I later learnt that enthusiasm, followed by disillusionment and rejection, was a behaviour pattern Peter had re-enacted with his therapists over the course of many years.

Dr Bendit is like my superiors at Cambridge, too easy going. People seem to be taken in by my facade, not realising that I need a lot of pushing and jerking around. April 1949

It's dreadfully slow. Dr Hind isn't provocative enough. Am beginning to think he isn't the man for my money. I wrote him a 7 page letter criticising his methods. I think a man like Dr Howe would be better. October 1949

In 1985, he received the following letter from his therapist in London:

Dear Mr O'Connell, I suppose that if you see our meetings as pleasurable reminiscing you would be right to stop seeing me. My own feeling is that careful construction of the way the past lives on in the present can be enormously liberating, but you must decide whether or not my approach has anything to offer you. Yours sincerely, Dr Lane.

I was in my late twenties when I first started seeing a psychotherapist, and received mixed reactions from my parents. My mother was horrified, insisting that I wasn't a crazy person and expressing alarm at what her Swiss family would think if they knew. Dad was shocked and said, rather sadly: 'I always thought you were the one thing I'd done right in my life'.

1949 was a difficult year for my grandfather. He had invested a thousand pounds with a man in Harlesden who subsequently vanished without trace. In an effort to recoup some of his money, Harry began placing bets at the London Greyhound stadiums.

Dr Hind encouraged Peter to channel his efforts into expressing appropriate anger towards his father. Lea, however, was of the opinion that Peter should be open with Harry about his feelings of sadness and disappointment.

In his autobiography, *Timebends*, Arthur Miller makes the observation that many successful male writers, including Hemingway, Steinbeck and Whitman, had fathers who were either defeated by life, or whose sons regarded them as failures. Peter's anger masked a longing to impress. He yearned to feel the grip of his father's hand on his shoulder and to experience Harry's pride in his achievements. In 1954 Peter wrote to his father with the news that an article he had written was to be published in an American journal. Harry's response was: *Soon you'll be writing successful crime novels and living in Hawaii with a dolly secretary.* Peter's literary ambitions stretched far beyond the trivia of Father Brown or indeed the clichés of Waikiki Beach. His companion, too, needed to be much more than a secretary; he was searching for a soul mate, a woman who was not only beautiful but well-read, gracious and intelligent.

These boys, whom I taught in my very first term, are blood of my blood and flesh of my flesh, and I feel like Rachel mourning for her first born. July 1948

In post war England, boys' boarding schools were austere, monastic, Christian-led institutions, full of bachelor masters. Peter had a capacity for great love and devotion. God and his father were inaccessible to him, and after his mother died, he chose to dedicate himself to the boys at Highfield. He was quick to recognise signs of struggle and isolation: *I found poor little Havers being attacked by a gang of boys. I put my arm around him to protect him. Tears sprang to my eyes at the tragedy of that poor, suffering, unloved and bewildered creature. How I should love to have my own home to take him to; to adopt him.*

My father believed in self-improvement and was constantly seeking ways to become a better teacher. He taught himself the Greek alphabet and studied the cycles of the moon. During the school holidays, he collected booklets, maps and photographs from the offices of colonial governments, overseas food corporations and church missionary societies: *These will interest the boys and add colour and definition to our geography class.* As a way of helping his pupils understand the difference between fact and opinion, he gathered articles from a selection of newspapers reporting on the same topic. The Headmaster approved of this idea in principle, although he insisted that the Communist 'Daily Worker' be removed from O'Connell's press collection. My father never shied away from controversy and chose to include, in his repertoire, any subject that might engage the boys' minds – from the Kontiki Expedition to Flying Saucers. He taught them about the Catholic Church in the 15th century, read them Robert Scott's journals and, every Trafalgar Day, he talked to them about Admiral Nelson and read relevant excerpts from Shakespeare's plays and Churchill's speeches. When the School Inspectors visited in October of 1949, Mr O'Connell was congratulated on the high quality of his teaching, which they considered to be *very modern*.

At weekends Peter took the boys bug-hunting and black-berry-picking. They cooked fried bread over bonfires and pretended to be 'Red Indians'. In the winter, they had snowball fights on the playing fields and gathered holly for the classroom. On Sunday walks small fingers would slip into the kind master's hand and the older boys would jump on his back. He was also in charge of the school plays, and following a production of *The Stolen Prince*, one master remarked that it was the most polished performance he had ever seen at Highfield. *The boys loved it – that is my main satisfaction* wrote Peter in his diary. At the end of the school year Wheatley burst into tears at the thought of not returning to Mr O'Connell's class in the autumn. His mother, embarrassed by her son's sobbing, told him to pull himself together, but Peter was quick to come to the boy's defence declaring that he had: *an affectionate nature and great courage – a happy combination.*

Internally, however, Peter was struggling: *I am so unable to plan or think ahead that most hours are a real dread to me. Today, I felt controlled and calm, and although the lesson did not go as intended and wandered around atomic fission and Russian slave camps, the eager interest of the boys, my own happy feeling of release and mastery, the easy light-hearted five minutes chatting to them at the end, all indicated that the hour had been a great success. Atherton indeed said later that it was the most interesting geography hour he had ever had.*

My irritation was nearer the surface today. I snapped at the boys and gave many impositions. I have now forgotten to whom I gave them! Another example of my repressed emotion. November 1949.

At the age of twelve, I was sent to Ashford School for Girls. Pupils were divided into four sets according to their abilities in English, Maths and French. I was in the top two sets for

French and English, but relegated to div. four for Maths. My teacher, Miss O'Halloran, was a tiny Irishwoman with a frizzy halo of orange hair, who wore houndstooth suits in winter and rockabilly dresses in summer. Miss O'Halloran and I took an instant dislike to one another, and, as we were destined to move up the school forms together, our relationship deteriorated over the ensuing four years. Her despairing cry, uttered with ever greater frequency was: 'Oh, look at Susan O'Connell, can't you do anything now?'

If pupils were naughty in class, teachers had the right to issue 'a stripe'; similarly if they did well, they might be awarded a star. Every morning, at the end of Assembly, girls with stars and stripes rose from their seats, walked down the aisle, and handed their slips of paper to the Senior Prefect, who delivered them to the headmistress on the stage. If a pupil had been exceptionally wicked, she might be given a double stripe, which invariably resulted in a follow-up meeting with the headmistress. In the unlikely event that a girl accumulated nine stripes during a single term, Ashford School had the right to expel her. One morning, Miss O'Halloran's frustration peaked, and, in a cloudburst of spit and fury, she declared that she was issuing me with three double stripes. The room went silent and we all watched, open-mouthed as she aggressively attacked the stripe book with her fountain pen. I was stunned, but also curious to discover the nature of my misdemeanour, which was noted as: *failure to pay attention in class*. The following morning, I walked up to the front of the assembly hall with my six stripes, and they were duly handed to the headmistress. Miss Thompson flinched, peered down from the stage and in an even voice invited me to visit her study before first period.

She was surprisingly low-key and told me I should listen to Miss O'Halloran in future and pay better attention in Maths. I was puzzled by the leniency of my punishment, which was really just a mild reprimand. Expulsion wasn't even mentioned.

Many years later, I took our daughters to an Ashford School Founders' Day. Polly and Lucy were seven and eight years old at the time, and as my Miss O'Halloran stories were among their favourites, they were particularly keen to meet her. I approached her, rather warily, with the opening remark: 'You probably don't remember me, Miss O'Halloran', but she did. After we'd broken the ice and I'd introduced the girls, I said, a little hesitantly: 'I wasn't very good at Maths, was I, Miss O'Halloran?'. Without missing a beat she replied: 'No, dear, but you were very good at languages'.

Polly and Lucy thought Miss O'Halloran was charming, and I have to admit I thought she was too. Claire O'Halloran died in 2014, and her obituary remembers her as kind, welcoming, full of praise and devoted to her students. Miss O'Halloran, just like the rest of us, was a medley of contradictions, neither a wholly good woman, nor an entirely bad one. Perhaps Claire, like Peter, had imagined a rather different life for herself. A life back in Ireland, married to a young man from Galway with children of her own, children whom she could have raised to be Maths geniuses. On that summer afternoon in 1998, Miss O'Halloran was kind to my children, and by praising rather than shaming me, she included me in her kindness. I shall always be grateful to her for that.

Amongst my father's papers, I discovered a collection of letters addressed to him in America. Written on airmail paper, scrap paper and embossed headed notepaper, they were sent from Highfield School, Eton College and Sandhurst Military Academy. Some of the pages are almost illegible, others are badly stained. All are tender and funny.

I hope you are enjoying life in America. I can imagine you living in a luxurious suite of rooms, and pressing button B for ice cream. (Peter Humphrey)

Dear Mr O'Connell, I went to the dockside to see you off, but as I was late for the boat I did not see you. Did you see me? I waved my green cap. ('Butch' Woolmer).

Mr Lumb(ago) takes us for English. He is very Victorian. We are reading Hamlet, a lovely story. But it is not as good as 12th night. Do posh Americans go around with cigars in their mouths? (Philip Darley)

I hope you like it in the Eton of America. I suppose you know about King George's death. In the middle of writing an essay, we were called to the Headmaster's dining room. When he told us, I jolly nearly fainted. I could not finish my essay after that. (Nicholas Walkinshaw).

I'm terribly sorry I have not written. I have no excuse, Sir. I'm glad you like America. I can just imagine you trekking across the USA wearing one of those sun helmets, cursing the heat and flies. Sorry about messy letter. No excuse. Very bad. Rub out. Do again and see you after six. (John Cox)

In the year following Grace's death, Harry and his new partner, Joyce Allen, moved to a flat near Hyde Park. Harry chose not to marry again, and this decision forced Joyce into the role of his mistress. Mr Allen refused to recognise his daughter's relationship with the bankrupt, whisky-drinking, two-timing spoiled priest, and, on high days and holidays, Joyce would make the journey alone to visit her family in Dover. Every Wednesday evening, following his appointment with Dr Hind, Peter would walk from Harley St to Seymour Place and have supper with his father and Joyce, before catching the last train back to Highfield. Harry rarely travelled further than the Harcourt Arms public house, and Peter soon slipped back into his role of friendly companion and now dutiful 'step' son. He took Joyce to the pictures, to the Lyons Corner House for chicken suppers and for Sunday walks in Regent's Park. He also bought her flowers and cologne. She, in turn, darned his socks and arranged his travel to Switzerland to visit Lea. Beneath Peter's kindly generosity, however, crouched resentment: *Every time Joyce calls Dad 'Darling', something inside me is wrenched and hurts intolerably. Their happiness and gaiety together makes me want to cry out in pain. And the pain comes from the division. One part of me rejoices in their happiness; Dad particularly is a different man. But the ghosts of the past are not yet laid and I feel the deep stirrings of stifled resentment at Mother's agony.*

When I first started reading my father's diaries, they made me so angry that I considered burning them. I was appalled by his narcissism and careless cruelty to women and I didn't want Polly and Lucy to know how selfish and insensitive their grandfather had been. I didn't destroy them but I did banish them to a far corner of the attic for fifteen years. Today, I am relieved that I kept them, because without access to my father's diaries, my own writing would have deviated from a larger truth. I have learnt too, from my mother's journal and letters, that she had her own part to play in the story, and that the roles of victim and offender were not as clearly defined as I had imagined.

Why are all my girlfriends foreigners and live hundreds of miles away? Perhaps I am afraid of women and prefer mild flirtations by post?

In 1949 Peter accepted Lea's invitation to spend Christmas with her family in Biel. Nothing was too much trouble for Lea's gentleman friend – he was wined and dined all over town and taken on a skiing holiday to Wengen. In quieter moments, Frau Kummer took Peter aside and told him, in some detail, about all the ghastly things Lea had been through with Hans: *It has warped her whole outlook, even though the man has proved himself weak and foolish and is still in love with her. This 'human bondage' is a frightening thing. I suppose a relationship which has the power to raise one to heaven, must, by the nature of things, bring one to hell when it goes wrong.*

In January 1950, Lea accepted a position caring for small children at a boarding school in Rottingdean, near Brighton. Dr Mordasini, her tuberculosis consultant, however, vetoed the move to England, saying that she was still too ill to take on such a challenging job in a foreign country. Lea told him to 'go to hell' and Peter praised her determination: *these damned medicos seem to resent any patient becoming independent of them. It's worse than having a confessor.* Privately, however, he was somewhat concerned about his own role as Lea's apparent back-up plan, should 'the damned medicos' prove to be right:

I wish I could feel Lea more vividly – my letters to her are so much like those to Mother, particularly in the later years. I know sort of intellectually that I love her but cannot feel it and enter into the richness of it. Perhaps this means that I don't really love her fully, am only fond of her, sorry for her, grateful for her love. On the other hand, perhaps it means I am still just frozen and the lyricism will follow the release. At the moment however, there is no doubt that she loves me with a passion and depth of which I am incapable.

In March of 1950, Peter received a letter from his cousin Harry O'Connell, announcing his engagement to Peggy Lee. Peggy had struggled with tuberculosis for almost a decade, and when her second lung became infected, the doctors sent her home to die. Peggy's father worked at the post office, and, with five children to support, there was no question of sending his daughter to convalesce in Switzerland. Instead, Mr Lee built Peggy a shed in the garden. Harry visited her every day. Peggy loved him, but she was concerned that his motivations might derive from heroic duty rather than feelings of true love. Together they read Stefan Zweig's novel, *Beware of Pity*, the powerful story of a man who mistook sympathy for love, with disastrous consequences. Harry had heard about Streptomycin, the new wonder drug in America, and Peggy's doctor eventually agreed that if they could get hold of it, he would administer it, but, they were to tell no-one. Mr Lee had a brother in America and friends at the sorting office in Dublin, and, over the course of six months, one hundred and eight bottles of Streptomycin were shipped to Ireland in parcels marked *Perfume from America*. Eight months after she was discharged, the hospital requested a copy of Peggy's death certificate, and, astonished to hear that the patient was still alive, she was called in for an examination. The specialist was baffled to discover that the tuberculosis had almost entirely vanished: 'Another bloody Catholic miracle!' he exclaimed. In spite of fierce opposition from Harry's widowed mother, who was dead against her only child marrying a consumptive, Harry O'Connell and Peggy Lee were married on September 25th, 1950. 'Harry and I had a great life and a very great love', Peggy reflected during an interview with Radio Eireann in 1999. Harry died at the age of seventy-one and Peggy died in 2014, just a few months shy of her ninetieth birthday.

Whenever Lea felt Peter ebbing away from her, she would give his Achilles heel a quick jab. In spite of his kindness, she felt his ambivalence: *Lea senses that our relationship is not permanent and is torturing herself with the thought of 'afterwards', asking me not to drop her as suddenly as Hans did.* Peter, the knight in shining armour, ready to do battle with weak-willed scoundrels, realised that he could not love Lea in the way she wished to be loved. However, one lesson his mother and the Wallington Bible Institute had taught him, was the importance of crushing evil. On February 7th 1950, he wrote:

My darling Lea,
I forgive you for comparing me to a man who took your gift of love and threw it on the scrap heap in exchange for money and social position – his three pieces of silver. The difference is that Judas did at least have the grace to go out and hang himself afterwards. I am sorry to speak like that of someone

you loved, darling, but the more complete and final your separation from that bounder, the better. His influence is malignant and evil and by God I hate him. He is not just selfish and money-loving, he is a destroyer. Jesus, when I think of it I get so wild I could come over and beat him up now. One can argue that a man must have some good features to have been loved so deeply by a woman of your quality but the devil has corrupted his soul with a thoroughness and viciousness which makes me believe that perhaps Lucifer does exist after all.

I can promise you that I'll not let you down. I love you my sweetheart and I am not a fickle person. All I ask you to remember is that I'm in a very unstable emotional state and until that is resolved, I cannot know my own deepest heart nor make plans for the far future. But, darling, <u>everything</u> is going to work out well and, fear not, I will be your companion in that joyful journey from the valley of the shadow on to the sunlit uplands where the wind blows sweet.

His diary entries, however, reveal a rather different picture:

Lea will need support for many months and I feel a great sense of responsibility. I am fond of her but in a vague, rather protective way and yet, I have to pretend to be so much in love with her. At times I feel like marrying her – determined to love and cherish her, but realise this is mock heroics and doomed to failure. She is spending 2-3 days in Paris with an Olympic oarsman – a handsome fellow who I think is fond of her. Feel now that the happiest thing that could happen would be for her to marry him – but would I if it happened?'

In spite of their muddled relationship, Peter and Lea wrote to each other several times a week. Lea was enjoying her life at the boarding school: *The food is bad and the portions are small but I am managing to gain weight*, she writes. Dr Hind, however, was not at all happy with the situation and noted a distinct deterioration in his client's psychological condition. He advised Peter to leave Highfield, move to London and increase the frequency of his visits. He also suggested he end the toxic relationship with his consumptive Swiss girlfriend. In his diary, Peter writes: *I cannot as she is so dependent on me. She fears that I will leave her.* Frau Kummer joined the conversation too, sending Peter cigarettes, chocolate and money to buy books. In a letter Rosa writes: *'Mama', Lea used to say to me, 'My greatest wish is to join my dear dead father'. You are such a good man, dear Peter, and God will reward your kind-heartedness.*

At the end of July, Lea and Peter took a holiday together on the Isle of Wight. They stayed at the Torland Hotel, swam in Colwell Bay, marvelled at the dolphins and the giant seaplanes, collected coloured sand in glass jars and enjoyed cakes and cornets in Freshwater tearooms. Peter bought a copy of Francois Mauriac's *The Desert of Love* in an old bookshop and read to my mother on a sheltered cliff overlooking the bay. Mauriac's novel is an odd yet fitting choice, a tale of estrangement between father and son, a profile of obsession and the search for peace in the arms of God. The inscription on the inside cover reads: *With love to an audience of one, beside the murmuring sea, who made reading a delight.* One night, they climbed to the top of Headon Head: *We stood in the rich purple heather and watched the full moon rise in the east. The flashing buoys and lighthouses and the silent passage of an ocean liner over the darkening waters painted an impressive picture. As we walked home in the moonlight, Lea whispered – No-one will ever love you as much as I do – and I believe she's right. If she isn't, then I am to be a very lucky man.*

Peter had made up his mind that he didn't wish to be: *committed or bound to any one person or policy, religion or career* until he had released his demons. Lea was understanding and said that she knew he was not in love with her, but was gambling on the possibility that he might be some day. She told Peter about Hans' pathological jealousy, and the fact that his father had recently been committed to a psychiatric hospital. In his diary, Peter writes: *Lea insists that I am the finest character she has ever met and that I am good and strong. I wish I felt even one of them.*

In August, they spent a day in Brighton, strolling along the seafront, picnicking in the rain and having their fortunes told on the Pier: *What a delight it is to see Lea so free and joyful, a magnificent victory over the twin ogres of Balmer and Dr. Mordasini.*

In September, Lea returned to Switzerland: *We made our adieus at Waterloo to the tune of hissing steam and recorded waltzes. It reminded me of 'Brief Encounter' and I was glad Lea had not seen the film or the parallel would have been too painful. As it was, she showed great courage and determination, stifling her grief and anxiety. She is the salt of the earth, and it is a bitter irony that I cannot love her as she wants to be loved. It may come but I am doubtful. I'd like to take a whip to Balmer. Why are the best women ensnared by such worthless men?* Lea's much-improved appearance was the subject of great delight amongst family and friends, whilst the gossip circles of Biel chewed greedily on the bones of speculation. What, they wondered, had happened to Fraulein Kummer in England? To Peter she writes: *I find Biel a different place, one no longer haunted by evil ghosts. I feel your presence strengthening me and when I passed Hans with his wife and son on the Nidaugasse last week, I felt nothing.* Things continued to go swimmingly until the early months of 1951, when everything began to unravel. In her journal, Lea writes:

I am seeing Hans again. Re-uniting after three years brought back so many memories. Our unending love, buried deep, has re-surfaced and is blossoming again. Why did it have to turn out this way? It was all so simple back then, so completely clear. Today it is dreadfully complicated. Hans regrets his decision and says he will free himself from the ties that bind him.

Educated Americans are the most charming and vital people I know.
Peter's diary, May 2nd, 1949

Peter and Alan Pifer had met as students at Cambridge. Alan was from Massachusetts and had attended Groton School and Harvard. By 1950, he was Director of the Fulbright Commission in London. Alan knew that Peter was interested in working in America, and offered to write to Jack Crocker, the Headmaster at Groton, recommending his friend for a teaching position at the school.

By January of 1951, Peter was feeling sufficiently healthy in body and mind to mail his letter of application to the Reverend Crocker. He was surprisingly frank about his emotional difficulties: *I mention these because I know Groton has high standards and I don't want to risk letting you down.* Four days later, Peter received a letter from America inviting him to Groton to teach English. Later the same month he met Robert Moss, the school's divinity master, in London: *Moss sank three large gins and smoked a great deal. A good sign that Groton isn't too stuffy in its religion.* Peter was successful in his application for a Fulbright travel grant, the hospital signed him off as tuber-culosis-free and the US Embassy issued him with a work visa. He was off to the United States of America!

In spite of his two years in psychotherapy, Peter's progress had been slow. In the spring of 1951, therefore, Dr. Hind offered him a series of Pentathol injections. Thiopental sodium, also known as 'the truth drug', was injected intravenously and produced an immediate state of hypnosis. My father liked to refer to these sessions as his 'LSD trips'. As a twenty-something student, I found this embarrassing as well as distressing, in part because I was experimenting with marijuana at the time, a drug far less daring than 'acid'. Peter's first session was a great success: *a delicious feeling of drowsiness like the early stages of drunkenness came over me, and I was able to remember and associate fairly freely.* The drug, however, set a precedent and Peter subsequently considered his non-Pentathol sessions to be rather flat in comparison. Dr Hind, on the other hand, was most encouraged by the great thaw that had apparently taken place in his most challenging patient: *Hind has given me a firm promise that I will be able to tackle anything by the time I get to Groton in September.*

There are certain things in life over which we have no choice. As long as I live, I shall never be Taiwanese or a triplet. In view of my age and physical limitations, it is unlikely that I shall ever sail solo across the Atlantic or leave Earth for Space, but other aspects of my life do offer me choice. As a former smoker, I choose to deny myself the occasional cigarette and a paralysing fear of debt leads me to avoid using a credit card to purchase something I cannot afford to buy outright. When Hans Balmer left my mother for Kathy Kellenberg, Lea had no choice in the matter. When Hans returned, however, she did have a choice. His offer was a poisoned chalice and yet she accepted it. Lea believed him when he told her he loved her. She also had faith in the gods when they promised her the future hand of a divorced man in marriage.

During the spring of 1951, Lea and Hans, with the help of a go-between, met several times a month: *We went to Bern, to Wengi and Scheunenberg and to Rapperswil, where, many years ago, we had been on a cycling holiday together*. By the time she was in her sixties, Lea's mobility was severely reduced, and she relied entirely on my father. When the weather was fine, she would ask him to take her for drives – along the Lake of Biel and through the villages and vineyards to her favourite restaurants. I imagine my mother gazing through the passenger window, her grief gasping inaudibly through the cracks of her broken heart as she remembered those stolen nights with Hans, recalling a time when she still had choices and hope.

When Lea left the nursery school in Rottingdean to return to Switzerland, her friend Vreni replaced her. Peter, ever the gentleman, was kind to Vreni, inviting her to Highfield to watch the cricket and taking her to the theatre in London. She mistook his stolen kisses in the moonlight as a sign of attraction and decided to extend her visa: *I hope this decision has nothing to do with me*, wrote Peter, rather disingenuously, in his diary. Vreni would have known about Lea's rehabilitated relationship with Hans and probably decided that a good man was hard to find and she wasn't going to let this one go to waste. Peter, meanwhile, concluded that the best course of action was to explain himself, as casually as possible, in a letter to Lea. Her reply, which she chose to write in French, was cold and firm. He must be absolutely clear with Vreni and under no circumstances could news of his indiscretion get back to Biel. I was shocked when I read Lea's letter and the magnitude of her duplicity suddenly dawned on me. Peter was her Plan B, her safeguard against a life of shame and loneliness. Hans was pathologically jealous and his renewed interest in Lea coincided with rumours of her handsome and brilliant Cambridge beau. If it was discovered that Lea's marvellous catch was nothing but a two-timing cad, the town gossips could enjoy a second wave of loose-lipped chatter. There could be no creases in Peter's poster-boy image. He was the bait to haul in her prize catch. If her plans for Hans failed then Peter was the back up.

Hans had promised divorce, but Lea recognised that there were countless personal, business and financial impediments that would make this extremely difficult: *I am unsure whether Hans has the strength and courage to start divorce proceedings. And yet, I would so dearly love to believe in him. Peter is another problem – he wishes to be free of all ties before he leaves for America. He is a kind, dependable and devoted man and I know that a life with him would be one of quiet contentment. A life with Hans would be much more tempestuous, full of heartache and sorrow, but I would be willing to commit myself to whatever lies ahead, if only love would unite us forever.*

In the spring of 1951 Lea decided to return to England, possibly with the intention of provoking Hans. Peter, meanwhile, was quite unaware that Balmer was back in the picture: *I cannot think why Lea hasn't written. I fear I may have wounded her hypersensitive soul. My letters usually go by return, but I sometimes have the feeling of being captive.*

Lea was offered work as a nanny to Christabel McDowall, whose brothers were pupils at Highfield. On April 21st, the day before she left Biel, Lea writes in her diary: *Peter's psychological state appears to have grown worse. He tells me over and over again how much he loves me and how much he would like to make me happy as a way of compensating for all the suffering 'that Balmer swine' has caused me! Oh God, Peter, I can't share this with you because you wouldn't understand. You have never loved anyone the way Hans and I love each other. In a different way, yes, you loved your mother over and above everyone and everything else; but this mother-love has robbed you of your soul and your inner peace. May God help you finally recover from your loss. Last year I was able to help you through your hours of darkness – today I must admit defeat. I feel sorry for you, but my heart cannot be dictated to or restrained. Will I be made to pay for my unfaithfulness? Dear God, help us in our hour of need!*

Rosa too was beginning to lose her grip on the situation, and in early April, she wrote to Peter, telling him very emphatically that Lea was not doing well in Biel. She thanked him for his kindness in finding her a position with the McDowalls. When Lea arrived in England, Peter felt she looked sad and strained: *She is carefully avoiding endearing names and close embraces and I am conscious of a self-protecting selfishness which is to save me but, I pray, not at her expense.* Their relationship limped on through a long summer of indecision as Peter continued to wrestle his angels: *I must keep my eye unwaveringly on the goal – working, working, again working, never slacking or idling or killing time.*

In public, Peter and Lea were the perfect couple. She often took the bus to Highfield at weekends to watch him umpire the cricket and join him for tea with the boys. They visited Cowdray Park, and lay under an ancient oak tree where he read her Paul Gallico's *The Snow Goose*. They saw Margot Fonteyn at the Royal Ballet, went to plays and concerts together and in July Frau Kummer arrived from Switzerland to say a final farewell to Peter, whom she feared she would never see again following his departure for America. The McDowalls invited Peter and Rosa to join their holiday party on the Isle of Wight. In pictures taken at Seaview, Lea is in a pretty cotton dress and cat's eye sunglasses and beside her stand Peter and little Christabel. The three of them look the epitome of a happy family, enjoying a day at the beach.

In February of 2017 I visited Christabel at her home in Hampshire and she gave me a photograph of herself and my mother sitting together on a bench. The little girl's hand is resting on Lea's lap and their fingers are gently entwined. Christabel described my mother as her rock and I think of how difficult it must have been for Lea, caring for a little girl who, in different circumstances, might have been her own. She was thirty-four years old, and her personal life was in a dreadful muddle. She might marry one of two men, but then again, she might not marry either of them. She might have children of her own someday, but her age and the side effects of her tuberculosis would have seriously reduced her chances of a successful pregnancy. And yet, Lea's courage and determination, her generous heart and her ability to stand steady when the ground beneath her was shaking so violently, were the qualities that little Christabel had recognised and appreciated.

Lea, Peter and Christabel, Isle of Wight, 1951

August 12ᵗʰ, 1951
My darling Peter,
There are many things I don't understand. It is touching that you see me as a beloved sister. I wanted to be more than a sister to you and more than just one of all your nice girlfriends. It is nice to admire the roses in other people's gardens, but it is sweeter to have just one rosebush in one's <u>own</u> garden and to know that it is <u>yours</u>. You don't know that yet, but I pray for you that you will one day.
I did love two men in my life. Hans does love me as I wanted you so much to do - you couldn't, my Darling, it is not your fault. But he is still having that deep painful love for me, as

he always had. His life is spoilt and hell to live, with a wife he hates. He deserves it and I am not sorry for him. But the root of the great love he planted in my heart 10 years ago is still there. I don't mind to wait for the man I love. Life for me until then will be wonderful and hell at the same time but I need his love more than ever now. Please, Peter Darling, don't misunderstand me, this is not a threat. You can't help it that you are not in love with me. I did love you deeply, you've done so very much for me. I loved you, therefore I don't want you to think that I am better than I really am.

Who knows, perhaps in many years when I shall be married to Hans at last and you to someone you love, I might ask you to come and stay with us? We will look at each other and see love and happiness and peace for both of us. We'll celebrate it with Beaujolais and champagne, and all the misery of the past will be forgotten and you will say: 'I am happy now, because I see that you are happy,' and I shall say the same to you. Peter, this will be the happiest day of my life. God bless you. Lea'.

My heart aches whenever I read this letter. As a teenager and as a young adult, I often experienced my mother's artful manipulation; a clumsy attempt, I now realise, at self-preservation. This final letter to my father, however, feels neither devious nor self-pitying. It speaks to a truth that acknowledges the depth of the bond between them whilst recognising that their relationship must be allowed to die. Lea allows herself one small step into thin air as she envisions her future home, a sanctuary of love and happiness. I imagine Peter, together with his English, possibly Irish, maybe American wife, unpacking their bags after a long journey. They have come to visit Peter's dear friend, Lea.

They knew each other long ago and, if he's honest, he still loves her a little and harbours a slight regret that he didn't pursue her more wholeheartedly when he had the opportunity. The four grown-ups drink Bollinger and Beaujolais and they laugh and enjoy the delicious food that Lea has prepared. She is happy that Peter has found true love at last and she thanks God for her life with Hans.

After months, indeed years of considering different exit strategies, Peter had finally been offered a graceful way out of his predicament. Lea had ended their relationship. In three short weeks he would be leaving for a new life in America and she would be returning to Switzerland.

Peter replied to Lea's letter by return:

My Darling Lea,

Your letter upset me greatly at first: then everything became peaceful and clear. The answer appeared like a sign in the sky. Darling, will you marry me? I can imagine all the objections you will make and none of them is valid. You'll say I don't love you – but I do. I think you are the loveliest person in the world. Marry me next year and we'll be so happy together. I will come back at the end of my Groton year or, if a good job opens up there, you may like to come out to the States for a while. In any case by then I shall be fully free and able to give myself to you entirely. The point is we should get engaged now. Come up as soon as you can and we'll choose the ring and have a celebration together.

It would be a good idea, perhaps, if you stayed with the McDowalls a little longer. As for having anything more to do with Balmer – it's preposterous. Nothing but disaster can

come of that, so if you really want to go back to Biel for a few months, do something drastic to keep him from annoying you. Darling Lea, don't mistake this for pity or any lesser emotion than love. I love you and want you to be my wife. Will you say Yes? Please do.
I long for your reply. God bless you.
With love and tenderness,
Peter

In his diary, he writes: *Lea's letter distressed me deeply. Suddenly I realised the depth of sorrow that lies before her and that the obvious path for me is to marry her. This decision was hard to make, for I was afraid of false motives and bogus heroism. I had to search my mind to see how sincere I was. Came to the decision, wrote and posted the letter. Strange peace came over me; it's a practical step towards maturity and the shedding of adolescent illusions and fantasies. I shall become happy in making Lea happy. But, will she accept me now? Had an excellent dinner at The Grapes in Shepherd Market and bought a very good suitcase for 4gns – bargain, worth double.*

Lea took a day to consider Peter's proposal, then sent her reply:

Peter, my Darling,
How shall I start, what shall I say or do? I only know that you are wonderful, with the warmest heart I've ever seen. One big and happy 'Yes' would be my only answer if I were really sure that you don't sacrifice yourself for my sake. Is it only because you want to avoid that I wait and marry Hans that you ask me to marry you? Is it, darling? Peter, sweetheart, I know how

good you are and can very well imagine you doing so. Your sudden reaction frightens me somehow. Do you really mean to marry me? So very many things are against me, darling, you know them all. I would rather die than knowing that you sacrifice yourself for me. Perhaps you regret your question already? Oh, it's too wonderful to be true. Darling, think it over and if you regret it, I'll understand. If you don't, send a wire please.
It's you I really love,
Lea.

PS. Your letter is the compensation for all my painful years. It was worth suffering to have a letter like this – even if you have changed your mind in the meantime.

Peter's mind <u>was</u> changing and his feet were already cold. He wired her, although not to confirm his proposal but to suggest that they meet and talk. In his diary, he admits that *the Balmer rat* is one of the strongest impulses urging him to intervene, as he cannot see Lea sacrificed to *that bag of selfish guts*.

He sought the advice of several women friends, all of whom considered his marriage proposal to have been a big mistake and recommended that he extricate himself as quickly as possible: *Far better pain and trouble now than long, drawn-out misery later,* advised one. *It would be wrong to marry Lea if you don't love her – wrong to her as much as to you,* declared another.

My Darling,
Just received your letter. We must talk it over if you are worried for my sake. I know you better than you know yourself. I trust

you completely, Peter. You are never going to be the light-hearted man you are worried of, you couldn't. Darling, if we are going to be engaged, which I do hope now from all my heart, it will be like a rock in the sea for you in big America. I have no other wish in the world than to make you happy. I shall be very happy knowing that your wonderful heart belongs to me, that's all I am hoping for. Darling Peter, do you think your mother would like us to get married? I think of her so much and feel her big eyes on me with a sweet smile on her face. Do you think she loved me as much as I loved her? I even think she is twinkling at me saying: 'Hold him!' God bless her.

God <u>will</u> help us, I am certain of it.

All my love to you, Lea

They met in London the following week. Their discussion ended inconclusively. No ring was purchased, no party planned and a veil of silence fell over the subject of marriage. There was one awkward moment when Frau Kummer wrote to Peter, excited and delighted by the news, but Lea soon set her straight. On September 6th Peter left for America. Harry accompanied him to the station and Lea met him at the jetty in Southampton: *She came up to the visitors' gallery and waved but did not wait for sailing time. Thank God. She was brave and sweet. Still I felt nothing.*

My favourite story, as I was growing up, was of Mum and Dad and the *QEII*. My father's rendition was very romantic and I imagined Mum on the quayside in a swing dress and high heels, waving her red handkerchief while Dad stood on deck in a white cricket jersey, holding a rolled copy of the

Times and calling: 'Goodbye, Goodbye'. It is a tender image, and convinced me that there had once been a time when my parents were very much in love with each other. In fact, it was 'Butch' Woolmer with his green Highfield cap who was doing all the waving, and, at no-one in particular, because he wasn't quite sure whether Mr O'Connell had spotted him.

Chapter Four

Fly low but don't land.

On his first night aboard, Peter found himself at table *with a negro and an American couple who, horrified at the humiliation, ran away.* After dinner he inadvertently discovered the emergency stairs which offered him unchecked access to First Class. He was bowled over by the luxury of his surroundings as well as the beauty of Elizabeth Ehrenberg, a college student whom he met playing cards: *Flirting mildly with Elizabeth was a splendid distraction from the heaving, plunging ship.*

The Queen Elizabeth sailed into New York harbour on September 11th, 1951. Fifty years later, at about the same time in the morning, two hijacked aircraft flew into the Twin Towers of the World Trade Centre, killing nearly three thousand people.

The city customs official was a tad suspicious of the Anglo-Irish immigrant with his one bargain suitcase of personal effects and five tea chests of books. He insisted on prising them open, one by one. By the time he reached the third chest, he had taken rather a liking to my father and decided that his story about the books was probably true: *OK, Peter, we're done. Welcome to America. Now get outta here...*Peter fell in love, right there and then: *Where else, but in the United States, would a government official call you Peter?* He spent a few days with Alan's parents in Shirley, Massachusetts and then Claude Pifer drove him to

Groton, where he was greeted on the steps of Hundred House by the Reverend Jack Crocker.

The two greatest forces in America are Niagara Falls and Endicott Peabody.
Old Groton legend

Endicott Peabody was educated at Cheltenham School and Trinity College, Cambridge. In 1884 he founded Groton, which he modelled on the public schools of England. His goal, he said was *to instil high-minded principles in the offspring of the most successful American entrepreneurs of the Gilded Age*. Peabody was born into one of the wealthiest families in America. He studied theology, and in 1882 was sent on pastoral assignment to Tombstone, a town which, three months earlier, had witnessed the Gunfight at the OK Corral. The young seminarian was not shy about entering the saloons and asking for donations from poker games, and it is said that Wyatt Earp contributed a pew to Endicott's new Episcopal church. Groton and Peabody were synonymous and the school was created in his image. Former alumnus and President of the United States, Franklin Delano Roosevelt declared that apart from his parents, Endicott Peabody was the strongest influence in his life.

Peter was struck by the lack of inflated egotism amongst the boys: *Nor is there much snobbery, though quite a few families appear to be descended from American presidents. At supper last night I spoke to three boys, all of whom were direct descendants of Coolidge, Taft and Roosevelt.*

There is tradition at Groton that when a new President takes office, he is invited to write a letter to the school, offering words of wisdom and encouragement to the students. In 1962 President Kennedy wrote: *There was a period when it seemed as though a Groton graduate might be President more or less permanently. I am sorry that the best I have been able to do is make a Grotonian Secretary of the Treasury.* In 1970, Richard Nixon misunderstood the purpose of the letter and sent a signed photograph, saying how flattered he was by Headmaster Wright's request. President Obama's letter encourages Groton students to dedicate their energy and talents to their classrooms and communities.

Reverend Peabody considered Groton to be an extension of the family. Meals were taken at tables with a master and his wife and there were Bible readings and prayers before bed. When Reverend Crocker succeeded Reverend Peabody in 1940, he reinforced the adviser system which made individual masters accountable for the academic and social progress of the boys: 'We are engaged in teaching both the skills of existence and the meaning of existence', Crocker told the faculty. Ironically, the fathers of two of Peter's advisees in his first year at Groton were eminent theologians – Reinhold Niebuhr, whom President Obama has described as his favourite philosopher, and Walter H. Gray, the Bishop of Connecticut.

Groton School lies thirty-five miles west of Boston, with views across the Nashua River valley and the mountains of Wachusett. The campus is arranged in a circle, and Schoolhouse, with its white columns and gold cupola, faces Hundred House and its Palladian windows: *What a beautiful place this is! The buildings, the setting, the interiors, everything is lavish and tasteful. My small dorm and my flat are attractive and very comfortable. I have a big open fireplace in the sitting room and a telephone.*

Many of the staff have been to Oxford or Cambridge, the chapel is modelled on Magdalene, there is a full peal of bells in the tower and the complete volumes of Punch *in the Library.* Peter considered the boys to be polite and interested, although not as academically advanced as his pupils at Highfield. He appreciated the religious life at Groton and found both Morning Chapel and House Prayers to be friendly and relaxed: *Sunday Chapel is more formal and the choir wear red cassocks, but aesthetically it is a very happy experience with the organ, bell and voice music. The religious meaning remains elusive, yet I respect the religious life at Groton in a way I did not at Highfield.*

One of Peter's responsibilities was to coach the soccer team and he was relieved to discover that the standard was so low he could almost pose as an expert. In spite of a weak understanding of the rules, Peter's band of brothers showed tremendous enthusiasm: *They're dead keen and go flat out, never grumbling or being silly.* He began an active campaign on behalf of soccer, fighting to raise its status in the school, and encouraging more spectators to attend practice games. At the end of the season, to show their appreciation for Mr O'Connell's efforts, the boys presented him with a small silver football engraved with the words: *PO'C Coach GS 1951.* The following season, a newly arrived first-former approached Peter, and asked whether the rumour he had heard was true, namely that Mr O'Connell had once been invited to play for a professional soccer team in England: *How the Highfield folk would have laughed at that!*

In the classroom Peter felt comfortable and self-assured as he continued to seek original ways of engaging the boys' interest. Horrified to discover how little his sixth formers knew of Shakespeare, he kick-started them with Hamlet, inviting their opinions of the Prince of Denmark, then confusing them by criticising Hamlet and defending Polonius. He gave them the task of summarising the play and then rewriting it in the Shavian idiom: *transposing Shaw into the 16th century and making him revolutionary, didactic and progressive but in an entirely different context.* He then asked them to write a new version of the first soliloquy by *Shawspeare. I hope to have more fun with Shakeshaw tomorrow.* The boys' views were certainly provoked and there was much lively discussion in Mr O'Connell's English class.

Arthur Miller once described Hamlet as a dilemma which is both obvious and insoluble and Peter would certainly have agreed with him: *I sympathise so much with Hamlet, the man who could not make up his mind, caught in a web of conflicting loyalties, weakened by intellectualism - 'sicklied o'er with the pale cast of thought' - and torn by ambivalent emotions. Substitute mother for father and there is the core of my problem. I am Hamlet without his genius; without his simple way out too.*

Peter's highly developed intellect and strong moral beliefs were wrapped in a fragile sensitivity which hobbled his perceived ability to act swiftly and decisively. In fact my father, like Hamlet, was a man very capable of decisive action, as his sudden marriage proposal to my mother had proven: Hamlet kills Polonius with comparable swiftness. Peter wanted to avenge the broken life of his mother, but recognised that he also loved and admired the man he blamed for her suffering. Then, there was God, who came at him from both sides – the loving, vengeful God of his mother and the hypocritical, long-ago abandoned God of his father. Which version should he trust? Peter reasoned relentlessly with himself and each time he reached the point where he recognised what needed to be done, his sympathies would flip, filling him once again with remorse and self-reproach. Like Hamlet, he saw himself as *pigeon-liver'd*. Murder wasn't an option, although it surfaced in his dreams; neither was suicide, because there was always that nagging possibility that God, if he existed, could send him to Hell for all eternity.

When I was a student at the University of Reading, my father suggested I read *A Portrait of the Artist as a Young Man* by James Joyce, and he directed me to the rector's sermon on the nature of Hell. It remains one of the most terrifying passages in literature that I have ever read. It was not so much the physical images that filled my heart with dread – the boiling brains, the molten eyeballs, the stench of damned flesh – but the description of eternity. I was invited to imagine a mountain of sand reaching to the farthest heavens, a million miles broad and a million miles thick, then to multiply every grain of sand by every leaf on every tree, feather on every bird, scale on every fish, hair on every animal. At the end of every million years, a little bird arrives at the foot of the mountain of sand and carries away a single grain. After millions of centuries have passed and the bird has finally removed the entire mountain, we are apparently no nearer the end than we were at the beginning. Eternity, we are told, has scarcely even begun. As I had not been raised in the Christian faith, the concept of being spurned by God and cast into the fires of Hell did not disturb me unduly. However, the terror of being held captive by my life, of having no way out of the powerlessness I felt as a child and later as an adult, literally took my breath away. My sanctuary was my imagination, an internal landscape where I could wander unseen and undisturbed. I had taught myself to close my eyelids, by day as well as by night, and make the world go away. But, I needed the promise of hope, the assurance that each tick of the clock, each sunset and sunrise brought me a step closer to my release from captivity. I truly and completely believed that one day, the door dividing my inner and outer landscapes would dissolve, and I would be set free, the caretaker of my own life. I could be patient, very patient, but this concept of eternity was something new to me. I had never conceived of the idea that I could travel across my whole life, from its beginning to its end, and still find myself standing, like the little bird, at the bottom of a perpetually replenishing mountain. It was the most frightening idea I could have imagined for myself.

Peter had been at Groton for less than a month when he received a letter from his father with the news that Joyce had been diagnosed with leukaemia: *Poor Dad, he must be suffering terribly. I regret being so far from home at this time.* A few days later, a letter arrived from Dr Hind, urging his former patient to remain in America, in spite of the difficulties at home.

Endicott and his wife, Fannie, had died several years before Peter arrived at Groton, but their two unmarried daughters, Elizabeth and Margery, still lived on campus and continued the family tradition of hosting tea parties and cocktail evenings. The Peabody Sisters reminded me of Miss Emily and Miss Mamie in *The Waltons*, a popular American television series in the 1970s. Betsy and Marge never disagreed with anyone about anything, an impartial attitude which ensured that, like the Queen, they never got embroiled in anything tricky or delicate. Betsy's favourite expression and one that found its way into the received wisdom of our family was: *he's just as nice as he can be*. As I got older, I realised that this is a perceptive observation because it recognises that people are doing the best they can: if it were possible for him to be nicer, then it was assumed that he would be. The closest Betsy ever came to open criticism was in a letter she wrote to my father in 1974: *We don't like the way that all things, political and economic, are going on both sides of the Atlantic, do we? We can only hope that 1975 will be a better year for all mankind.* She was referring, I imagine, to the Watergate scandal in America, and the IRA bombings in England.

In spite of their diplomacy, there was nothing dull or insipid about Betsy and Marge, who were universally considered to be good listeners and delightful companions. The sisters were well-educated and well-travelled. In 1925 they spent five months in China and Japan, and during WWII Marge served as a nurse in Australia. Betsy had a degree in Psychology from Columbia and taught remedial reading at Groton from 1932 until shortly before her death in 1976.

In October of 1951 the Misses Peabody invited Peter to dinner and introduced him to Serena, their English houseguest and member of the English aristocracy: *She's an attractive girl but rather gauche and given to superlatives. I found her dull.* Peter had pretty much forgotten his half-hearted commitment to Lea, so although they continued to write to each other, the news he shared with her could sometimes be rather thoughtless: *Extraordinary letter from Lea, accusing me of 'sadism' in my last letter. Cannot remember what I could have said.* The outburst was caused by his references to Serena, which Lea considered to be vain and boastful. In spite of his departure for the New World, Rosa had not entirely given up on Peter and when Lea's niece was born, she wrote, describing her daughter's heart-breaking cry: *Oh, that she were mine!* Lea's friend Gillie wrote too, begging Peter to marry Lea. He wrote back saying that he couldn't: *not yet.*

When I was a little girl, Uncle Bobi used to take me to the Seeteufel, a small private zoo near Biel. In the far corner of the estate lived three African lions. Their enclosure was tiny, and the male paced up and down, day after day, year after year. I used to try to catch his eye in the hope of offering him a caring smile, but he was caught by something else, a memory perhaps of the Serengeti Plains. Years later, I went back to the Seeteufel with our own daughters, Polly and Lucy, and the lion was still pacing, still walking his memory across the grasslands of Africa. Between 1951 and 1955, Lea too was trapped by her life in Switzerland. She saw Hans once a month, and remained ever hopeful that he might still keep his promise to her. While she waited, his wife gave birth to a second child. A couple of years later, the Balmers welcomed their third child. Meanwhile, Kellenberg AG continued to grow from strength to strength as Hans dedicated himself to the successful expansion of his father-in-law's business.

In 1952 Lea was working as a dental assistant in Bern and her mother wrote her the following letter:

Dear Leneli,
You want Hans back at all costs, but he won't come back because he's stuck and he can't leave. He will be punished, sooner or later. I am convinced, however, that you will

find happiness again one day. Be patient: God gives us the courage to bear our burdens. He helped me when I found life so unendingly difficult and He will help you too. Don't lose heart, don't try and force anything and The Good Lord will lay his crown upon your head. Everything in life is fate, and maybe, one day you will thank God for the way things turned out. For now, keep praying, be patient and don't wish any ill will on Hans and Kathy. God alone knows what He's doing.

In 1974 my mother and I were in a fabric shop in Biel. We were the only customers and Mum began a conversation with the sales assistant. Suddenly, the woman began to sob uncontrollably and, embarrassed, I moved away, feigning an interest in sewing patterns. When we were back on the street, I asked my mother how she knew the woman and why she was crying: 'She's Hans Balmer's widow', Mum replied. I was astonished, both by my mother's courage and by her empathy. Had I been in Lea's shoes, I would have taken great pains to avoid my rival, and I most certainly wouldn't have initiated a conversation with her. What if I had simply stood there, listening to their exchange – what might I have discovered about these two women who had loved the same man? I asked my mother if she had ever regretted not marrying Hans, to which she replied: 'If I'd married Hans, I would have been a widow at fifty'. This was certainly true, but it didn't really answer my question. It was not until many years later that I discovered the two women were not rivals, but allies.

Peter was much loved at Groton. He was an intelligent and thoughtful companion and soon became a regular at the supper tables of faculty families. Gina Murray and Edie Hardcastle enjoyed his mildly flirtatious manner and Peter successfully avoided offending their husbands by openly complimenting Jack and Fitz on the loveliness of their wives. He was a favourite with the children too and little Phoebe Bowditch, out in the vegetable patch with Peter one day, declared: 'We invite you to dinner, Peter, because we love you'. He attended birthday parties and school plays, and when he was away from Groton, he sent the children postcards. When Peter wasn't being wined and dined by the Murrays, the Bowditches and the Peabodys, he was at the Bull Run with Corky Nichols and Jim Hawkes, enjoying a duckling and ice cream supper: *what a contrast with the shabby old Highfield sitting room and tea at nine o'clock from cracked cups out of a metal teapot.* He spent Thanksgiving with the Pifers, where he went horseback riding and tasted his first pumpkin pie. In December a visiting headmaster from Texas offered him a position teaching history at a school in Dallas and within the week, Jack Crocker had invited Peter to his study and guaranteed him a position for the following academic year. He was doing a fine job, Jack declared. Everybody said so.

In the week before Christmas, Peter joined Norris Getty and Jack Murray on a trip to New York. They shared a room at The Paramount Hotel on Times Square and while his colleagues attended a teachers' convention, Peter explored the city and its bookshops. Norris and Jack took Peter to see his first musical: Mary Martin in *South Pacific,* and thirty years later when *Dallas* was a smash hit on British TV, Dad would delight in telling us that he had seen Larry Hagman's mother on Broadway in

1951. As he left the room, he would sing a song about washing a man out of his hair and sending him on his way. Perhaps the lyrics reminded him of his victory over the abominable Balmer.

Peter spent Christmas with the Pifers and then caught the train to Far Hills, New Jersey, where he had been invited to stay with Groton parents, Hughie and 'Cocky' Hyde. He went pond-skating and danced with an array of beautiful women at a party given by Henry Ford's brother-in-law: *They are simple, decent folk, of good incomes, the wives well-turned out and attractive, the men unassuming and straight forward. There was no buffoon or elegant poseur present as at similar gatherings in England.* On New Year's Eve he attended the Hunt Club Ball, founded by Hughie's grandfather, where he danced with a cousin to the future Queen of England. It was a glamorous life and my father was enchanted by it.

In March of 1952 Peter proposed the introduction of a literary society at Groton as a way of encouraging boys to read for enjoyment. At each meeting a student would deliver a paper on a subject of his choice. There was general astonishment at O'Connell's idea and very little enthusiasm from the faculty. Undeterred, he raised the subject again and Jack Crocker decided to authorise it on a trial basis. A group of six senior boys gathered for an informal meeting in Mr O'Connell's study and fifty turned up to the second meeting, listening with: *deadpan or small smiling expressions. After my impassioned harangue, not a soul spoke or had questions to ask.* Jim Amory delivered the first paper on the subject of the harpsichord, *marred only by too many 'ums.* Jim later went to Mr O'Connell's study for tea, where he complained about the general lack of enthusiasm amongst the faculty. Peter defended his colleagues, but was secretly pleased that his newly-formed society had launched so successfully. In March 2017 Jim Amory, now in his late seventies wrote: *I bet Mr O'Connell made a hell of a schoolmaster. He was a man with passions, and he wasn't afraid to express them.*

To my father's great disappointment, I showed no obvious interest in books. When I was twelve, I casually picked up an historical novel in a petrol station, and Dad, spotting an opportunity, offered to buy it for me, declaring he would give me twenty pounds if I read it within a month. Twenty pounds in 1971 was a lot of money, four weeks was a long time and the book was relatively short. In spite of the odds in my favour I failed the challenge. When I was in Switzerland during the school holidays, however, I would ask Uncle Bobi to take me to the English bookshop in Biel where I bought as many Enid Blytons as I could afford. I didn't tell my father about this, because he considered Blyton's books to be poorly written and insufficiently challenging. When Lucy discovered the *Malory Towers* series, I was delighted. Her English teacher was less enthusiastic, declaring that she really should be reading books of greater literary merit. Reading, as far as I was concerned, was reading, especially when you are nine years old and English is not your first language.

Peter began to attend Groton's Drama and Debating society meetings but found the tone overly earnest and the material too factual. He also went along to Jim Hawkes' play rehearsals and offered much unsolicited advice: *I told Jim I thought the boys were poor – bad speech, lack of imaginative insight, no inspiration.* Surprisingly perhaps, Jim was not offended and invited further suggestions: *I succeeded in diagnosing some of the main complaints. Peter Nitze intones on final consonants and turns simple vowel sounds into dipthongs. I also got the boys to laugh. The tavern scenes are going to be dull without laughter.*

In March 2017 Edward Gammons, cast in the role of Falstaff in Groton's 1952 production of *Henry IV* wrote:

Mr Hawkes gave me over into the care of Mr O'Connell. For weeks we went over every line that Falstaff spoke, every gesture. We talked much about Elizabethan theatre. This led to other discussions about English history, heroes and literature. My passions for Shakespeare, Elizabethan drama/ literature and for the theater in general can be, at least in part, traced to Peter O'Connell. It is one of the happiest memories of my Groton education.

Tom McNealy, a good-looking lad from Chicago, has taken me under his wing and is very charming in his efforts to make life easier for me.

In the summer of 1952, my father was invited to stay with the McNealys at their home on the shores of Lake Michigan. A decade later, Tom wrote to Peter: *I have frequently dreamed back over all that you managed to instil into our circle of adolescent indifference. My very best to you, Peter, and I think of you often with warmth and respect. Yours, as ever, Tom McNealy.*

In December 2000 a letter addressed to my father arrived at his address in Folkestone. It was from Tom, and he enclosed a faded photograph of Peter on the campus at Groton. It was, he wrote, one of his most treasured possessions, and had lived on the door of his fridge for more than forty years. I wrote back and told him that Peter had died in 1998. I made a copy of the photograph and returned the original to him, as it seemed to be something inordinately precious to this now late-middle-aged man. Thomas McNealy died three years later in 2003 at the age of sixty-nine.

As the Easter holidays approached, invitations were extended to the bachelor master from England. He spent a week in Dayton, Ohio and was set to return to Far Hills, New Jersey to stay with Cocky Hyde, but with Hughie away on business, it was felt that Peter's visit might provoke unnecessary gossip. The invitation was, therefore withdrawn, with much regret and some embarrassment. Instead, Peter went to New York where he looked up Elizabeth Ehrenberg, his young friend from the *QEII*, and accepted several dinner invitations from Groton parents.

By the start of the summer term, however, Peter was struggling once again: *I feel tired and dispirited and am conscious of intense spiritual loneliness and emotional starvation. I am so depressed by the ease with which I can charm women and am afraid my stone heart might lead to another Lea episode. I am incredibly inhibited, unable to feel any spontaneous impulse, a prey to anxiety and doubts. And, in spite of all these disabilities, women fall in love with me and I am never refused. I get glimpses of freedom when great gusts of passionate poetry blow through me like a Pentecostal revelation and give me a feeling of almost divine competence. Immediately my Puritan conscience asserts itself, calling this attitude vanity. I snap my fingers at it, but I also embrace the idea that when I am free, I shall owe a huge moral debt to those who are suffering from the pains and sorrows that I have myself*

endured. I hope I shall be wise and good enough to resist self-in-
dulgence and choose service to those still standing in the shadows.

It was in his relationship with the boys that Peter felt most alive, perhaps because what he felt for them was instinctive and uncomplicated. In spite of its academic brilliance and attention to morality and manners, Groton School remained, by its very nature, a holding pen for the sons of wealthy and eminent men. The Groton Boy had no regular contact with his father and little opportunity to share with him his scholastic and athletic successes. He was denied the opportunity to learn from, talk to, or be angry with his father on a daily basis. Peter knew what father-hunger felt like, and he had an intuitive capacity to tap into the hearts of those boys who, like him, missed their fathers' physical and emotional presence.

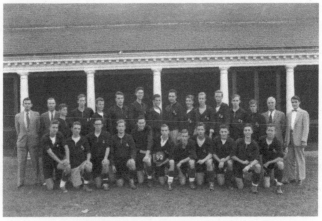

Peter and the Groton School soccer team, 1953
Image reproduced with kind permission of Groton School

Peter decided not to return to England that summer, but to find a job in America, and Jack Crocker offered to write to his friend, Francis 'Duke' Sedgwick.

Dear Duke,
This is a long shot but we have a very attractive and able young Englishman teaching here, who is eager to get himself a job this summer. He is a good soccer player, is very adapt-able and has an excellent head on his shoulders. He would be prepared either to tutor or take a job on a ranch, or both. Minty is in good form and Mary joins me in sending you and Alice our love.

The Sedgwicks, related by marriage to the Peabodys, had a long tradition of sending their sons to Groton. Francis, known as 'Minty', was a student at the school in 1952, as was his brother Jonathan. Bobby had graduated to Harvard a few years earlier.

Unfortunately, Mr Sedgwick had nothing to offer Peter, but, in early June, a letter arrived from William Wood-Prince, President of the Union Stock Yard and Transit Company of Chicago, offering my father a summer job as a yardsman.

On the Greyhound bus from Boston to Cincinnati, Peter read Upton Sinclair's *The Jungle,* a horrifying account of life and practices in the early Chicago stockyards. Following publication of *The Jungle,* President Theodore Roosevelt began investiga-tions which resulted in the Meat Inspection Act of 1906. On July 2nd 1952, Peter met Mr Wood-Prince and his Vice chair-man, Mr O'Connor from County Kerry, who subsequently arranged a three-hour tour of the stockyards: *a wonderful organisation capable of handling thousands of cattle and hogs a day.* The following morning, Peter punched his card and reported for work at A3 weighing scale.

On his second night in Chicago, my father got very drunk with a Republican politician: *We ate and drank so much that I was only semi-conscious, but remembered Hacker's bodyguard telling me that Chicago police deal with pickpockets by breaking their fingers. I got Hacker very wild by praising Eisenhower.* The 4th of July was a national holiday and Peter's arrival in Chicago coincided with the Republican and Democratic nominating conventions for the Presidency: *Today's proceedings were a mixture of a Cup Final and Bertram Mills' Circus. There were bands and processions, charabancs and rosettes. Everything that could carry a favour was pressed into service – helicopters, an elephant (which went berserk), banners, flags, buildings. When the full moon rose, I half expected to see 'I Like Ike' painted on it. I came home through the coloured area, still awake at 2am.*

Just as I could never imagine my mother as a carefree young girl, neither could I envisage my father in denims and a cowboy hat, driving cattle in the Chicago Stockyards. Peter disliked physical activity because it invariably meant time away from his beloved books. Judging by his diary, however, he worked uncomplainingly as a yardsman for six hot weeks: *17,000 cattle came through today and it all began with a torrential rainstorm. I blessed my plastic suit. Then came the sun and it felt like a Turkish bath. I worked for twelve hours and spent most of the day at the weighing scale, driving the cattle to their pens and then loading them into railroad cars. I was blinded with sweat, but it was very satisfying work, and I held the vision of a cold bath and a gin sling at the end of my shift. The following day temperatures fell to*

60 degrees: extraordinary change – yesterday cattle died of heat, today one calf died of cold.

In a letter to Jack, he writes: *I came to meet people and see things in this great heartland of America and by Jove I've met and seen both. The yards themselves are a great American enterprise but it's the men who work here that delight me most – they're as fine a bunch as you'd find in a month of Independence Days – genial, warm-hearted, cheerful (and blasphemous!), always willing to judge tolerantly. I have also met people from every walk of life outside the yards and I've been impressed there too with the same kindness and friendly hospitality. The last vestige of formality remaining in 'Peter' has disappeared – I'm 'Pete' to all in Chicago.* I am stunned by this revelation, by the thought that anyone would call my father Pete. No-one called him Pete. Not ever.

It is clear that Pete's position as a yardsman was somewhat unique. I doubt that every new employee was given a three-hour tour of the plant on his first day. This was followed by a cocktail party where he met the divorced wife of Adlai Stevenson. Stevenson was then Governor of Illinois and a dark horse for the presidency. Peter also received an employee pass which gave him free access to the Convention centre. He attended a reception for Eisenhower, heard many of the nominating speeches and met people from all over the Union. General Eisenhower won the Republican nomination and Richard Nixon was his Vice President. After the five-day party was over, Peter felt flat and dispirited: *The light of common day seems very dull.* He enjoyed working on the scales and didn't mind shovelling dung in the terrific heat, but he found the weekends lonely and longed for company: *I must get married and have my own folk on whom to lavish this intense yearning to love.*

On July 21st, the Democrats arrived in town: *I enjoyed Eleanor Roosevelt's speech and Stevenson looks like the man, but there's a dullness about the Democrats.* During the convention, Peter met a young woman selling raffle tickets who invited him home for tea: *Tea in America is an engaging euphemism for hard liquor.* After a few dry martinis at Ken and Helen's Lake Shore Drive apartment, they took Peter to the Racquet Club for dinner, then back home for more 'tea'. The Crowells began to include their newly-discovered Englishman on weekend trips to Kenilworth and pretty soon Peter's social life had regained its bounce. He and his new friends went to the Wisconsin State Fair in a cavalcade of convertibles. *The richer sort in America are refreshingly free from money-pride,* he writes in his journal. When Peter wasn't hanging out with the Crowells, the Southworths and the Hamiltons, he was arguing politics with Joe in the Tap Room at the Stock Yard Inn or visiting Fred's wife who was a dancer at a burlesque club.

In the spring of 2016, on a drive from New Glarus to Chicago, I decided to detour along Lake Michigan in order to visit the North Shore communities of Kenilworth and Winnetka. In 2011, Forbes ranked Kenilworth as the second most affluent neighbourhood in the United States. It is quaintly described as a 'village' and lies fifteen miles north of Chicago. I drove along wide avenues lined with turreted castles and mock Tudor mansions. It was eerily quiet, and the only people I saw were uniformed Mexican gardeners working out of landscaping trucks and a few lithe women walking small dogs. It all felt a little unreal, like a movie set waiting for the main actors to return from a break.

Happy, restful day in the suburbs. We had a barbeque supper with steak about a foot square and corn, broiled over charcoal braziers and, of course, buckets of whisky. I taught Bud and Bruce how to play darts. Bruce is a charming fellow, most unassuming though his father was VP of General Motors and his mother was a Dupont. I have been very impressed by the easy, warm-heartedness of everyone here: though Fayette Ann startled me by saying it was I who made these folk out to be so good. It was meant as a compliment but I hope the truth of it isn't that I'm indiscriminate.

Peter's nature precluded him from being openly discourteous, but he never hesitated in his felt obligation to comment on matters of moral importance. One of his bête noires was excessive drinking. *This evening I discussed, with Nat, the American lack of discrimination in drinking. The pre-dinner cocktails are always so crude, and so many that all sensibility is dulled. The food cannot be fairly savoured, and the development of a discriminating palate for wines is impossible.* Peter did not wish to appear haughty or ungrateful however, and he continued to join in the alcoholic merrymaking: *By bedtime, I felt very mellow from drinking whisky, wine, Benedictine and 'Stingers' (brandy and something).*

The only association I have with Kenilworth, apart from my father's wealthy Chicago friends, is Walker Evans, the documentary photographer known for his powerful images of rural Alabama during the Great Depression. Evans had lived in Kenilworth as a child. In 1983, I was staying with Gina Murray who had retired from Groton. She had a holiday home on Cranberry Island, Maine and at a supper party I was seated next to Isabelle Storey, the former Swiss wife of Walker Evans. She told me that in the late 1950s, at the age of 25, she had left her husband to marry Walker, who was thirty years her senior. In fact, I found Isabelle's stories less interesting than some of the others I heard around the dinner table that night. Cranberry is both beautiful and isolated and during July and August the island is popular with artists. One summer, an island boy fell in love with a girl from the mainland. He was angry and heartbroken when she ended the affair and returned to Boston. He was so angry in fact that he drove a bulldozer up to her parents' house and pushed it over a cliff into the sea.

I wonder what went through my grandfather's mind as he read Peter's letters telling him of his life in the Chicago suburbs, drinking milk punch with his millionaire friends. I expect he was happy for his son, relieved he'd got away and made such a good life for himself. Henry, Peter's grandfather, had been a cattle farmer in County Cavan, and had he lived in the rural Midwest, he too would have sent his cows for slaughter to the Union Stockyards. Cattle were in Peter's blood, and the summer he spent in Chicago was perhaps an unconscious bid to reconnect with his tenuous, but still felt, Irish roots. Ireland and Irishmen were never far from my father's mind: *Today I got picked up by a bum and taken for a lunch and three bottles of beer. Inevitably he was Irish.* In the Tap Room one night, Peter fell in with a party of tipsy waitresses saying farewell to Mary from Tipperary who was heading for New York: *We got on famously. She's had a hard time with a husband and I must be careful not to hurt her. I made a date with her for Sunday.*

As his time in Chicago came to an end, Peter began to spend what he referred to as: *gentleman's days in the stockyards, talking to the yardmasters and touring the Grain Exchange.* He never visited the killing beds or the packing houses though, and his journal, surprisingly, makes no mention of the sounds and smells of the Yards – the metallic odour of blood, the squealing of hogs and the braying of cattle. The French journalist, Jules Huret, writing in the Chicago Tribune in 1905, remarked that watching thousands of animals being driven to their destinies created: *a melancholy like that caused by the departure of armies.* I think of the men and women who lined the Slope Road in Folkestone to watch the million soldiers, my grandfather amongst them, march onto troop ships bound for the Killing Fields of WWI.

On August 25th, Peter flew to New York and immediately telephoned 'Tipperary Mary,' who was delighted to hear from him. Her Brooklyn landlady, however, strongly disapproved of my father and insisted that Audrey, a family friend, act as their chaperone. Audrey felt sorry for the couple and agreed to take care of Corinne, Mary's little girl, so the two of them could go to the movies and out to dinner. Unfortunately Peter had already decided that the relationship had no future. Mary's tears and declarations of love left him feeling guilty and he agreed he would write to her from Groton: *Mary thinks I am moody; rebutted this – but is it true? I wonder what causes such strong variations in mood and emotions?*

I have sometimes wondered whether my father's behaviour was related to a more serious mood disorder. The fact that he was so high functioning, so articulate and self-aware only served to deflect from the potential severity of his condition. He dismissed his psychiatrists with such regularity that they were perhaps never in a position to fully recognise the magnitude of his difficulties.

While he was in New York, Peter had a brainwave. He realised that his situation at Groton would always be tenuous, because permanent positions rarely occurred, save through death or retirement. He decided, therefore, to set himself up as an 'Alistair Cooke in reverse'. Cooke was an Englishman who had started his career as a correspondent with the Manchester Guardian. After he moved to America in 1937, he became the equivalent of a national treasure, known for his weekly Letter from America on BBC Radio, which was broadcast over a period of fifty-eight years. The formula was simple but unique and drew heavily on personal experiences of casual conversations with ordinary people. In 1952, 'The Letter' had just won a Peabody Award, radio's equivalent of an Oscar.

Peter wrote Cooke a letter, outlining his idea of teaching Americans about England and Cooke invited him to his apartment on 5th Avenue for a drink: *He was friendly, witty, entertaining and perhaps a little egotistical. If I want to go ahead with this, it will mean a clear-cut policy and high pressure salesmanship.* Nat Hamilton from Chicago put Peter in touch with Herb von Metzler, an investment banker on Wall Street. Herb liked Peter's Cooke idea and promised to introduce him to the right people once he had concrete proposals.

The morning after his meeting with von Metzler, Peter awoke feeling: *gloomy and depressed.* He had planned to start work on his new idea, but instead spent the day in *the neurotic, spirit-draining sleep of anxiety.* I don't think my father would have made a very good 'Alistair Cooke in reverse'. He was too partial and too affected by the opinions of others. He would have got distracted from his own remit, either by another, equally interesting idea, or by the renewed conviction of his own incompetence.

In an attempt to widen the horizons of both students and faculty, Jack Crocker had begun inviting distinguished speakers to the school. Over the years, these included Eleanor Roosevelt, Martin Luther King Jr., Robert Frost, Reinhold Niebuhr and Kurt Hahn, founder of the Outward Bound movement. Peter decided to invite Alistair Cooke to speak to the boys, and on November 11th 1952, Cooke travelled the two hundred miles to Groton from New York. His talk was: *urbane and fluent – fluent to the point of glibness. All found him most entertaining.*

On his last day in New York, Peter went to the police station in search of two books he had left in a taxi. Here he witnessed what he referred to as: *an interesting scene. A coloured man and a white man had been brought in on an indecency charge. The two men were being interviewed by a detective and while he took the white man's finger prints, he talked to him, calling him a 'degenerate fuck' and threatening to 'punch his fucking jaw' if he didn't cooperate more. The detective seemed a pleasant chap and I wondered at his manner.*

The test of Groton is what its graduates will be like as human beings when they are your age and mine and even older.
Jack Crocker in a talk to the Faculty, April 1961

A Groton boy was deemed to be in service to God and his fellow man, and the school has always challenged its students to assume the mantle of social responsibility. Hiram Anthony Bingham, known as Tony, was Peter's advisee and Dorm prefect, and he taught my father how to play a strategic game of chequers. I was struck by the boy's name, and wondered whether he was any relation to Hiram Bingham, the explorer who discovered Macchu Picchu in 1911. Tony died in 2008 and his obituary is a template for the ideal Groton student. He founded a company promoting renewable energy and clean technology, and was a generous supporter and patron of the Waldorf schools. Tony Bingham's grandmother was an heiress to the Tiffany fortune and his grandfather had indeed discovered The Lost City of the Incas. The Binghams, however, recognised that great wealth carried great responsibility. Tony's father, Hiram Bingham IV, known as Harry, was the US Vice Consul in Marseilles during WWII and in 1940, he disobeyed orders from Washington, and issued more than two and a half thousand exit visas to Jewish refugees escaping to the United States. When the war ended, so did his career with the State Department. Unlike Paul Grueninger, however, Harry Bingham was financially secure. He and his wife Rose, who worked as a teacher, retired to the family farm in Connecticut and raised their eleven children, of which Tony was the eldest. It was not until Harry Bingham died in 1988, that the full extent of his humanitarian work during WWII was discovered, and he was subsequently honoured by Yad Vashem.

For several years Jack Crocker had been giving serious consideration to the question of admitting African Americans to Groton. He was well aware that the school was not living up to its Christian ideals by limiting what it offered only to wealthy white boys. In September 1952, two years before the United States Supreme Court ruled that racially separate educational facilities were inherently unequal, Roscoe Lewis from Washington DC became the school's first black student. In February 1957, Peter, who had left Groton and was teaching back in England, received an anonymous letter addressed to all parents and faculty, announcing the school's intention to: *increase the number of negroes from a few students to not less than a quarter of its total enrolment. Groton pledges, if necessary, the full use of its entire endowment fund towards scholarships for the purpose.* It turned out to be a hoax and following an in-depth investigation, the agitator was exposed as Duke Sedgwick. He explained that he wished only to spare African American students the disappointment of being denied the ability to date and marry the sisters of their white classmates.

In November 1952, Groton was back in the news when the Austin Motor Company launched an advertisement with the caption: *I am sending my son to Groton on the money I saved by buying an Austin.* Jack was furious at this crude attempt to combine snobbery and economy at Groton's expense.

That winter, Peter bought a car: Perhaps he should have chosen an Austin, because his 1941 Buick convertible ended up costing him a great deal of money in repairs. He needed a car in order to drive to Cambridge for appointments with his new therapist. Psychology was coming of age in the 1950s, and many schools in America were appointing resident psychiatrists.

Reverend Crocker was reluctant to do this, because he disagreed with Freud's theory that religion was a neurosis and that man should rely, not on God for his salvation, but on himself and his own efforts. He recognised, however, that Groton needed help, and so he contacted Dr Herbert Harris, a psychiatrist at The Massachusetts Institute of Technology. It was Jack who recommended Harris to Peter: *He's expensive – $25, but he said that if I was as free in future as I was today, three months might see me through.*

If all masters were like Mr O'Connell, school would be a wonderful place
Mr Kellog, quoting his son, Tony in a letter to Peter

Peter remained committed to purposeful and relevant teaching. In October of 1952, he took a group of boys to hear Adlai Stevenson speak in Boston, stopping en route to buy them milk shakes at Howard Johnson. A week later, he woke his dorm at one in the morning to hear the results of the presidential election. In History classes, Mr O'Connell used the coronation of Queen Elizabeth to teach his students about seventeenth century religious conflict in Ireland; in English, he recorded the boys reciting Hamlet's soliloquies, and then played them a tape of the same passages spoken by Laurence Olivier. Peter's intention was to inspire, but for some, the comparison served only to deflate. Parke Gray, son of the Bishop of Connecticut, so disliked the work in Mr O'Connell's class, that he complained to the Head of English and asked to be moved to another division.

Peter was known to be very pro-Irish and sensitive to any implied criticism of his father's people. In 2017, Jim Amory recalled a comment he had once made to Mr O'Connell about the bloodthirstiness of the Irish when compared to the relatively civilised behaviour of the Scots: *Mr O'Connell snorted and countered with - Well, the Irish fought for centuries to get the English out of their country, while the Scots satisfied their patriotism by dancing around a couple of swords. He got kind of hot under the collar.*

Peter also took time to speak to worried parents: *I spent two hours with Mr C at the Groton Inn, while he expressed his anxiety about his son. He has the most mixed-up attitude towards the poor boy – has even gone so far as to threaten him that if he doesn't 'do better' (by which he means make friends and become socially popular), then he won't go to Harvard. I tried to point out that you cannot compel a person to be popular, and that John is suffering now from over-tension and needs easy relaxed relations with his family.*

My father was away a lot when I was growing up: teaching, learning and making the world a better place. He felt guilty about his frequent absences, so he sent me postcards. These invariably contained educational quizzes intended to improve my mind, because a simple postcard would have been simply wasteful. Unlike Parke Gray, I couldn't move to another division. All I could do was refuse to give them my attention. I still balk at riddles. I simply will not engage with them, and I recognise, with some satisfaction, that my interrogator is entirely powerless in the face of my noncompliance.

Peter's desire, both to educate and be popular, occasionally undermined his good judgement. Once, on the way back to

Groton from a football game, he even put lives at risk: *I meant to be sedate, but when Fitz Hardcastle passed me I couldn't resist the temptation to repass, travelling at one point at 65mph. This is too fast with boys aboard and with one worn tyre.*

Douglas Brown is the Groton School archivist, still in post in 2020. In 1954 he was a student in Peter's English class and he recalls asking Mr O'Connell to raise his grade so he could remain on the honour roll. Peter agreed, but Doug subsequently regretted his request: *Mr O'Connell was the adult and the correct response should have been: This is the mark I believe you deserve and corresponds to your overall efforts and achievement. It will stand as it is.* He told me, a little sadly, that following this incident, his relationship with my father became more distant.

In 1953 Peter was still unmarried. He was handsome, intelligent and caring, so why, at the age of thirty-four, had he not settled down with a nice girl? An unofficial campaign was launched at Groton to find Mr O'Connell a wife, a movement which included the faculty wives, the boys and even the young Irish girl who cleaned Peter's rooms.

One of Cary Grant's four spouses allegedly divorced him on the grounds that she was incapable of being his perfect wife. My father's own definition of perfect was always just beyond his reach, but he was faithful in pursuing it whenever the opportunity presented itself. At Prize Day in 1953, Peter was introduced to Alice Sedgwick, Duke's eldest daughter who was a student at Radcliffe. He was smitten by her good looks and quick wit, and wrote to her with an invitation to have dinner with him. She was slow to respond, which surprised and irritated him, but when her letter eventually arrived it was charming. She was very busy and the only time she could see Peter was during the Christmas vacation. She suggested he come down to Washington and have supper with her there and she asked that he write to her again: *And I shall undoubtedly do so*. He was mesmerised by what he described as her *artistic, impulsive and lively mind. I think I could easily fall in love with Alice Sedgwick.*

Impulsive and artistic were adjectives often used to describe Duke Sedgwick and his eight handsome children. Duke was a world renowned artist and sculptor. In his early twenties, he spent three months at a psychiatric hospital in Stockbridge, Massachusetts, following a manic-depressive episode. Two of his three sons followed in his footsteps: Minty took his own life at Silver Hill psychiatric hospital in 1964. Bobby was institutionalised for depression and on New Year's Eve 1965, he ran a red light and crashed his motorbike into the side of a bus. He never regained consciousness.

The best known of Duke's children was his seventh child, Edie, who was Andy Warhol's muse and Bob Dylan's some-time girlfriend when they lived at the Chelsea Hotel in New York. Edie's drug use and her excessive lifestyle accentuated her already fragile mental health and like Duke, Bobby and Minty, she spent time in psychiatric institutions and died in 1971 of a drug overdose. According to John Sedgwick, his cousin Alice, or 'Saucie' as she was known by the family, was the sensible one who picked up the pieces and tried to put them back together again. Duke was angry at his sons' deaths, and he blamed, not his beloved alma mater, but its headmaster. In a deeply offensive letter to Jack Crocker, he accused his good friend of failing to prevent Minty's suicide. Shortly before Duke's death in 1967, when the state of his own mental health had finally been acknowledged, he wrote a second letter to Jack, one as touching and sweet as the first one had been cruel and ugly. Jack Crocker replied with both a graciousness and a depth of understanding that confirmed all his Christian teachings on kindness and forgiveness. The fact that his own mother, like Minty, had died at Silver Hill may well have been an additional factor in Jack's generosity of spirit. The last time Francis 'Duke' Minturn Sedgwick appeared in public was to unveil his life-size statue of St Francis, receiving the Stigmata. Duke and his wife Alice gifted the artwork to the Old Mission in Santa Barbara in memory of their two deceased sons, Robert Minturn and Francis Minturn Sedgwick.

On December 22nd Peter took the train to Washington and went to collect Alice from her job at Brentano's bookstore. Unfortunately she had forgotten to tell him that it was her day off. He took a cab to her apartment and after dinner the evening developed into a party: *Young things started dropping by. Alice is engaging but sloppily dressed, and not as attractive as I had imagined her.* And that, was another end, to that.

In February of 1953, Betsy and Marge invited Peter to a cocktail party in honour of the third wife of Joseph Chamberlain. That night he met Jeannette who he describes as: *an attractive blonde, womanly and intelligent.* He invited her to the Groton School dance, and the Peabody sisters generously offered to cover the cost of her airfare from Poughkeepsie. To this day I remain puzzled that Peter was considered to be an appropriate match for these college girls. I suppose he was a good catch and a young girl attending one of the prestigious 'Seven Sisters' colleges would have made him a fine wife. At the age of nineteen I entered into a relationship with a man of thirty. My mother was initially suspicious and disapproving. My father believed that he would improve my mind and act as a steadying influence. Dad even went so far as to lend us the family car for a summer holiday in Italy, a gesture my mother considered to be impulsive and inappropriate.

Jeannette was different from the other young women Peter had met at Groton. She intended to break her engagement to an eminently suitable medic in her hometown of St Louis, not on Peter's account but in order to pursue a career in academia. For a Southern belle in the 1950s, this was highly unusual thinking. Jeannette considered Peter to be quaint rather than attractive and, in her letters, she refers to him as *brother*, a term he found endearing but confusing. In early May he drove his convertible across country to visit her at Vassar where he was astonished to see: *girls coming into the lecture hall, wearing Bermuda shorts and blue jeans and chewing bubble gum.* That evening at supper, he was the only man in a dining hall of sixty women: *I sat at table with eight pretty girls and had coffee in the housemother's sitting room, where I felt like Harun al Rashid in the 1001 Nights.* Jeannette was wise beyond her twenty-one years and told Peter that he needed to think less about himself and more about others. She declared that she was fond of him, but didn't want to see: *someone so brilliant waste his time working on a problem that might take years to solve.*

Dr Harris had suggested that Peter leave the monastic community of Groton and apply for a teaching job at Bennington, an all-women's liberal arts college in Vermont.

Fortunately, he was happy at Groton and had the foresight to recognise that escaping to a women's college, where he would be permanently surrounded by young Scheherazades, could only serve to exacerbate his difficulties.

I saw Jack Crocker as a god-like figure.
Douglas Brown

In 2016 during an afternoon spent with Doug in the archives of Hundred House I asked him about the changing nature of religious faith at Groton. It is no longer promoted as a Christian school and Sacred Studies has been replaced by Ethics. Some form of worship, however, is compulsory and chapel remains mandatory four mornings a week: *You can claim you hate it,* said Doug, *you can refuse to sing or say amen but you're in there four or five days a week, and over time it will have an effect on you. It becomes a spiritual experience, however you choose to interpret it.*

It was through Jack Crocker that Peter first experienced religious faith as a source of consolation rather than punishment. Whenever his belief, either in himself or in God, began to falter, it was Jack who gave him renewed courage; it was talking to Jack that temporarily chased away the devil snapping at his heels.

The Reverend Crocker was a tall, imposing man with a hearty laugh. He wore a collar at all times, robes in chapel and was widely respected as a preacher. Sometimes he spoke to the inner world of the Groton boy, sometimes he spoke of the society that surrounded it, but his sermons were always relevant and important. Jack's intention was to prepare students and faculty to meet failure without losing heart, and to handle success without being corrupted by it. These were particular issues that haunted my father. He struggled to accept the possibility of a middle way, one that might include both human and divine rapture: *My faith in a hereafter is so very small, whereas my conviction that this is a very sweet world is powerful and probably exaggerated by my inability to savour it.* Jack considered Peter to be *essentially religious* because he was attuned to the feelings of others, especially to the boys who struggled under the pressure of life at Groton. An awestruck pupil at Highfield had once declared that listening to Mr O'Connell read the gospel was like listening to Jesus himself.

In the Gospel according to Matthew, Simon Peter is assured that he will be safe from the waves that threaten him as long as his eyes remain fixed on Jesus. In her book, Auntie Dorrie is more admonishing: *Oh you Peters who are reading this. Don't try to save yourselves. It is a hopeless task and will only end in despair. Do what Peter did – cry to the Saviour, cry to Him with all your might: 'Lord, save me'.*

After four months with Dr Harris, Peter decided to abandon therapy and approach his problem from a religious perspective, with Jack as his spiritual adviser. Harris described Peter's relationship with his mother as *pathological* and declared that it was the most acute case he had ever come across. Peter responded with the observation that it was: *no more pathological than jumping in to a river to save a drowning man.*

In gratitude for Peter's kindness to his son, Reinhold Niebuhr gave my father a signed copy of his book *The Irony of American History.* In his thank-you letter, Peter took the opportunity to seek Niebuhr's advice regarding his own religious hairballs, and he received a thoughtful and gracious reply:

May 7th 1952

Dear Mr O'Connell,
I deeply appreciate your letter, if for no other reason than it gives me an opportunity to thank you for your great kindness and help to Christopher. I meant my copy of the book to be a token of my gratitude, but it is a poor token indeed. I find as a matter of fact that parents are so deeply indebted to teachers who take an interest in their children that there is no adequate way of expressing gratitude.
The issues which you raise in your letter have concerned me all of my life, but I have reached rather different conclusions. I believe, for instance, that in a world where, as Pascal said, justice must be enforced by power, the voluntary abnegation of power by a few Christians is not as valuable as the wielding of power 'with fear and trembling' in the way that every business man and every Government official must wield it. Whether on the question of powerlessness or poverty, it seems to me that the Christian has to choose essentially between the Monastic-perfectionist principle of goodness and an essentially Protestant one. According to the one, he seeks to free himself from the evils of the world, but he does not seriously affect the struggle in the world for a tolerable justice and brotherhood. According to the other, he never escapes guilt because he is involved in all the various forms of guilt in the social life of man, but he regards this as a concomitant of 'an ethic of responsibility' in contrast to 'an ethic of perfection'. I know

this is a very sketchy way of stating a very ultimate problem
with which I have been wrestling, as it were, all my life.
With cordial personal regards, Reinhold Niebuhr.

Niebuhr spent thirteen years as a pastor in Detroit, where he was highly vocal in his criticisms of Henry Ford and the American automobile industry in the days before labour was protected by unions. His own humility and lack of social pretension established him as a figure of enormous respect amongst politicians, students and civil rights activists. Martin Luther King Jr. studied Niebuhr while he was writing his doctoral thesis and later praised him as a theologian of great prophetic vision. In 1965 King invited him to join the march from Selma to Montgomery and only a severe stroke prevented him from accepting the invitation. Niebuhr is perhaps best known for writing *The Serenity Prayer* which was later adopted by Alcoholics Anonymous.

In 1957 Peter received a letter from Christopher Niebuhr in Stuttgart, where he was stationed with the Medical division. Army teaching, he writes, is poor and: *it is nice to remember the days of instruction I had under you.* He also refers to the new US ambassador to the UK, former Groton alumnus, John Hay Whitney: *His stepdaughter is going to be his hostess. I think it is quite ironic that a Roosevelt will be the American hostess under a Republican administration.*

A man is trapped in his home by rising flood waters. He stands on the roof of his house and prays fervently to God to rescue him. A boat sails past and offers to take him onboard, but he declines, saying: *God will save me.* A little later, a helicopter flies overhead and the pilot offers him a lift: *No thank you,* replies the man, *I'm waiting for God.* Eventually, the man drowns, and when he arrives before the Almighty, he complains bitterly: *I prayed so hard and you didn't help me,* to which God replies: *I sent you a boat and a helicopter.*

It is a great pity that Reinhold Niebuhr, Jack Crocker and even the long shadow cast by the mighty Reverend Peabody, could not rescue my father from the turbulent waters of his evangelical childhood, and the guilt and doubt that consumed his adult life. He had the tremendous good fortune to meet two wise and principled religious thinkers who offered him a meaningful alternative to Grace and Dorrie's *vile, helpless, hopeless sinners* model of theology. His religion, however, remained rooted, not in awe, not in wonder of God's love, but in an unrelenting fear of punishment and eternity in Hell.

In my first year at Reading University, I met Fiona. She was a Christian; not a closet Christian and not a member of the campus God squad, but someone who lived openly and proudly according to Christian values. She did not lead with her faith and never sought to criticise or convert those who were not on the path to God. I began to ask her questions about what it meant and felt like to be a Christian and she suggested I attend a fellowship meeting. The hall was packed and the atmosphere was tense with anticipation. People were invited to come to the front if they felt Jesus moving inside them and to the front they went, one after the other, waving their arms and weeping. At first, I was embarrassed. What if someone I knew put their head round the door to see what all the noise was about? How would I explain myself? Perhaps I should just leave? Then, something strange happened. I suddenly wanted to feel God's love flooding my chest. I wanted to be saved by the Holy Spirit, so that at the hour of my death, I too would go straight to Heaven, just like my grandmother and my Auntie Dorrie. But nothing happened, and I left feeling physically underwhelmed and spiritually disappointed. I quickly recovered from my misadventure and soon forgot about my failure to speak to God or have Him speak to me. For my father, however, the weight of His silence was a constant and excruciating burden that he carried throughout his life.

On April 12th 1953, Joyce died of leukaemia. When Peter received the news, he immediately wrote a long letter of condolence to his father, cancelled his plans to go out West for the summer and booked a passage home to England. Shortly afterwards, a letter arrived from Lea with the news that she had broken with Hans and this time, she declared, there would be no going back. In her journal she says she feels *numb and bewildered*, and in his diary Peter confesses to feeling *ambushed and uneasy*. He cautions himself to tread carefully with her when they meet again in London.

I am reading The Cruel Sea by Nicholas Monsarrat. I did not a stroke of work before I'd finished it and very little after. There is a very satisfying sense of sound moral values; it's tough, realistic and in places horrifying, but there's no trace of nihilism.

In 2014 my cousin, Anne-Isabelle Fleming, sent me a book entitled *What Cares the Sea?* by Kenneth Cooke, with a note telling me that John Turney Arnold, one of the heroes of the story, was Peter's and her father Toby's first cousin.

On March 19th, 1943 a merchant ship, the SS Lulworth Hill, was torpedoed by an enemy submarine in the South Atlantic. The ship sank in ninety seconds and of the fifty-seven men on board only fourteen survived the attack. After fifty days at sea, the raft was spotted by a British destroyer and two survivors were rescued, one of whom was Kenneth Cooke. In 1960 he published his account of those seven weeks adrift.

Many of the men suffered terrible injuries from the initial explosion; one had lost both his feet, and three others were badly burnt. Their bodies, covered in saltwater boils, began to split like pieces of raw beef; their tongues went black and the air was filled with the sickly, sweet smell of gangrene. John Arnold, a seventeen-year-old apprentice, was one of the survivors. He was a deeply religious young man, and each night, he offered up a prayer to God on behalf of the small party of men. On April 12th, 'Little John', as he was known, told Cooke that he was preparing to die. God had spoken to him, he said, and told him that some of the men would survive and that Cooke would be one of them. As he lay in the older man's arms, John offered up a final prayer, thanking God for Cooke's friendship, and asking his friend for one last favour: to tell his parents that he died a good Christian.

After John died, there were no more prayers. Some of the men committed suicide by rolling overboard to be eaten by sharks; others went insane from the effects of drinking sea water. Twenty-two years later, Kenneth Cooke was invited to speak to John Arnold's bible study class in Surrey. He told the assembled group that it was the face of Little John that had kept him sane; it was the memory of what John had said to him that had given him hope, again and again: *His example and his presence saved and altered my life. I have never met anyone like him, and the day it is my turn to go, I truly believe that I will meet Little John again.*

I was very moved by Cooke's story, both by the book and the 1965 recording of his talk, which survives in the archives of David Arnold, John's half-brother. I was astonished that I had never heard of this young man. It seems that Peter too was unaware of the fact that his first cousin, his mother's nephew, had been a young man of such physical and spiritual courage.

Memorial Day in America marks the beginning of the long summer vacation, and Peter describes it as a day of: *relaxed, easy and democratic marching, parading and remembering. It is a pity the Russians cannot rid themselves of some of their obsessions on American warmongering. Nothing could look less aggressive, less arrogant or less full of military pride than the school band and the rows of easy-swinging lads in their white ducks, blue coats and overseas caps, followed by a ragged little detachment of Boy Scouts and Brownies, led by Jack Crocker on a rather restless horse.*

My father used to say that if you weren't a Communist in your twenties, then you had no heart and if you were still a Communist in your thirties, then you had no brain. During my university years, I favoured the 'better red than dead' ideology, and in October 1981 my housemates and I attended a nuclear disarmament rally in London. We spray-painted a sheet with the slogan: '44 Basingstoke Road Against the Bomb', attached it to a couple of broomsticks and marched down St James. Dad had bought the house on Basingstoke Road, in part to off-set his tax bill, but also because he wanted me to learn how to manage money. As we marched, a reporter with a notebook slipped in alongside us, and asked why we were demonstrating and whether Number 44 was a commune. On Monday morning, our neighbour at Number 42 excitedly handed us his copy of the now defunct Communist newspaper *Morning Star*. The headline read:

> *'No missiles wanted here' sang marchers.*
>
> *A lone guardsman stomping up and down outside the Queen Mother's bomb shelter at Clarence House looked on blank faced. On this occasion, the richest old age pensioner in the land was not amused and she did not appear at a window to wave. Obviously she felt safe.*
>
> *But Suseli O'Connell didn't. Her banner declared, '44 Basingstoke Road Against the Bomb'. Number 44 is a small terraced house in Reading, and it is Ms. O'Connell's only home. Holding the other pole, her lodger, Ian Mather said: 'It's our fall-out shelter.'*

I phoned home to tell my father the exciting news, that I was not only a good but also a publicly-named Communist. He was interested, although a little perplexed. My mother was aghast. She told me that my name would now be recorded in government files and that I would have trouble finding a decent job, not to mention a professional husband who embraced the right politics. After I graduated from Reading, I applied for a visa to study in the United States. The US Embassy rejected my application and that nailed it for my mother. She blamed my father and his stupid ideas and told me that even if I now lied on my customs form when answering the question: *Are you now or have you ever been a member of the Communist party?* the authorities would have all the proof they needed. They could track me down and God only knows where that might lead, because just look at what happened to all those Communists under Senator McCarthy. The whole thing took ages to calm down, by which time I had laid aside my half-hearted interest in Bolshevism in favour of more frivolous concerns.

On June 17th, 1953 Peter met his cousin Toby Fleming for a drink in New York, before setting sail for England aboard the Liberté.

My cabin companions seem pleasant – a doctor, a professor and a college boy. At table there are four girls, one from Smith and four men.

Thursday 18th June
Played bridge all morning and then sat on deck and got a very red nose. Steamy heat: they say it's because we're going through the Gulf Stream. After the movie this evening, I went dancing in the Winter Garden. Joined an attractive party of girls from the South and basked in their warm, Southern voices. Went out alone and listened to the wind shrieking through the rigging, and watched the masthead keeping steady course across the stars. Felt moved by the magic of ocean travel – this mighty ship, thrusting towards England at 30 mph. And by contrast the ghosts of other ships, other

sailors, who ventured forth in cockleshells and spent months to cover the distance this giant liner traverses in 5 days. What a staggering example of man's conquest of his environment, of the massive achievements of Western Europeans in the realm of science and technology. And in social organisation: how little like steerage is this tourist class.

Friday June 19th
After lunch, our table went along to Cabin Sports deck to watch the crew boxing tournament. The ring was set up aft in view of the great creamy wake stretching towards the western horizon. The sea was blue and calm. Later, gate-crashed Cabin swimming pool with Fran and then explored 1st class where she has a steward pal. After supper, a singsong in the sundeck lounge and Virginia reel on the Sports deck (to pipe music played by a Princeton man), followed by dancing in the Winter Garden until 2am. Won 50 cigarettes in a variation of musical chairs, known as musical knees.

Saturday June 20th
This afternoon I tried to have another swim in the Cabin pool, but the attendant had had pressure put on him and refused me admission. Felt sore, especially as the others managed to lie their way in. To bed about 2am – my stable companions all tucked up as usual.

Sunday 21st
Our 'table gang' has developed a strong esprit de corps. We spent the morning playing deck tennis and ping pong, and the afternoon writing and rehearsing a melodrama – The

Lighthouse, *the main humour of which came in walking round and round in the crouching position gradually straightening up. We rehearsed in the 1st class Press Room. I was the villain – an odd reversal of roles for me. The audience reacted correctly with cheers and hisses, drowning the last lines in laughter. We danced in the heavy roll until 2 and sang Auld Lang Syne. Then, we all trooped off to 1st Class. To bed at 3am.*

Liberté was the most glamorous of all the great liners and in 1953, it was the setting for the Hollywood movie *The French Line*, starring Jane Russell. It was so raunchy that the Archbishop of St Louis wrote a letter, which was read in Catholic churches, declaring that whoever saw *The French Line* would fall under penalty of mortal sin. Jane Russell, rather like my father, led a bit of a double life. She had found the Lord at the age of five and she insisted He had chosen her path to Hollywood. What she did, therefore, could not possibly be seen as the work of the devil. 'Christians have bosoms too,' she once snapped at a reporter. At the age of thirty, Russell turned her back on Hollywood and took up fund-raising and evangelism.

Monday 22nd June
Last day aboard. After lunch we spotted the coast of England and for several hours watched the Isle of Wight materialise out of the mist. The sun shone forth and made a gay homecoming. Southampton water never looked more beautiful to me. We passed very near Seaview and I could make out the place from which Lea and I used to watch the big ships passing by. The softness of the light, the freshness of the air, the dramatic

clouds, all spoke of home. It has been a delightful crossing in weather and in society. It was remarkable how ten such different persons at one table could blend so harmoniously: American college girls and boys, a young Frenchman and two middle-aged Englishmen. Each contributed something to the group and every one of us grew genuinely fond of the other nine in those five days.

As a child I loved to hear my father's stories of life on the ocean wave: the dining and dancing, the moonlit walks and the daily adjusting of wristwatches: 'We never suffered from jetlag', he used to say. I swatted away the things I found confusing, such as the mention of so many young women, and the unmistakeable disobedience my father had demonstrated by using First class facilities when he had only paid for those provided in Tourist. In 2004 instead of flying to Boston to see Dan, I decided to follow in my father's footsteps and sail to New York on *QEII*. Cunard wrote to me, listing the many delights that awaited me, including the promise that, as a woman travelling alone, I would be provided with: *a gentleman dance host.* I was horrified. I wanted to meet exciting strangers with whom I could go on rip-roaring adventures; a kind of adult version of Enid Blyton's *The Famous Five*. Ocean travel in the Noughties had clearly drifted a long way from what it had been in the Fifties and, reluctantly, I went back to flying *Virgin Atlantic*.

Chapter Five

A Foot in Two Camps

I begin to feel touches of love which up to now has been a strong though stifled hatred. God and my father both create these ambivalent emotions in me.

Shortly before Peter left for England, he had a powerful dream. He describes it as similar in content to many others, namely the conflict between his parents: *but it differed in that for the first time Dad was seen with some sympathy. At the same time, I was less inhibited and felt resentment towards him. I said I couldn't stand the conflict any longer. In the next sequence he had killed himself. In Harris's interpretation this means I killed him, and violently too.* During the two months that Peter was home from America, he and his father spoke about many things, including religion: *Dad now expresses a strong, though rather inchoate, religious conviction as a desire and a need to keep God always as a partner – a God who is interested only in spiritual growth. He has taken up a constructive, even creative response to his grief and has gained in tranquillity and depth of understanding. His health and his financial situation, however, worry me.*

In July Harry and Peter took a holiday together. They visited the family of one of Peter's former pupils at Highfield: *Entertained to see how well Dad and Mr K got on. He showed us all round the garden, a thing he rarely does for people, and chatted and laughed most affably with Dad.* Lea had booked a flight to London to coincide with Peter's visit home and, perhaps inspired by the success of his holiday with Harry, she began arranging a trip of her own: *Lea tells Gillie that she and I are going to the seaside together for a few days. I must squelch that notion.*

Peter avoided Lea as much as possible that summer but agreed to a short holiday in the week before she returned to Switzerland. Their relationship, however, remained strained: *Lea says she is disappointed in me, claims I am less thoughtful than formerly, but she loves me just the same. I do love and admire her without bounds, but am nearly certain that I cannot be in love with her.* He drove her to London Airport and they said their farewells in the departure hall: *I wonder when we shall meet again and in what circumstances. It seems a cruel fate and I wonder how much is in our stars and how much in ourselves.*

After Lea left, Peter invited his father to spend a few days in Oxford, an invitation Harry declined. Peter was disappointed, and decided instead to visit three former Highfielders who were, by then, students at Radley and Eton. He took them to lunch in Abingdon and then the four of them rowed down the Thames to Sutton Courtenay for tea: *The boys are quite unchanged and utterly delightful. The exquisite courteousness of all three of them shook me. I had forgotten the charm of it.* The following week, he received a thank-you letter: *Dear Mr O'Connell, It was wonderful to see you again after 3 years. I have not had such a cracking good day out from school since my first leave-out from Highfield and that is true, it's not just that it's the thing to say. I cannot thank you enough for wasting some of your limited and valuable time to take me, Philip and Peter out. Yours truly, John Cox.*

Inspired by his trip to Eton, Peter decided to visit Dulwich College, his own alma mater and a place he had avoided for twenty years: *It was a powerful experience and I got a glimpse of the emotional forces that are so conflicting in me and of their origin and composition.* The memory of his sudden dismissal, only weeks before his final examinations, lingered like a festering wound. His mother and her family had made it possible for him to attend Dulwich; his father had made it impossible for him to remain there. Peter was angry and humiliated and in spite of his many successes in life, he could never shake the belief that, in comparison to his peers, he just wasn't quite up to scratch.

Shortly before he returned to America, Peter had dinner with the family of Jan Van Roijen, a fourth former at Groton. Herman van Roijen had been instrumental in negotiating Indonesian independence and in 1953 he was the Dutch Ambassador to Washington. Peter, inspired by their conversation that night, decided to write a letter to Winston Churchill – if American Presidents could offer words of encouragement to the boys at Groton, then why not British Prime Ministers?

My father was singularly unimpressed by celebrity and had no patience with people who sought only to distinguish themselves. He believed in excellence, collaboration and good role models. In 1968, the year Cliff Richard almost won the Eurovision Song Contest, my father invited him down to Folkestone to sing to our students at The School of English Studies. I was only nine years old, but even I thought this was a bit of stretch. Dad, however, considered that Cliff had a good voice, was wholesome and quintessentially English, and he thought the students would enjoy the concert. Peter never received a reply to his invitation. In 1988, however, Stephan and I, who had started our own promotional watch company, were approached by the Cliff Richard Fan Club and asked to design a timepiece for his thirtieth anniversary in show business. The organiser wanted a likeness of Sir Cliff on the dial. My father considered this to be the height of vulgarity. The fans liked it though, and the club put in an order for one hundred watches.

I only once saw my father impressed by fame. He returned home from London one evening and said, with a flourish: 'Guess who I saw today?' I didn't want to guess and so I waited. A taxi, he told me, had pulled up in front of him, and 'four long-haired louts' had got out. 'Guess who they were', he continued. I waited. 'Mick Jagger and the Rolling Stones!' he announced, straightening his back and rolling his shoulders slightly: 'the seat of the cab was still warm when I sat down'. Uncle Leonard's granddaughter, my cousin Sally, had worked as a Norland Nanny to the Jagger family, and later became the band's tour manager. I was utterly obsessed with The Rolling Stones, and my father was convinced that his brush with rock royalty would impress me. He was right, although I considered the experience to have been entirely wasted on a non-believer. Mick Jagger was a legend, not a long haired lout!

During his final weeks in England Peter spent as much time as possible with his father: *Our relationship has undergone a quite remarkable change. His awakened religious faith has contributed to this improved understanding, and my own greater ease and confidence has also helped. We parted today with genuine regret.*

I sometimes wonder how Peter's life might have unfolded had Grace survived Harry. I suspect he would have abandoned all thoughts of an independent life and lived as his mother's companion, mirroring the life of his cousin 'Bunch' who cared for Grace's sister, Ruby: *I took Bunch out to supper at the Chicken Inn and listened to accounts of her peregrinations with her mother and of jobs started and abandoned to suit the whims of that egotistical old bitch. She's a sweet, unselfish girl and never stops to ask herself if she's happy or not. She's a true saint.*

In August, Lea wrote to Peter saying that she wanted no further contact with him. This could only mean one thing Peter concluded: she had returned to Balmer. He ignored her request and she responded. *I'm confused. She says she recognises that she will never mean more to me than she does now, but she wants to continue as 'friends'.*

Groton School is perfectly incomprehensible to those who have not belonged to it.
William Amory Gardner, teacher, 1884 – 1930.

I recognise that I have an idealised view of Groton School, due, in part, to the fact that I have never belonged to its student body. It was, however, a close call. In 1975, twenty-three years after the school accepted its first African American student, Groton opened its doors to girls. It was around this time that my parents, alarmed by my increasingly difficult behaviour, sought the advice of their general practitioner. Dr Whittaker diagnosed me as neurotic, and prescribed valium to calm my nerves. My parents were reluctant to pursue this route to healing and my father considered sending me to boarding school. The three contenders were A.S. Neill's Summerhill, St Christopher, Letchworth and Groton. In a letter sent to me from Massachusetts in 1974, Dad writes: *I have spoken to the Director of Admissions about you. He's impressed! You're too young for 1975 as a 6th Former but he'll take you in 1976 for one year as a non-diploma candidate (no worry about exams!). Or, you can come next year as a 5th Former, stay for two years and take a Groton School Diploma (very highly regarded). I have just seen the Groton film – if you saw it you'd be lining up for a place! All those handsome boys and lots of fun amongst the hard work.* I am astonished by my father's liberal use of the exclamation mark, a form of punctuation he generally considered to be a sign of lazy writing!

Dad was enthusiastic about the possibility of my going to Groton, but Mum was dead against it. She said I'd fall in love with an American and never come back, which, to me, felt more like a promise than a threat. Twenty-five years later, when Stephan was offered a position with an American watch company in New Jersey, I wrote to the headmaster and inquired about the possibility of enrolling Polly and Lucy at Groton. Bill Polk had been a pupil of Peter's and expressed delight at the prospect of _two_ O'Connells walking the hallways of Hundred House. In the end, we moved to London, and the girls became day pupils at St Christopher School, Letchworth.

There is, of course, another side to Groton. Alan Pifer, honoured as a *Distinguished Grotonian* and a guest speaker at the school's one hundredth birthday, had been unhappy there and chose to educate his three sons elsewhere. Amos Booth, who spent three years at Groton as a bachelor in the 1950s and then returned in 1973 with his young family, wrote: *More than did your father, I ran across a disaffected minority who were – and remain – victims, unsung, and still hurting. Foremost on my list and conscience are my own children, hapless victims of my benighted ignorance and witness to my involvement in the lives of other people's children. In the 'old days' faculty brats were farmed out to other boarding schools.* Amos' wife, Jeannine grew to hate Groton. In 1978, in a letter to my father, Amos wrote: *Nanie is working for $3 an hour in a dress shop which at least gets her out of the incestuous atmosphere of the 'family school' and its hallowed halls.*

In the summer of 1968, my favourite song in the UK charts was *Massachusetts* by the Bee Gees. The Gibb brothers sang about 'going home' to Massachusetts and whenever I heard the opening bars of the song, the walls of my heart would grow soft and wide and I experienced a great longing for a place I had never seen.

In the spring of 2017, I travelled to Massachusetts with the intention of digging deeper into the mystery and the magic that is Groton School. I arrived at eight o'clock on a May morning, expecting to negotiate locked gates and an intercom system, but there was only Herm, the security guard, standing outside the chapel. He listened with interest to my story and then said: 'If your dad was here in the 1950s, then you best talk to Mr Sackett. He's coming up the path behind you'. Hugh Sackett had arrived at Groton the year my father left, but had visited Peter and Lea in England in 1958.

The Chapel talks at Groton have become a rite of passage for students in their senior year, and the best ones are published in the Groton School Quarterly. I heard three talks during the four days I spent on campus, and was surprised by their revelatory content. School policy is not to censor nor even to read the chapel talks in advance and students are left with the consequences of what they choose to share. The Groton hallmark, however, remains: life isn't simply about following your heart, it's about using your silver spoon to live a life that has purpose and meaning. After chapel I sat for a while on a bench outside Schoolhouse. The hot pinks and soft corals of cherry and rhododendron blossomed beneath a cobalt blue sky and as the sunlight hit the white porticos and the golden cupola, I experienced a great yearning to step back in time and walk into my father's long ago life at Groton.

Soccer squad shaping up well. Kermit Roosevelt is a useful recruit.
Peter's diary.

Between 1899 and 1961, twenty members of the Roosevelt family graduated from Groton. Kermit was the great-grandson of President Theodore and Kermit's father, Kermit 'Kim' Jr. led the 1953 coup which brought Shah Reza Pahlavi to power in Iran. Kermit, who was on Peter's soccer team, chose to send his own son, Kermit to a private school in Washington DC. The last Roosevelt to graduate from Groton in 1961 was Theodore

IV, the great-great-grandson of the twenty-sixth President of the United States. Groton's most famous Roosevelt was Franklin Delano, the first and only President in American history to be elected to four consecutive terms. Franklin, an only child and used to solitary pursuits, did not thrive at the school, although he sent his eldest son John, to Groton. In 1934 on the occasion of John's graduation, Betsy Pifer marched the then thirteen-year-old Alan up to FDR and said: 'Mr President, I would like you to meet my son, Alan'. Betsy, like Sara Delano, had an intuition that her son was destined for greatness. Perhaps she hoped that one day, upon hearing the name Alan Pifer, the President might recall the day he had been formally introduced to the young man at Groton.

During the four days I spent at Groton, I sat in on a History class, joined the students for milk and cookies in The Sackett Forum and toured the dormitories of Hundred House. The wood panelled cubicles with their single beds are long gone, and the dorm masters' studies and bedrooms have been converted into student lounges. On the day I returned to England I thought about all the stories my father had so lovingly shared with me as I was growing up, stories which I had embellished in my own imagination. Groton, although alien in many ways, is not *perfectly incomprehensible* to me. My father's love affair with the school has become mine and, as long as I live, I think I shall view Groton as practically perfect in every way.

Peter's diary entries in his last year at the school seem less burdened, more joyful, even witty. Shortly before term started, one hundred and twenty clergymen from the Diocese of Massachusetts gathered on campus for an Episcopalian convention. Peter was asked to guide them to their cubicles, a duty he described as: *reminiscent of my job last year in the Stockyards of Chicago!* During his fireside chats with Jack Crocker, Peter no longer pursued theological issues. Instead, he talked about Harry, telling Jack about his father's recovered faith and his plans to write a book on religions of the world.

I had a letter from Dad this morning. He admitted that the barriers of reserve were high between us and said a few more months might have enabled us to get to know one another. He was cheerful, his finances are sounder, and he was emphatic that I should not make plans that took account of him. Today I felt relaxed, happy and confident. In every way I felt that life was worth living.

Peter arrived at Groton in 1951 to replace 'Zu' Zahner who had gone to Beirut for a year to teach at the American University. Every spring Peter, and others like him, would wait for notification of available positions for the following year and if a post suited a master's skill set, he could apply. During my father's four years at Groton, he taught English, History, German, Latin and American Government, but in 1954 there were no suitable vacancies and he was forced to look for work elsewhere. In Switzerland meanwhile, Lea was struggling, and after several months of no contact, Peter received a letter from her saying that she had *broken finally* with Balmer. Life had been extremely difficult, but she was making new friends and had joined the English Club in Biel.

I don't know what prompted my father to propose to my mother a second time. Lea had broken with Hans so many times that perhaps he felt it was his duty, as a gentleman, to deliver her from evil, once and for all. In January 1955 he wrote asking her to marry him. Peter was preparing for a new life at Noble and Greenough School in Dedham near Boston and, in spite of his reservations, he recognised that Lea would make the ideal schoolmaster's wife. She was warm, kind and dedicated. She loved other people's children and, unlike a college bride, she would not be at risk of itchy feet. Lea was the one woman in Peter's life who had withstood the test of time and he knew that Grace would have approved the match. And so the matter was settled. Whatever misgivings my mother might have had about a second marriage proposal, tendered across a three-thousand-mile stretch of water, she agreed to become Peter's wife.

My darling Lea,
I feel joyful and confident at the thought of having you by my side — both to look after and to love and be loved by. Together we will explore worlds of wonder and together we will make a success of life. When I got your cable I began to tell a few people. They were amazed of course and then very enthusiastic, especially when they saw your photograph! The Crockers brushed away the tears in their eyes as they exclaimed: This is the most wonderful thing that's happened, this is just perfect; isn't she just lovely and what's her name and tell us all about her.

Groton was stunned. No-one, it seems, had ever heard of Lea Kummer. After years of creative and thoughtful match-making, Peter, it turned out, had a girl over there in Europe the whole time.

The following week, he received a letter from Bill Westgate, Headmaster of St Bernard's School in New York: *I write quickly a line of affectionate and enthusiastic congratulation to you on the news of your engagement. You are so manifestly a good and wise man that I know you must have chosen a really good and lovely girl.*

Of course Lea wasn't a 'girl' but a thirty-eight-year-old woman, approaching what, in the nineteen fifties, would have been considered middle age. Lea's advancing years, together with her medical history, would certainly have been indicators of a conceivably childless marriage. In his letter of January 15th, 1955, Peter writes that although he misses England and feels responsible for his father, a future in America would offer greater possibilities: *Now I've got you to inspire me I feel I shall be able to discover my talents. There's a good chance we can come back to Groton in a few years. And Dad would have a home here too.*

Yes, darling, relax and trust your feelings. It's been a long tough road for us both, but the future will compensate for it all. Write to me, pour out your heart, and let that big, overcharged and sorely wounded organ have a holiday.

God Bless. With warmest love, Peter

It was agreed that they would marry in Switzerland during the summer and then return to America together. A medical examination however, revealed Lea's tuberculosis, and the American Consulate in Zurich denied her an immigrant visa. In spite of this disappointing news, Peter and Lea were married on July 1st, 1955 at the reformed church in Biglen, near Bern. The wedding party consisted of just six guests: Rosa, Bertha, Bobi and his wife, Heidi and two Swiss cousins. Earlier in the year Lea had sent out a great many engagement notices announcing her forthcoming marriage to *Peter O'Connell of*

Boston, Mass, U.S.A. What the party lacked in size, therefore, was counterbalanced by the enormous number of cards and telegrams the couple received.

Peter and Lea on their wedding day, June 1955

At the wedding breakfast, the guests enjoyed oxtail soup, trout, champagne sorbet, filet mignon and a 'Bombe Prince Bueckler' for dessert. In photographs my mother looks beautiful in a bronze silk rockabilly dress, small veil and white gloves. She wears her trademark stilettos and carries a white cake-tin handbag. My father is wearing his St John's College tie and Rosa, Bertha and Heidi are dressed from head to toe in black. Everyone looks a bit grim, as though they've fought a long battle but haven't yet won the war. The visa issue remained unresolved, and Peter was to return to America in August without his wife. The newlyweds spent their wedding night at the Waldstaetterhof Hotel in Luzern, before taking the train to Melide for their honeymoon. Within forty-eight hours Peter had lost his wedding ring while swimming in Lake Lugano. He never replaced it, which I always thought was a shame: he had beautiful hands and a gold band on his wedding finger would have suited him.

Peter received wide-ranging support in his efforts to bring his new bride to America. Martin Hill, a contact at the United Nations, tried to find Lea a job with the Swiss Mission, but the department only employed unmarried women. The High Commission for Refugees had no vacancies. The most encouraging idea was put forward by the Auchincloss family. The Auchinclosses, like the Roosevelts, were dyed-in-the-wool Grotonians. Kenneth was in the Class of '55 and his grandfather, James C. Auchincloss represented New Jersey's Third Congressional District in the House of Representatives. Congressman Auchincloss was a seasoned politician who served a total of nine terms over an eighteen-year period. His suggestion, therefore, to introduce a private bill to Congress requesting that Mrs Lea O'Connell be granted permanent residence in the United States, was met with excitement and a great deal of relief. Bill number 9705 was to be presented to the House on March 1st, 1956 during the 2nd Session of the 84th Congress.

The application form asked for the names of relatives residing in the United States: Peter listed his cousin, Toby Fleming and Lea recorded her Aunt Elise in Wisconsin. In terms of people who could vouch for them, Peter offered John Mason Brown, a well-known New York drama critic, Dr Van Roijan, William Wood-Prince, President of the Union Stockyards of Chicago, and Congressman Auchincloss himself. My mother knew no-one of influence and so she left this section blank.

In anticipation of moving to America, she had resigned from her job at Omega in Biel and moved back in with her mother. There was nothing to do but wait for her visa to be issued.

Dan and I were married on August 18th, 2012 in Baraboo, Wisconsin. Unfortunately the immigration rules had changed just one month earlier, which left us stranded in America with incomplete documentation. We spent the first part of our honeymoon in a Bed and Breakfast in New Glarus, and made daily calls to our lawyer in London, who was herself confused by the new regulations and had to refer many of our queries to an Immigration hotline for clarification. In the evenings, we would venture out to eat fondue and drown our sorrows in Fechy, a brand of white wine I had never before encountered outside Switzerland. Across the state border in Chicago, Pat Quinn, an old school friend of Dan's and then Governor of Illinois, offered to contact the Immigration Authorities in New York, but even he was unable to make headway or fast-track our application. Eventually I returned to England without Dan. I often thought of my parents during this time, and although our visa difficulties were resolved by November, the uncertainty was distressing. Was it simply a matter of time, or would our case be rejected altogether, and, if it was, what on earth would we do?

After Mr O'Connell explained that even after the knights have been slain in battle their sweet-hearts marry them, Treadwell remarks: Boy, that's really dragging them to the altar.
School Notes, Nobleman, June 1956

I first visited Noble and Greenough School in 2016. My father always spoke easily and expansively about Groton, but he rarely mentioned Nobles. I used to think his sadness was due to the fact that he and my mother were separated that year, but, as I grew older, I began to sense that the grief he felt was more complex and largely unrelated to Lea. A few years before he died, Dad told me that there was a part of him that had always regretted the life he had been forced to leave behind in America. He would, he said, willingly have exchanged the affluence and the accolades for a humbler career as an English master, soccer coach and drama teacher at Nobles.

You may find your shift from Groton to Nobles like stepping out of a palace and into a cottage
Sidney Eaton, letter of April 6th, 1955.

In the spring of 1955, Peter received a letter from Sidney Eaton, a senior member of the English department: *Eliot Putnam tells me that you are to be with us next year and I write to extend the inky hand of welcome. I feel as if I know you already and I have an intuition that you will be good for us. We are small and we are traditional (though I hope thoughtfully so).*

In 1958, a young Englishman, who had been offered teaching positions at both Nobles and Groton, wrote to my father requesting an insider's view of both schools. Peter replied:

Dear Mr Pennington,
Let me say that you are a very lucky man if you go to teach at Nobles. It is in every way a first-class school. It is, in fact,

the best school I have ever come across – the most united, the happiest, one of the most beautiful. It has a tradition of hard work and good academic standards. It is not in the same class academically as Groton, but the boys are very well prepared for college intellectually and in every way. Faculty, parents, graduates, trustees and the boys themselves are all devoted to the school. Nothing is gold-plated and the boys are not spoilt. As in many institutions, much of this virtue flows down from the top. Eliot Putnam is an outstanding headmaster; in fact, he is the perfect headmaster. He always stresses the positive in school life, encouraging the boys to better efforts by praising their achievements individually and collectively. There is nothing of the mealy-mouthed or easily pleased about this as he has very high standards. The boys themselves are easy and natural but with a startling, almost Arnold-of-Rugby idealism in their approach to school life. Nobles is the only school in England or America that I know of where a definition of the gentleman hangs on the walls, is frequently read by the Headmaster in the morning assembly, and is quoted with no trace of satire or self-consciousness by the boys themselves. Relations amongst faculty are harmonious with none of the cliques so often found in schools.

As to Groton, I spent four very happy years there and thought it the best school in the world until I went to Nobles. They are not strictly comparable, Groton being 100% boarding and Nobles having only one third boarding and the boys nearly all go home at weekends. I preferred Nobles because I think a really good day school is preferable to the best boarding school. Nobles has all of Groton's undoubted school spirit, without the stresses and strains that inevitably flow from the artificial and unnatural life of a segregated boys boarding school.

Michael Pennington chose Noble and Greenough.

Peter arrived at Nobles in September of 1955 and moved into 'The Castle' as a dorm master. In the 1950s and 60s, Nobles had a reputation as a bit of a jock school and although today it is highly ranked academically, its playing fields and sports halls testify to a strong athletic legacy. Joseph Kennedy Jr and his younger brother, John F. Kennedy, were students at Nobles between 1924 and 1926.

Over the course of my life, I had managed to gather a cluster of seemingly unrelated facts about my father's year at Nobles: there was an outbreak of polio in the school and two children died. The football team, highly ranked and generally undefeated on New England's varsity circuit, failed to win a single match during that season. And then, there was the school play: Thornton Wilder's *Our Town,* which my father produced and directed in April of 1956. None of these things added up to very much.

I arrived at Nobles shortly before 9.00am on October 6th 2016, and, in spite of receiving a friendly welcome, I felt rather out of place. I had no hook upon which to hang any memories; there was no Doug Brown or Hugh Sackett on campus, and there was nothing about the school that I recognised. Nobles was a blank canvas and I wondered whether I might simply be visiting just one more private, privileged high school in twenty-first century America. Then the bell rang for Morning Assembly: it wasn't the high-pitched electronic shriek so often heard in school corridors, but the rich, deep sound of a bell cast in a foundry. My father would call his students to class in the same way, walking through the building ringing the SES handbell.

Morning Assembly, although less formal than at Groton,

was inspiring and on the day I visited, a reference was made to Eliot Putnam's favourite reading:

A gentleman is a man who never looks up to the rich or down to the poor, who can lose without whimpering, who can win without bragging, who is considerate of all women, children and old people – or those who are weaker or less fortunate than he is; a man who is too brave to lie, too generous to cheat; whose pride will not let him loaf, and who insists on doing his share of work in any capacity. A man who thinks of his neighbour before he thinks of himself and asks only to share equally with all men the blessings which God has showered upon us.

Charles Wiggins II, Headmaster 1920 – 1943

While I was waiting to see Isa Schaff, the archivist, I read Robert Henderson's Letter from the Head in the school magazine. Nobles was marking the first anniversary of the death of one of its students, sixteen-year-old Casey Dunne, who had collapsed and died from a brain haemorrhage on October 9th, 2015. The school was no stranger to tragedy, Mr Henderson reflected. Almost exactly sixty years earlier, on October 7th, 1955, eleven-year-old Arthur Putnam, had died in tragic circumstances. It had been a difficult year for the headmaster's family, Henderson continued, as Arthur was the second Putnam child to die that year. The beginning of the autumn term had also seen an outbreak of polio: *Great communities are at their best when things are at their worst,* concluded Mr Henderson.

The school was founded by George Washington Copp Noble in 1866, and eight years later, Mr Noble and his wife lost two children to scarlet fever. In 1921, the school purchased the family home of a railroad magnate, who had built himself a castle on land adjoining the Charles River in Dedham. Eliot Putnam arrived in 1931 to teach French and coach football. He and his wife, Laura moved into The Castle where they lived, together with their ever growing family – Eliot Jr, Rita, Betsy, Arthur and Charlie.

We lived together, studied together, played together, ate together, skated together. The ice was thick then. Safe.
from the play *Betsy and Arthur* by Jesse Putnam

Eliot Putnam had been a star quarterback on the football team at Harvard, and his eldest son, Eliot Jr. remembers him as a man: *without ego, strong, loyal, fair and humble.* Charlie Putnam describes his father as: *a worldly and sensitive man who respected good intellect, good sportsmanship and character most of all.* Mr Putnam coached the Nobles football team for twenty years, producing not only first-class athletes but also gentlemen on the field. He taught his boys the importance of gracious behaviour and of never, ever booing the opposing, generally losing, team. 'History is just the slow process of learning to be kind,' he used to tell his students.

Eliot Putnam cared deeply about the school. He aspired to make Nobles more accessible to the local community, and after days spent in the classroom, coaching football and even driving the school bus, Putnam would knock on doors in the neighbourhood, introducing himself and inviting Dedham families to send their sons and grandsons to Nobles. Laura Putnam was beautiful, and much loved by her husband. Every year, in the week before the annual school dance, Mr Putnam would give the boys a pep talk. Bob Chellis, Class of '55 recalls the Headmaster sitting on a desk, tapping ash from a cigarette into the cuff of his trousers and speaking to the boys about the importance of treating girls with the utmost respect, as if they were standing on a pedestal.

In the winter of 1952, Laura and Eliot Putnam's ten-year-old daughter, Betsy, began to complain of a sore foot. The local doctor said that the pain was caused by a form of arthritis associated with early adolescence. It failed to improve, however, and Betsy subsequently developed chronic fatigue. Eventually she was hospitalised and the doctors diagnosed Ewing's Sarcoma. Betsy Putnam was thirteen years old when she died on July 31st, 1955, and the whole school mourned her loss. The night the boarders returned in September, Eliot Putnam read them The 23rd Psalm: *The Lord is my shepherd; I shall not want -Yea, though I walk through the valley of the shadow of death, I will fear no evil; for Thou art with me -*

In May 2017 I attended my fortieth high school reunion. An abiding memory I have of my time at Ashford is the death of a girl in my year: Rosie Holloway was a boarder, she had long blonde hair and she died of leukaemia at the age of fourteen. That was all I ever remembered, and it was all I never forgot. As a clutch of women in their late fifties gathered on the lawn outside Schoolhouse for a photo opportunity, someone mentioned Rosie Holloway. I felt an odd sense of relief to hear her name spoken out loud after so many years, and I asked some of the former boarders who had known Rosie well about their recollections of how the school had dealt with her death.

It was never mentioned, they all agreed. Rosie had vanished and we all just carried on. Perhaps it was felt that openly addressing the young girl's death might upset us, and so a blind eye was turned to the truth.

In 1955 shortly after the first football game of the season at Nobles, four members of the varsity team contracted polio. The boys were hospitalised and two were placed in iron lungs. The Head met with the board of trustees and, in an attempt to contain the virus, a decision was taken to close the school and send all the boys home. Polio was a ruthless and highly contagious disease which, like a shark in shallow waters, spread fear and panic through a community. No one really knew where it came from, nor why most of its victims were children, but, in the United States in the early 1950s, polio was responsible for more than fifteen thousand cases of paralysis each year. With the school closed, the board of trustees encouraged Eliot and Laura to spend some time off campus in order to recover, both from the polio crisis and the loss, just two months earlier, of their daughter Betsy. On October 7th, they returned home to yet another tragedy. The Putnams' eleven-year-old son, Arthur, had, that very afternoon, been playing with his classmate Peter on a sandbank overlooking the playing fields, and a huge tree stump broke loose from an overhang. It rolled over Arthur, carrying him down the bank and killing him instantly.

In October, Richard Flood, the Assistant Headmaster, wrote to Peter:

You have had a rough baptism into life at Noble and Greenough School, but I have been impressed with the job you have done. It is quite evident that you are a real school man and we are all fortunate to have you with us. I want you to know the confidence I have in you and the comfort it is to know that someone so new to Nobles can do an especially good job for us. With repeated thanks, Sincerely, Dick Flood

Peter's eight months at Nobles were forged by unspeakable loss and an exceptional sense of community. Lea, meanwhile, three thousand miles away and still swimming against a tide of red tape, was unavoidably excluded from the bonds of trauma and loyalty that were forged in Dedham that year:

My darling Peter,
Thank you for your letters and postcard. It was a good change to your business letters of the last months. At least they had a human touch. It is all very difficult for me just as much as it is for you.

Many years later, Charlie Putnam expressed astonishment at the way in which his parents dealt with the deaths of their two children: *They were largely there to support and hold one another together*, he said. As well as finding consolation in each other, Laura and Eliot were supported by St Paul's Church in Dedham: *If it hadn't been for the Church,* Laura Putnam once remarked, *I'd have gone to the nuthouse.*

In July of 2017 I was contacted by our local breast screening unit and asked to attend for a scan and biopsy. There is no history of cancer in my family, so I wasn't especially worried.

Five days later, a nurse called to confirm that I had tested positive for Triple Negative breast cancer. As Dan and I were leaving for a family wedding in Wisconsin the following day, an appointment was scheduled with the consultant for mid-August. It would make absolutely no difference, the nurse assured me, whether I saw the surgeon then or three weeks later: 'Forget all about it and have a lovely holiday in America,' she offered brightly. I tried, unsuccessfully, to follow her advice. My imagination had no boundaries as I struggled to make sense of what she'd told me: Was the disease so advanced that seeing a consultant was no longer a matter of urgency, or, was it a slow growing tumour and a few more weeks wouldn't make any difference?

We broke our journey to Chicago in Winthrop, Massachusetts. The following morning I woke early and as I watched the sun rise over the Boston skyline, I reflected on the beauty of nature and the suffering of humankind. I decided to go to Mass with Dan, and we walked along the shoreline to the Holy Rosary Catholic Church. The priest spoke about God's mercy and the healing power of Jesus Christ, and my attention was drawn to the six foot cross beside the altar. It was constructed from badly splintered timber, and its arms were wrapped in coils of fraying rope. Six-inch nails had been strategically hammered into the wood and the words: *Blood of Jesus, Cover Me* were splashed across it in red paint. I felt disheartened. You can't fake faith, and, in the eyes of card-carrying Christians, I have no invisible means of support. God cures the sick, but only if they believe in His majesty and mercy. Unlike Grace, Dorrie and Laura, I could not offer up my despair into the healing hands of God, because He would realise right away that I was a fraud. Auntie Dorrie tells me that a personal knowledge of the Lord is essential to my salvation: *One can no more grow naturally into a child of God, than a sow wallowing in the mire can turn into a butterfly. This idea of the natural growth into spirituality is an absolute delusion.* Time might be running out, and if I showed up at the gates of Heaven any time soon, the Lord would take one look at me and say: 'I know you not'.

As a student, I studied Jean-Paul Sartre's play *Huis Clos (No Exit)*, which tells the story of three people sealed inside a room without doors or windows. The lights are never switched off and the prisoners have no eyelids. This idea of being unable to close one's eyes had a haunting effect on my imagination. Like Garcin, Inez and Estelle, I couldn't escape the world or my situation. I had stepped into a life without eyelids, without God and, in the dead of night when all the lights inside my head were switched on, the only source of consolation was my ability to self-soothe. I had always hoped to remain alive for at least as long as my parents, who both died at the age of seventy-nine. But here I was at fifty-eight years old, neatly posted between my grandfather, Ernst who had taken his own life at the age of fifty-four and my Uncle Bobi who had suffered a fatal heart attack at fifty-nine. If death had indeed turned my corner, I too wanted to walk through the valley of its shadow and fear no evil. The night before my mother died, she asked me to switch on all the lights in the house, saying that she wanted to enjoy the brightness before she walked forever into darkness. I didn't want to walk forever into darkness.

After the deaths of Betsy and Arthur, Eliot Putman, the great Harvard athlete, never again took part in sport. He stopped coaching the Nobles football team, and he no longer skied, skated or played games in the backyard with his sons. Instead, he burned leaves and took up wood carving. The Nobles yearbook of 1956 makes no direct mention of the three tragedies that struck the school that year, and the clues are discreetly scattered. In *The Story of Noble and Greenough School*, the timeline for 1956 refers simply to the fact that: *Mr Putnam gave up coaching football*. In light of the full story, it is no wonder that the team lost almost every game that year. The bodies of four boys had been temporarily paralysed and the hearts of the entire squad had broken for their beloved headmaster, coach and mentor.

Perhaps the most poignant line in the yearbook reads: *Mr and Mrs Putnam have two boys and one girl*. Just one year earlier, the sentence would have read: *Mr and Mrs Putnam have three boys and two girls*.

The Class of 1956 dedicated the school yearbook to their headmaster: *With gratitude and affection to Mr Eliot T. Putnam for his understanding leadership and courageous spirit, for his faith in us, and for the inspiration we have received from him.* Mr Putnam responded with a message of his own, never mentioning the unimaginable losses suffered by his own family and referring only to his profound admiration for the boys:

It is unlikely that we shall again see a class quite like this one. Throughout their years at Nobles, these boys have deservedly earned our affection and respect, but never to such a degree as in their final year. I do not recall a time when misfortune has struck a group of boys in more varied ways or with greater impact. Their response to these blows has been spontaneous and magnificent. The standard of leadership which the Class of 1956 passes on to their younger brothers was born of a fundamental bigness of character, the ingredients of which are spiritual depth, complete sincerity, and unflinching courage. Their lives will be richer for the service they have performed for the school. 'United we stand' seems to have been their motto, and our farewell to them can only be said with a heavy and grateful heart.

The Class of '56 remains one of the most tightly-bonded year groups at Nobles. They have stayed in touch for more than sixty years, their reunion attendance is excellent and they regularly reach one hundred percent participation in the annual Nobles fundraiser. In the late fall of that year, they united in their efforts to offer the school a practical gift. The result was 'The Path of '56'.

We could have pooled our resources to buy something like a bench. But when the option of turning a washed-out gully into a real, usable path was put forth, the whole class jumped on the idea unanimously. We wanted our legacy to be something that would be used by students and faculty, forever and ever. Class President, Fred Wells '56

Every Sunday that Spring, the boys devoted their time to building the path and laying the wooden railway ties that would serve as its steps for more than fifty years. At the foot of the path is a plaque which reads: *56 Path. These 28 steps constructed by the 28 members of the Class of 1956 as their gift to the school.* Beneath it is a second plaque: *56 Path. Built by the Class of 1956. Rebuilt by the Class of 1980 as their gift to the school.*

EMILY: Do any human beings ever realize life while they live it? --- every, every minute?

STAGE MANAGER: No. (Pause). The saints and poets, maybe --- they do some.
Our Town Act III by Thornton Wilder

I first saw a performance of *Our Town* at the Lyceum Theatre on Broadway in 1988. My friend Karen was working backstage and she gave me a free ticket. I knew nothing about the play, other than that my father had directed it in the 1950s. This particular production, with Spalding Gray in the role of Stage Manager, has been heralded as one of the most accomplished and original interpretations ever produced. In 2004, Gray committed suicide by jumping into New York's East River. His body was not recovered from the water until two months later.

STAGE MANAGER: Now there are some things we all know, but we don't take'm out and look at'm very often. We all know that *something* is eternal. And it ain't houses and it ain't names, and it ain't earth, and it ain't even the stars ... everybody knows in their bones that *something* is eternal, and that something has to do with human beings. All the greatest people ever lived have been telling us that for five thousand years and yet you'd be surprised how people are always losing hold of it. There's something way down deep that's eternal about every human being.
Our Town Act III

Our Town is set in Grover's Corners, a fictional New Hampshire community, at the turn of the twentieth century. It's a little like Dylan Thomas's *Under Milk Wood* but set over the course of a twelve-year period rather than a single day. I am interested in plays that speak about the complexity of family and I go to the theatre not to be distracted or entertained, but to witness stories that deal with family trauma. Having read a synopsis of *Our Town*, I anticipated a gentle play about life in small-town America. I was immediately enthralled by the story of the endearing Emily Webb, who grows up to marry the kindly George Gibbs in Act II, only to die in childbirth in Act III. I was also surprised and a little embarrassed by the depth of my emotion: I couldn't stop crying.

Thornton Wilder's Pulitzer prize-winning play has been translated into many languages, and is performed at least once a day somewhere in the world. *Our Town* is neither a nostalgic slice of rural Americana, nor is it light-heartedly sentimental. The playwright Edward Albee described *Our Town* as one of the toughest, saddest plays ever written. In the final Act, Emily decides to return to the living for just one day. Her fellow souls in the graveyard discourage her from going back, but she is determined. In his folksy, engaging manner, the Stage Manager reflects on the fact that, as human beings, we so often ignore the important things we know to be true; those things that are eternal. Emily soon finds life among the living too painful to endure and resumes her place in the graveyard. Her pain awakens in us the realisation that we struggle to truly appreciate life until we are close to death, just as we fail to fully cherish the living until they are no longer with us.

At Nobles in 1956, Peter was working with an all-male cast, but it was Loring Conant Jr. in the role of Emily, who faced the greatest challenge to authenticity. Following the single performance of *Our Town* which took place on Saturday April 7th, Sid Eaton wrote to Peter.

Sunday a.m. April 8, 1956
Dear Peter,
May a grateful and admiring colleague put down a few flying thoughts on the play last night? It was a banner job, a glory to you all, especially to you. Your courageous tastefulness in its selection and your unsparing devotion to making it effective and affective have been impressive. That it included so many boys, a number of them lads who have been wanting in this sort of spiritual endeavour, is extremely valuable. I think that 'Our Town' matches the best we have achieved. You accomplished wonderful things too with Loring Conant. He was authentic and moving beyond dream last night. How good he was receives testimony from the not-one-snicker when he threw his arms around Gage's neck. If the spell had not really been woven, that's an inevitable spot for a school-audience horselaugh. It wasn't that your audience was on its good behaviour. Your performance had them.
The entire cemetery and revisiting scene were 'terrific' beyond the schoolboy jargon.
I can't tell you how grateful I am for your willingness and your success. This seems to me the most important education we've achieved all year, as it inevitably will be when we select meaningful plays and have directors with passion.
Yours, Sid

In August, 2017, Loring Conant sent me a page taken from the script he had used in 1956. It was Emily's seminal speech: *the most moving lines I have had the privilege of delivering,* he wrote. In the margin are my father's directional notes: *Not too fast.*

Thornton Wilder's nephew, Amos Tappan Wilder, played the role of Professor Willard in *Our Town*. Doubtless inspired by the family connection, Peter wrote to Tappan's uncle, inviting him to come to the play. Unable to attend, Thornton Wilder sent a telegram of congratulation: *To Peter O'Connell. Best Wishes for tomorrow night. Please give my thanks and these greetings to the actors and technical assistance. Cordial regards, Thornton Wilder.*

In May, Peter wrote to Mr Wilder and received the following reply:

Dear Mr O'Connell,
I've shrunk from answering your letter simply because I was scared to. From time to time editors here and abroad have written to me asking me to contribute to those 'what I believe' collections.
Each one of us is different. I find myself often admiring the credos of others; but I seem to belong to that group that feels no need of any precision in the statement of those great subjects. In the last act of Our Town *I merely 'borrowed' the picture of the waiting dead and some of its idea-background from Dante's Purgatory. I felt I was more using it as a means to say something about life than about death!*
I remember giving glad assent to some things Goethe said about the afterlife (I wish I could remember the exact reference

— ie. the day — in the conversation with Eckermann). He too was hesitant to give, receive, or even seek for any very precise conclusion. But with his constant belief in doing, making, creating, striving he ever so modestly (and what a gracious and modest book it is) suggests to young E. that he cannot imagine that this ever-creative nature puts an abrupt stop to the creativity of its children-instruments.

This is no answer; I would like to feel that gradually you would come to find that you are in less need of an answer on that subject.

Many thanks for your letter with the vivid picture of the work and the performance and many regards,

Sincerely yours,

Thornton Wilder

Not exactly Grover's Corners. Imagine you live in a Castle -
From *Betsy and Arthur* by Jesse Putnam

The grandson of Eliot T. Putnam is a playwright, and for much of his life, Jesse Putnam knew little more than the names of the two children who had died so tragically in 1955; children, who, had they grown to adulthood, would have been his Aunt Betsy and his Uncle Arthur. In 1990 his Uncle Charlie found a diary that had belonged to Betsy, and a decade later Jesse met Peter Ward, who had been with Arthur on the hill the day he died: *I don't recall anyone speaking with me about who Arthur was in any detail prior to that. His life and his sister's life were very much mysteries; shrouded, one could say, in the hush of deep grief,* says Putnam.

The years passed, and although Jesse never forgot about his aunt and uncle, he held back: *perhaps waiting for the moment when inspiration overcame the burden of inherited hesitancy.* That moment came in 2014 when, after fifteen months of detailed research into the lives of Betsy and Arthur Putnam, Jesse wrote two plays. He was inspired, he said, by Spalding Gray's filmed production of *Our Town. I stitched them together into one production with some theatrical elements that paid homage to Thornton Wilder's story.*

Betsy and Arthur was performed at Nobles on December 19th, 2015. Jesse took the role of his grandfather, the school's former headmaster. Betsy Putnam Matthew was cast in the role of her great aunt and Eliot Putnam Jr, who had played Mrs Gibbs in the 1956 production of *Our Town,* was the play's Carpenter, Chauffeur and Ambassador.

Jesse dedicated his play to the memory of Casey Dunne, the Nobles student who died in 2015: *with love and understanding from the Putnam family to the Dunne family.*

Charlie Putnam later said that the play: *seemed to me to be a love letter of sorts from my brother and sister to all of us. After more than half a century I have been given an opportunity to know Betsy and Arthur to a degree I could never have imagined. The limitation of childhood memory is gone, and a veil has been lifted.*

Chapter Six

Slipstreams and Coat-tails

Congressman Auchincloss' private bill for Lea's relief was not acted on during the 84th Congress and lapsed at adjournment in August. He promised to submit it again the following year. In the meantime, Peter arranged a one-year teaching exchange with Paul Longland, an English master at St Paul's School in London. In June 1956, after five years in America, my father reluctantly packed a suitcase and returned to England, leaving most of his belongings behind to await his return.

Peter had rented a house in Surrey, and in a letter Lea writes: *I am looking forward to September 6th when we shall be in our own home, receive friends there and at last be alone together.* She liked Peter's suggestion of renting a house on Cape Cod when they returned to America: *I am sure I would like a little house at Barnstable. How nice it would be to have a home of our own on the Atlantic. Have you taken any photos?* My mother, who had a lifelong interest in people of wealth and consequence, would have been delighted to know that the Kennedy Compound at Hyannis Port was just a stone's throw from Barnstable. Her letter continues: *I wonder what Betsy (Peabody) could find out about Dean Acheson – I am much too small for a great man like he is.* Dean Acheson was educated at Groton and served as Secretary of State under President Truman. My mother, in spite of certain language barriers and a modest academic background, had strong social skills and was a gracious and charming companion. She knew that if she felt out of her depth in a social situation, the best thing to do was to ask a great many questions, with an expression of unwavering interest on her face. At a dinner party in London she was once seated next to a pompous bore, who didn't ask her a single question the entire evening. He was later overheard saying to a colleague: 'That Mrs O'Connell is a highly intelligent woman'. If Dean Acheson had ever had the good fortune to meet my mother, I'm sure he would have been equally charmed by her grace and intelligence.

Lea wished, above all things, to have a place of her own. It was what she had envisaged with Hans but that dream had been dug up and reburied too many times. Now it was over, and she had gathered up what remained of her still unbroken eggs and laid them in Peter's basket. When he arrived back in England on June 22nd, she decided not to meet him at the dock: *I still love you and we will have a happy year together,* she writes. I am saddened by my mother's use of the word *still*. She and my father had been married for less than a year and their letters to each during their time apart had not been especially joyful or loving. Peter writes: *I said I was struggling, trying to fight my way through to sanity and an appreciation of your mature beauty and loveliness of spirit. Only disaster can follow an attempt to repress my less amiable emotions, pretend they don't exist and rely on a sense of duty to keep our marriage going. I am drawing off the pus from my soul – a painful sight, but leading, I hope, to health and spiritual well-being.*

The two of them had arranged a marriage which they hoped would eventually work out well. Peter had invited Lea to accept the role of a boarding school master's wife in a country far away. She had accepted the offer because it enabled her to break free of the unrelenting heartache of life in Hans Balmer's slipstream. Although Lea still loved Hans with most of her broken heart, she had come to realise that they would never marry.

On June 3rd, 1956 Lea writes to Peter in German: *Thank you for your nice long letter. Now and again, there are small rays of hope that shine between us, and I am grateful for these. My somewhat inhibited feelings are released and I feel touched by tenderness. It is very hard for me, Peter. I'm giving up everything here in Switzerland in order to seek happiness in a new country. My future is uncertain – the hope I cherish is that it will all go well and that we will find a way to each other's hearts. I dearly hope that when the time comes for me to leave my family, my friends and my country, I will be able to convince them that I am heading for a good life by your side in America. This would make my departure much easier. I feel weighed down by the uncertainty but I'm sure it will all turn out well, darling, as long as we help each other bear the load. All my love, your Lea.*

My darling Lea,
Believe me when I say I want to give you the love you deserve. I am aware of the strong streak of unmitigated original sin that lies in my heart. Perhaps that is why what you call a 'religious' solution is necessary. I am in the stage of hating the very word religion, but something that will explain life and its meaning is necessary. My conscious will is on your side and I am fighting hard for the joy and the privilege of loving you. And oh Lea, do believe me, it's a struggle. You

often say how much you suffer. I am suffering too and in the
dark moments of night, the thought that this is something I
must learn to live with and accept all my life is nightmarish.
You deserve passionate, tremendous, annihilating love and
only the most inflexible fate has denied it you up to now – at
least since Balmer lost his mind and his sense of values.
With my warmest love and some genuine tenderness, Peter

My dear Lea,
Now you are a real bride and I am very happy for you. You
have made a good choice. The two of you are made for each
other and that cannot be said of every married couple. May
God bless you both. M. Meier.

When I found this handwritten note, I assumed that it
belonged with the cards and telegrams sent to my parents
on their wedding day, but then, I noticed the date: New
Year's Eve, 1943. Who was M. Meier and why was he or she
referring to my mother as a bride? I decided to contact the
Registrar in Hoechstetten and request the date of my mother's marriage. If she had married more than once, the clerk
would ask for clarification, and so confirm what M. Meier
was implying, namely that Lea had married Hans in 1943.
I took a deep breath and dialled the number. The woman at
the other end of the line was civil but cool. Why did I need
this information? What was I planning to do with it? Why
wasn't my mother calling herself? I danced courteously around
her questions, even declaring a willingness to pay whatever
fee she might ask of me. Finally, she painted herself into a
corner when she declared, rather hotly, that I had no right to

this information because I wasn't, strictly speaking, related to Lea O'Connell. There was a pause and I wondered what she was going to say next: 'Well', she said eventually, 'she's your mother, so I suppose you are related'. 'I suppose I am', I agreed. A few days later, I received an email confirming that Lea Kummer had married Peter O'Connell on July 1st, 1955 in Biglen. I felt strangely relieved.

St Paul's School was founded in 1509 and Old Paulines include Samuel Pepys and John Milton. Its mission statement is to provide: *a dynamic, academic experience for bright, inquisitive boys aged 7 – 18.* I'm not sure how my mother occupied her time while my father was teaching in London. She would have been grateful to have her own home, but it must have been lonely and dull for her in the suburbs. Rosa's letters, answering requests for recipes and promising to send cheese, suggest that mother and daughter wrote to each other a good deal. Telephone calls at that time would have been prohibitively expensive, and out of the question for a couple saving for a new life in America. Rosa expresses her delight at Lea's happiness, and is relieved to hear that everything is running so smoothly for her in England.

On October 25th, 1956 the unthinkable happened: Hans Balmer's wife died. Her obituary in the *Bieler Tagblatt* reads: *Early this morning, my kind-hearted wife, our dear mother, daughter and sister, died in her 31st year. She had a strong religious faith and yet her passing was unexpected.* My mother has drawn a thick blue pen line under the words *kind-hearted*. I know nothing of Kathy Balmer-Kellenberg, other than her name and the names of her three children. Her death was *unexpected* and remains unexplained.

What went through Lea's mind when she heard the news? Did she see the long years of excruciating heartache suddenly vanish into scorched earth? Did she believe that the Scales of Justice had finally tipped in her favour and that, at long last, she and Hans could be together? These might have been her first reactions, but once the euphoria had settled she would have recognised the impossibility of such a life. Lea was married to another man and in 1956 the laws governing divorce were complicated and expensive. In Switzerland, Hans's father was in a psychiatric hospital and removal of the Balmer children from the family home would have been a distinct possibility. Lea was stuck in suburban Surrey, and in her heart she must have known that Mr and Mrs Kellenberg would never allow their son-in-law's first love to become a step-mother to their dead daughter's children. As Peter had pointed out, Hans had lost both his mind and his sense of values, and it seems unlikely that he could have mobilised the moral courage and the determination required to fight for my mother.

Hans Balmer was to die less than nine years later, leaving his second wife, Elizabeth, and their little girl, Connie. It was Elizabeth I had met with my mother in the fabric shop in Biel, and I wonder about the circumstances of her marriage to Hans. I know, from speaking to former Verdingkinder, that second marriages were often entered into for practical reasons. An unmarried woman might agree to care for her predecessor's offspring, on the understanding that she did so as a second wife with the promise, God willing, of a child of her own.

I wonder whether Lea attended Hans's funeral in August of 1967. I imagine Mum in her Hermes scarf and sunglasses, slipping unnoticed into the back row of the chapel. The hope of re-uniting with Hans in her twilight years, when spouses might have died and children grown to independence, had been extinguished. I recognise too that had Hans Balmer's mind been more resolute and his sense of values stronger, my own place in this world would have been denied.

Peter and Lea left Surrey soon after Kathy Kellenberg's death and moved in with Harry on Seymour Place. This would have saved them money, but perhaps more importantly, my grandfather could keep an eye on Lea while Peter was at work. Photographs taken that first Christmas in London show my father carving the turkey in a tiny kitchen. My grandfather looks old. He is stooped and pale and a half-smoked cigar hangs from his mouth. He reminds me of the old man in the 'Elderly People Crossing' sign, but without the cane or the wife holding his hand. Grandpa has none of the straight-backed, dignified presence about him that I remember as a small child, and no-one would have thought to call him 'Colonel', which was his nickname at SES. At a guess, he could be ninety years old. In fact, he is just sixty-five.

If you could hear, at every jolt, the blood
Come gargling from froth-corrupted lungs,
Obscene as cancer, bitter as the cud
Of vile, incurable sores on innocent tongues

from '*Dulce et Decorum Est*' by Wilfred Owen

As I lay in my hospital bed, hooked up to tubes and needles, anticipating the first rush of drugs into my bloodstream, I asked the nurse about the origins of chemotherapy. She told me that it was first administered in the 1950s, but that research had been ongoing since WWII. 'It's derived from mustard gas,' she added.

Mustard gas was first used at the Second Battle of Ypres in April, 1915. It was perhaps the most feared of all weapons in WWI, because it descended without warning, cloaked in invisibility, devoid of sound or smell. There was nowhere to hide, and it killed indiscriminately; not quickly, but slowly and painfully, burning the body, destroying the lungs and liquefying the tissues. Rather like cancer, in fact.

In 1942, two Yale pharmacologists, Alfred Gilman and Louis Goodman, began to study chemical warfare agents and, in a derivative of mustard gas, they found the first effective chemotherapy for cancer. How ironic that a weapon of warfare used against millions of men, including my grandfather, was to be the source of my healing.

The Longlands are a major social hit, almost embarrassingly much in demand. They have succeeded in drawing down the envy of their confrères by securing an invitation to a South Carolina plantation, complete with coloured mammies and quail hunting. They have fitted in splendidly, writes Laura Putnam in a letter to Peter. At the end of the summer term, Paul and Helen Longland took a road trip to California in Peter's old Plymouth, and in September 1957, they sailed back to England.

If Peter ever felt that his Nobles friends had forgotten him amidst their enthusiasm for the Longlands, their letters proved otherwise. In January of 1957 Eliot Putnam writes:

We have thought of you constantly. I cannot hide the fact that you are the key figure in my planning for next year. The Nobles family is counting on you 100%. This letter then is in the form of a question, to which I pray you will give me an affirmative answer. Happy New Year to you. All you have to do to make it happy for us is to book a summer passage on the Liberté.

Sid Eaton adds his own thoughts in a note to Lea: *With Peter we're strong, without him we're a shaky outfit (this is no reflection on Paul, who's doing rich things for us). I mean in the long run. Trying to fill the gap if the plan for return fell through would be painful and make-shift, unthinkable, unfaceable.*

The boys too, wrote regularly: *Dear Mr O'Connell, Thank you for the wonderful telegram! Although we did lose 2-1, we were all tremendously glad to have heard from you. And I think we all played a harder and better game for it. I don't know whether you heard it or not, but we gave you a cheer after the game. I'm only sorry we couldn't put the icing on the cake and win. We do want you over here for two reasons: 1) we want to meet your wife, who must be charming and 2) we want our soccer coach back! Sincerely, Rip Henkels*

At the end of the season, Bob McElwain sent his former soccer coach a carefully prepared synopsis of the season's games. Written on a piece of lined paper, torn from an exercise book, McElwain neatly lists and registers the quality of each game, dividing it into its four quarters and assessing play according to his own exacting standards. It is practically a work of art. It is certainly a labour of love.

Leo Conant, Loring's mother, writes: *Everything those*

wonderful boys have accomplished and everything they do is for Nobles and for you Peter.

When I think of the many letters my father received from boys at Highfield, Groton, Nobles and St Paul's, letters he treasured all the days of his life, I recognise that there was a side to him I never knew, a side that failed to find expression because he fathered a girl rather than a boy. Even now, I cannot picture Dad as a highly regarded soccer coach, and a man who sent telegrams to America before games. Sometimes, when I see fathers and sons kicking a ball in the park, I feel a rush of tenderness, and have to restrain myself from calling out: 'That's a wonderful thing you're doing Sir and, in the name of all small sons, I thank you'. It's what Dad believed more Highfield and Groton fathers should have done – romp with their boys, take time out to kick a football across a stretch of grass. It's what my father might have done, had he and my mother not lost their first child, a son, to a miscarriage in the summer of 1957.

Two little dicky birds sitting on a wall. One named Peter. One named Paul. Fly away Peter. Fly away Paul. Come back Peter. Come back Paul
English nursery rhyme

By the spring of 1957, it looked increasingly unlikely that Lea would be permitted to enter the United States on a visa of any kind. Eliot, however, kept Peter's position: *unfilled in the hope that the one person we all pray for will find it possible to fill it. We need you as a teacher, as a person, and as a warm and very special friend, one who belongs in Dedham, Mass! Ever yours, El*

When Peter left St Paul's in July of 1957, the boys presented him with a dictionary entitled *Underworld Lingo*. The dedication reads: *To Mr P (Paddy) O'Connell from 6A as a small token of our appreciation to you for this year's work. We hope you will accept this small gift, and that it may prove useful to you if you decide to give up being a schoolmaster to become an American gangster.* The fly leaf carries the signatures of twenty-five boys.

The summer holidays created a financial challenge for many schoolmasters and in June Peter accepted a position teaching English to foreign students at a summer school in Essex. He and Lea were put in charge of a group of lively French teenagers, all of whom were mad for rock'n'roll. Every evening they would bring out their Elvis records and dance.

By the time I was six years old, I was occasionally allowed to join my father for the first hour of the English Vacation School dances at the Hotel Continental Wampach in Folkestone. The French still ruled the rock'n'roll roost and I loved watching the girls, hair and skirts flying, being lifted and thrown across the room ,where they landed deftly on two feet before reuniting with their partners. I envied their ability to disperse a crowd, like Moses parting the waves, and as I stood in the circle, holding my father's hand, I shared the awe of the crowd.

There was, however, a dark history to my fascination with the rock'n'roll dancers: in the summer of 1957, a French boy hurled his partner a little too vigorously across the dance floor and, unable to steady herself, the girl crashed into my mother, who was standing in the circle of spectators. Mrs O'Connell was rushed to the local hospital, but unfortunately her unborn baby did not survive the trauma of impact. Lea had just celebrated her 40th birthday and must have felt devastated by her loss. She was not, however, a woman easily defeated, and a heartfelt desire to have a child would have conquered whatever her biological clock or the emergency care physician told her that night.

I remember from an early age hearing about my little brother who died. My parents were going to name him Daniel. It was not, however, until I was six months pregnant with Polly that my mother told me the full story. After she miscarried, the attending doctor failed to conduct an internal examination to remove the pregnancy tissue. When I was born, less than two years later, Dr Aeschbacher, her gynaecologist in Switzerland, was forced to do an emergency Caesarean, because the tissue remains had reduced the available space in her womb, with potentially fatal results for me.

In January of 1958 Peter was invited back to St Paul's on a temporary contract. He and Lea were preparing to launch their own Summer School, and my father had secured Gilston Park, a country mansion in Essex where they offered: A *programme of English lessons, lectures, excursions, recreation, games and dancing.* Amos Booth, on his summer vacation from Groton, was to join Peter as Co-Principal. During the ten weeks of organised chaos that was the first English Vacation School, Amos found time to write to Gina Murray at Groton:

> *Dear Gina,*
> *Our lads and lasses laugh and chatter, sing and cry - eet ees very beautiful - and in three weeks we even begin to forget how much money they must have somewhere dans la poche de papa. Groton, Groton, Groton looms out of the mist... materialises,*

2 boys on motor bikes... Stu Auchincloss here on Friday, here on Saturday... home on Sunday; les soeurs Peabody - here five weeks ago; Hugh Sackett - here 4 weeks ago.

Gilston Park is huge and musty, chic and spectral, chrome and cobwebs, television and afternoon tea, children of eleven and teacher of thirty sharing the sublime and the ridiculous... thunderous rain roaring through the roof, bedroom, bed, ceilings and cellars - headmasters baling water from the castle roof and pushing and prodding at drains, inveighing against hotelier (not dead but sleeping), not mean, but 'working on a budget' - counting the lumps of sugar and the mouths, but not the shining in the eyes. Lea tidying rooms, writing in French, German and English, telephoning to Clermont Ferrand, hanging Swiss flags and keeping the show on the road - Israeli girls coming back rather than going to new places with papa and mama, dancing all Saturday night, talks on literature, visits to Stratford, talks with hotelier, talks about hotelier, talks. I take this down to office, bedroom, safe, library, faculty room - Much love, Amos.

Bill Polk, a future Groton headmaster himself, was appointed unofficial dorm prefect when he visited EVS that summer. Howard Corning and Temby Argall, former Grotonians and by then medical students at Columbia University also visited: *Your pseudo-gothic-Victorian pile will long remain a favourite memory,* wrote Temby from New York.

In September, Peter wrote in his diary:

Running a summer school for foreign students is one of the most enjoyable and exhausting ways of earning a living. One plays a variety of roles beyond that of the teacher – banker, taxi driver, psychiatrist, policeman, detective, interpreter and guide – and all these roles are played at the double. A summer school of 60–70 young people, aged 14 – 26, of both sexes and a dozen nationalities, is a highly unstable community. To make it a success and to create and maintain the right atmosphere, the staff has to live at a greatly speeded-up rate. If the orthodox schoolmaster is a rose grower, or even a forester, a summer school teacher is a cultivator of mushrooms. The whole thing comes up in the night. On 3rd July there was no 1958 summer school. By 4th July 50 young people had gathered in Gilston Park from China to Peru, and the school was in being. They have come thousands of miles to learn our language, to study our literature and institutions, to see something of our country, and to have a good time. Some knew no English, others were brilliant linguists. Some were just starting Lycée or Hochschule, others were university undergraduates (and one even a university lecturer). Some were very shy and reserved; others gave the impression of intending to take over the place.

They worked in small classes for 3 hours each morning and went on 2 excursions a week, one for the whole day. The rest of the time they were free to do what they liked, though there were many organised activities in which they were encouraged to join: baseball, football, tennis in the afternoon; debates, play readings, mock trials in the evening. Teaching was a delight, and it was impressive and encouraging to see how well the traditional enemies got on together – French with German, Lebanese with Israeli, German with Jew.

September 12th came, the date when the inhabitants of the

Tower of Babel were once more 'scattered abroad upon all the face of the earth'. The last train steamed out to the heartfelt strain of 'Auld Lang Syne' and left our Tower, like any other boarding school at the end of term – empty and hollow. Summer schools, like wine, are known for their years. 1958 was vintage.

Rosa came to Gilston Park that summer. She must have been dazzled by the magnificence of it all and by Lea's great good fortune, following her years of desperate disappointment. My grandmother had once foretold this time, assuring Lea in a letter that one day she would *thank God for the way things turned out.*

In January of 1959 Mr. Gilkes, the High Master of St Paul's offered Peter a full-time position. Lea was seven months pregnant and the couple had no money, no home of their own, and the situation with Lea's visa was no closer to resolution than it had been in 1956. However, there was talk of starting a year-round school on the south coast, so this offer created a sudden fork in the road. My mother could have erred on the side of caution and encouraged Peter to accept what was a prestigious job at St Paul's, but: *Lea had an unshakeable faith, in the future, and, above all, in me,* wrote my father many years later. Mr Gilkes was astonished to hear that O'Connell had other fish to fry, and whenever their paths crossed in subsequent years, he would jokingly refer to Peter as: 'the man who turned me down'. Looking back, I wonder whether my mother's decisiveness was motivated by an unrevealed desire to remain in England. Perhaps she wished to shape her own future rather than journey to America on Peter's coat-tails. Maybe she wished to be closer to her family, closer to Hans.

There is a tide in the affairs of men.
Which, taken at the flood, leads on to fortune
Julius Caesar Act 4, scene 3. William Shakespeare

This was one of my Great Uncle Leonard's favourite quotes, and he liked to reference it with regard to MK Electric, the company he founded in 1919. *My chief urge was to be creative and to do something useful,* he said in a 1966 interview. In the spring of 1959 Peter received a cheque from his uncle for one thousand pounds: *All you have to do is to send me an I.O.U. – no interest and the capital sum to be repaid within two years. I am always glad if I can help anyone with a creative urge and common sense. This particularly applies to you – son of my sister, Grace. It is now up to you. Your affectionate, Uncle Leonard.*

Lea is expecting a baby in March and wants to have it in her aseptic little country.
Letter to Alan Pifer, 19th September, 1958

In November, 1958 Lea left England for Biel and did not return for six months. In the early stages of her pregnancy, she suffered with morning sickness, and Dr Bell recommended a marvellous new drug, called Thalidomide. It was being prescribed to thousands of women all over the world, he explained, with amazing results. These results were ultimately to prove catastrophic: more than twenty thousand babies were born with severely foreshortened limbs and tiny hands and feet; some had no arms or legs at all. Thalidomide was a highly addictive sedative that offered users a real high, but it acted as a nerve poison on the unborn baby. Grunenthal, the company selling the drug, employed several former Nazi scientists, including Otto Ambros. He had been active in the development of the nerve gas Sarin during WWII, and was jailed for war crimes at the Nuremberg Trials. Grunenthal was promoting Thalidomide as entirely safe, even though the drug had not yet been tested on animals. When the British forces liberated Bergen-Belsen in 1945, they discovered babies whose mothers had undergone medical experiments in the concentration camp. Their children showed similar deformities to the thalidomide babies born in the late 1950s and early 1960s.

Lea took a withering view of people who relied on tablets to ease their aches and pains, and she warned me never to take over the counter drugs. Aspirin was only ever administered in cases of extreme emergency, and even then, Mum would crumble a tiny corner of a tablet into the palm of her hand, insisting that it was highly dangerous to swallow an entire pill. Most ailments in our house were treated either with local honey or a shot of Fernet Branca.

My mother always carried a small bottle of Fernet Branca in her handbag. I loathed the black liquid with its bitter, medicinal taste, but Mum insisted that it was made from herbs and was terribly good for me. I suspect the sense of eventual wellbeing it offered was due to the fact that the potion was thirty-nine percent alcohol. I finally took a stand against Fernet Branca when I was twelve years old. It was December 1971 and I was very excited about visiting America for the first time. We were to spend a week at Groton before flying to Milwaukee for Christmas. I felt ill on the flight to Boston, and just before we landed my mother took out the Fernet, insisting that if I took some, I would feel better. I promptly vomited in the aisle and had to be carried off the plane by my father. I spent most of the following week, lying in Fitch and Edie Hardcastle's spare room in Brooks House. It was, almost certainly, a bad case of the flu, but to this day, I blame the Fernet Branca for denying me my first experience of Groton School.

My mother was a great believer in the power of honey and we often drove into the Kent countryside in order to buy local honey. The beekeepers were an old couple who lived in a dark and spooky cottage on a lonely road. Mrs Fitall was gnarled and crippled with arthritis, and their garden was so overgrown that Dad frequently missed the Honey For Sale sign. Mum would collect up every last jar from the rickety garden table, and then knock on the front door of the cottage and ask for more. It was not until I was in my early twenties that I asked my mother about her unusual devotion to honey, and she told me this story:

In 1917 Rosa insisted on visiting a member of her family who was near death with the Spanish flu. Everyone advised against it, for her own safety but also for the sake of her unborn child. My grandmother chose to ignore the warnings and within a few days, she too had developed the deadly symptoms. My great-grandmother asked the advice of the family doctor who had a possible remedy, although not one he had ever tried himself. He told her to go out into the countryside and buy as much local honey as she could find. She was then to spoon-feed her daughter until she became physically sick. She followed his advice, and Rosa coughed up streams of thick black liquid. My great-grandmother continued to administer the honey until her daughter's lungs ran clear. Rosa survived and my mother was born on July 18th, 1917. At birth, Mum told me, her body was covered in a black film which wiped off as easily as coal dust. I loved this story but never thought to enquire about the details: Who was the family member who died of the Spanish Flu? She must have been much loved by my grandmother for her to have put herself and her unborn baby at such risk? I can find no recorded symptoms of the Spanish Flu that mention black liquid accumulating in the lungs, but perhaps no-one had ever tried the local honey cure? The moral of the story, however, was clear: generations of us are alive today as a direct result of the curative powers of honey. As Friedrich Nietzsche said: *It is the honey in my veins that makes my blood thicker, and my soul quieter.* Like Lea, my cupboards are full of honey: I spread it on my toast, put it in my tea and pack it in my luggage. Kent honey remains my favourite and although the tumbledown cottage in Smarden is long gone, I still have one of Mrs Fitall's jars in which I keep teabags.

By the time I was born, the die had pretty much been cast in favour of a life in England. In a letter to Alan, Peter writes:

> *We are planning to leave this flat in the spring and get a country place. My father's health is very bad and we are worried about him. Lea is already scanning Country Life for suitable places! We had many American visitors during the summer and the students found such pleasure in the polyglot community. Lea of course loves it all and I do not think we could leave it now even if there were not the problem of my father's health to consider. I regret Nobles but we have a useful and happy line of country before us here.*

Eliot Putnam writes:

I understand <u>completely</u> the reasons for your decision. I know how much you wanted to return to Nobles, and the fact that you have put your own interests second to that of your wife and father only increases my respect for you. It would be utterly unfair if I gave you the impression that I accepted your decision without considerable feeling. I don't know when I have been more deeply disappointed. Quite selfishly, I console myself with the possibility that a year or two hence we may have you back. Good luck, dear feller. I shall continue to think of you with very special affection. Ever yours, Eliot

Sid Eaton, remained optimistic but issued a warning:

The dream is to land you, young and vigorous, to fit and outgrow my shoes. This dream dovetails (eagle-feathers) with my old Ides of March warning – thou wast not built for administration, immortal boid. Thy place is near the lexicon, not the ledger; the dais not the dictaphone. You have Madison Ave. appeal too – the movie-America, big-time, coast-to-coast projection publicity gift. All I ask is that you never desert the classroom where the meanings are. Know within the inner recesses of your being that you are a teacher and must be. Best Wishes, highest hopes, Sid.

I was born by Caesarean section on March 21st, 1959 at the Bird Song clinic in the hills above Biel. As the midwife laid me in my father's arms, the church bells began to ring and Peter was delighted by this charming Swiss custom, extended to babies born on the first day of Spring. It was carefully explained to the Englishman that churches rang their bells at midday, every day. I was nothing special. My parents had given considerable thought to choosing names that could be easily pronounced in both English and German. Una was a good Irish name but the Swiss midwife had never heard of it: 'What's her middle name?' she inquired. Susan was a name she recognised and as babies in Switzerland are generally referred to in the diminutive, I was called 'Suseli' and Suseli I was to remain for the next forty years.

My father returned to London a week later and my mother remained in Biel until May. This may have been for medical reasons but I suspect that Lea also wished to showcase her baby and the new life she had so skilfully created for herself. At the age of twenty-six, she had suffered the scandal of her father's suicide, the humiliating and painful loss of her fiancé and the subsequent shame of tuberculosis. Sixteen years later, at the age of forty-two, she had secured, not only a highly personable, handsome and slightly younger husband but also a man clearly destined for business success. The cherry on Lea's cake was a baby of her very own, a little girl who would grow up to be her best friend, who would share hopes and dreams and secrets with her mother, just as Lea herself had done with Rosa. Unlike her aunts, Elise and Bertha, Lea would not be required to travel four-and-a-half thousand miles across the Atlantic in order to take up this wonderful new life. It lay, like a perfect jewel, just twenty miles across the English Channel from Calais and an easy train journey from her family and friends in Switzerland.

That summer, the English Vacation School was held at Grosvenor Hall, a former tuberculosis sanatorium in Kent and, without Amos' support, Peter struggled. In a letter to Sid, he writes: *During July I was near the end of my tether – I'm soft boiled, I guess, and I couldn't take the strain of mollifying hungry and indignant students and arguing and fighting behind the scenes. I found that with 14 classes to run I was getting almost no teaching, and then I thought more and more nostalgically of Nobles and the best teaching year of my life. The prospect of teaching at Nobles again is one which delights and tempts me, but, the family commitments are still strong, perhaps stronger since the birth of Una Susan. My father is devoted to her, and I could not consider at the moment leaving him to ever greater loneliness by carrying her off to the New World. And he is not the kind of elderly man who would fit in easily to the American scene. I am afraid, that, for the foreseeable future my fate is tied to this strange brand of teaching on these foggy shores.*

Chapter Seven

Closing the Circle

We are opening an all-year day school for foreign students in Folkestone and look forward to leaving the dirt of London and going to live in the bracing climate of the Kentish sea coast, excellent for the baby.
letter to Eliot Putnam, October 19th, 1959

We moved to Folkestone in the winter of 1959. Three weeks later, my parents left Pembury Lodge in the sole care of my grandfather and went to Adelboden for three months in order to run a combined course in English and Skiing. Unfortunately, the only applicant was an English Lord whose interest was skiing rather than the learning of English. For my mother, however, this extended period in her homeland would have been a rich and emotionally rewarding time as she invited family and friends to their little chalet in the mountains.

Our Una Susan has given us 7 months of pleasure, joy and amusement and we wonder how we ever lived without her. She is a lady about sleeping all night, eating whatever she is supposed to eat and spending her waking hours chuckling and squealing with joie de vivre. She made many friends in the summer school and now has a wardrobe that makes her mother jealous – full of Paris creations and Moroccan luxuries Peter in a letter to Eliot, 1959.

My father called himself Principal of The School of English Studies and when I was three years old, I asked him whether this made me a Princess. I was certainly treated like royalty and parents delivering their sons and daughters to the school would present Lea with Mini-Me designer dresses. My mother liked to dress me in frocks, frilly petticoats and hand-knitted cashmere cardigans and, from an early age, I was taught to curtsey whenever I met a stranger. This so delighted visitors that it became second nature to me.

When I was two, a Lebanese student gave me a doll with long, strawberry blonde hair, sewn, strand by strand, into her scalp. She stood two feet tall and her eyes, which opened and closed, were cornflower blue. She could walk and talk and she came with a designer dress of her very own. I loved Caroline more than I can say. She was my best friend, my sister, and I shared everything with her. Polly and Lucy loved Caroline too and one day, the sisters opened a hairdressing salon and their client was given a shampoo and set. Her head filled up with soapy water and no matter how much we shook her, the water sloshed around inside her like waves on a beach. She was never quite the same again. It didn't really matter though because Polly and Lucy were proper sisters and they didn't need Caroline in the same way as I had needed her when I was little.

Please give Reb Forte our warm good wishes and a very special kiss from Una Susan. She adored him and cried when he left. She has an obvious weakness for Americans and is not initialled U.S. for nothing.
Letter to Eliot Putnam

The 1956 Nobles yearbook photograph of Orville Willis Forte III shows a young man with perfect features and thick, glossy hair. It seems unlikely that my devotion to Reb was based on his movie star good looks, especially in view of the fact that, just a few months later, I was consumed with love for Abdullah, a thirty-something Saudi student with a wall eye and filthy fingernails. I managed to track down Reb, now in his mid seventies and living in California. His son, Will Forte, is a successful Hollywood actor whose career was launched on *Saturday Night Live*. It seems that Will had a very happy childhood with kind and loving parents so perhaps it was the embryonic 'good father' that drew me to Reb that summer.

Folkestone is one of the prettiest watering-holes on the south coast
Charles Dickens.

In the 1950s, Folkestone was still basking in a prestigious heritage. At the turn of the last century, The Prince of Wales, later to become King Edward VII, and his mistress, Alice Keppel were regular visitors to The Grand Hotel. A hundred years later, Mrs Keppel's great-granddaughter Camilla, would marry Charles, the current Prince of Wales. Winston Churchill and Agatha Christie also kept rooms at The Grand. H.G. Wells, Charles Dickens and Noel Coward all lived and wrote in Folkestone, Samuel Beckett married in Folkestone and Constable and Turner painted Folkestone. The Leas was considered to be: *one of the finest marine promenades in the world,* and the King of Belgium declared the town to be: *the prettiest place in existence.* It is sheltered from biting winds and, for all invalids suffering from nervous complaints or pulmonary infections, there was no place better to recover than Folkestone. We lived on a tree-lined boulevard beside a park with ornamental lily ponds and fountains. My father had undoubtedly done a good thing by moving the family out of London at a time when the country still relied on coal to heat its homes. Thousands of people were dying every year from respiratory illnesses. However, when the three of us left for Switzerland in December, I imagine my grandfather must have felt rather bereft in his new surroundings, handsome and wholesome though they were. Peter hoped that his father would take daily walks along the Leas, but I suspect that Grandpa either stayed home or walked only as far as The Central public house, his circuit of choice in the years we lived on Castle Hill Avenue.

In the days following my chemotherapy treatments, the exhaustion I felt was so debilitating that it even overrode my ability to sleep. Reading a book or watching television required a level of concentration I was unable to sustain, and the only solution I found that both held my attention and sent me to sleep, was listening to BBC Radio 4's *Homefront*. The drama, which was broadcast in eleven-minute episodes over a four-year period, explored the lives of those living on the home front during WWI. The series was poignant and engaging, but more importantly, it was set in Folkestone. My ability to fall asleep during the short episodes was, I suspect, linked to the soothing and familiar cry of seagulls and the mention of places that I know so well: The Leas, The Grand, Grimston Avenue and Bouverie Place.

There's rosemary, that's for remembrance. Pray you,
love, remember.
Ophelia, *Hamlet* Act 4, Scene 5.

As a child, my father told me that Grandpa had left for France from Folkestone in 1914, and that, after the war, rosemary bushes had been planted along the Road of Remembrance. Folkestone was the main port used by British troops on their way to the Western Front, and it is estimated that ten million soldiers marched down what was then known as The Slope and onto ships that took them to the killing fields of Flanders and Picardy.

Between August and October of 1914, one hundred thousand traumatised Belgian refugees arrived in Folkestone, fifteen thousand of whom settled in the town. At the end of the war, King Albert declared that the town had earned the admiration not only of the Belgians but of the whole world. Kitchener, who lived at Broome Park, nine miles from Folkestone, often came to watch his squadrons of volunteers marching on the Leas. The arriving recruits soon outgrew Shorncliffe Camp and soldiers were billeted in private homes and hotels. The Women's Army Auxiliary Corps took over the Metropole Hotel where seven thousand recruits were trained and sent to France to work as cooks, waitresses, mechanics and drivers. German submarines sunk ships in the Channel, often in full view of those walking on the Leas. On May 25th, 1917 the German Air Force bombed Tontine Street, killing seventy-one people and injuring ninety-six.

There were rest camps all along the Leas, and as many as nine thousand men passed through the camps each day.

The soldiers were English, Irish, Dominion and Colonial, American, French, Russian, Serbian, Indian, West Indian and Fijian. My grandfather not only left from Folkestone when he went to the Somme, he would have returned to Folkestone after he was wounded at Highwood. No wonder he didn't much care for bracing strolls along the seafront. To my knowledge, during the ten years Harry lived in Folkestone, he never once visited the Leas, nor walked down the Road of Remembrance to the Harbour.

Our Suseli is now rising four and is quite the most self-willed, cussed, cross-grained little critter I've ever met. At the same time she's also one of the most affectionate, engaging, amusing and jolly little buttons one could meet, and she has us all in rapidly oscillating moods of fury and fascination! She's going to school soon: maybe that will improve her.
letter to Eliot Putnam, December 8th, 1962

During the first few years of my life, I was entirely surrounded by adults and it was not until I was three years old that I made a friend of my own age. His name was Niall Finucane, and he and his parents, Kevin and Anne, lived next door at Pembury Cottage. Niall and I became inseparable and he endured my insufferable bossiness without complaint. We were often left to our own devices, but there were two rules we were required to follow: play quietly so as not to disturb the students and never go out onto the road. Every morning, an old man with a missing leg came by the house and Niall and I would stand on the swing gate and watch for him. We asked him about his leg and he told us that he had lost it during the war; the long-ago war, the one in which Grandpa had been a soldier. Sometimes, Mr Kenney would give us sherbet lemons, but this got us into trouble with the grown-ups and we were scolded for taking sweets from a stranger. We explained that Mr Kenney wasn't a stranger, he was our friend and we wanted to invite him to lunch. Dad said he would talk to the old man and we found him sitting on a bench on Castle Hill Avenue. My father spoke kindly to him, and Mr Kenney said he quite understood and promised not to give us any more sweets. Dad didn't mention anything about coming to lunch though. Standing beside my father, holding Niall's hand and listening to the two men talking, is one of my earliest memories, and I felt very sad without knowing why. After that, Mr Kenney didn't come by Pembury Lodge anymore. Niall and I waited by the gate, every day for weeks, but we never saw him again. For years, I used to look out for him when I was in the car with Dad, striving to recognise his face amongst the old men of the town.

Niall told me that his uncle was a famous fighter pilot and, not wishing to be outdone, I told him that my uncle could eat more sweets than anyone else in the whole world. Niall was staggered by this information and Uncle Paddy was never mentioned again. On his next visit to Folkestone, Uncle Bobi was surprised to discover that he was an object of enormous interest to the little boy next door. Niall no doubt imagined that a world champion consumer of confectionary must, by definition, carry plentiful supplies about his person.

I was lying, but Niall, it turned out, was telling the truth. Brendan 'Paddy' Finucane was not only a fighter pilot but, at twenty-one, the youngest ever wing commander in the RAF, and a hero on both sides of the Atlantic. Uncle Paddy shot down thirty-two enemy aircraft before he himself was killed over the Channel in 1942. He was profiled in both Life magazine and The New York Times and became known as: *The Flying Shamrock – terror of the Nazis*. Two and a half thousand people attended his memorial service at Westminster Abbey.

In a 2004 Irish radio documentary, Kevin Finucane spoke about his brother and his early life growing up in Ireland. Their father had fought as a volunteer alongside Eamon de Valera in the Easter Rising of 1916. Andy Finucane was a devout Catholic, and married an English woman who converted and raised all her children in the Catholic faith. When his sons left Ireland and joined the British Army, Andy didn't shun or banish them, and Kevin recalls that his father's greatest disappointment was that England and Ireland never fought on the same side against Hitler. Winston Churchill once declared that whenever he felt bitter about the Irish, the hands of heroes such as Paddy Finucane would stretch out and soothe the feeling away.

A great opportunity was lost when Mr Kenney slipped out of our lives. I imagine the conversation that might have unfolded over lunch: about what it meant to be English, Irish, Protestant, Catholic and a soldier in two World wars. Above all, however, I regret that I failed to bring home a friend for my grandfather. Somewhere inside my four-year-old imagination, I envisioned the two of them, sitting on a bench under the sycamore trees, sharing memories of their Irish homeland and of the terrible losses they had both experienced during the Great War.

Harry, Suseli and Peter, 1963

*26 Grimston Gardens – Large residence in red brick with
terracotta dressings, featuring an ornate two-storey loggia,
1908; the carved grapes hanging from its Doric capitals, add
a bacchanalian touch to a house built for the French mistress
of a London banker*
A guide to buildings in Folkestone and Sandgate by
Christopher Lumgair

My father bought Flowergate, 26 Grimston Gardens, in
1963. I grew up with the legend of the London banker, but
have since discovered that he was, in fact, a Harley Street doctor.
In 1920 Professor Mayo Collier, who had been the medical
officer in charge of the Dardanelles campaign during WWI,
purchased Kearsney Abbey near Dover as a country retreat. His
wife, Florence, was unaware that her husband had also acquired

a large Edwardian house in Folkestone, where he installed his French mistress. It is said that the elaborately designed copper fingerplates and door handles were imported from Paris. After Mayo Collier died, his wife sold the Abbey and moved into Flowergate, where she lived until 1947, having no doubt chased her husband's chatelaine back across the Channel.

If I had sat down and written out the ideal conditions for a school building, it would have described this house. Flowergate is perfect for our needs.
Peter in an undated letter to Uncle Leonard

The Castle at Nobles is a remarkable building. It is made from pink Quincy granite and Delaware brownstone, and its turrets and towers give it a distinctly Disney-esque quality. When I first stepped into the entrance hall, my heart missed a beat, and I gazed, slack-jawed, at the oak panelling, sweeping staircase, chandeliers and rope-carved tables. The Castle is an amplified, magnified version of the house in which I grew up! Flowergate is, undoubtedly a beautiful building, but, until I walked into The Castle all those years later, I never knew why it was the <u>perfect</u> building. By the early 1960s, Peter had given up all hope of returning to Massachusetts, and Flowergate and The School of English Studies provided him with the opportunity to re-create the body and the soul of his beloved Nobles on the south east coast of England.

In 1963, without consulting Lea, Peter bought the house, using Uncle Leonard's money as a down payment. We moved into the servants' quarters on the third floor, and the rest of the building belonged to the students. My parents went to local auction houses and gradually furnished the twenty-two rooms with oak tables, bookshelves, wingback chairs and mantel clocks. My mother's green fingers tended and revived the rose bushes in the walled garden, and for thirty years, the entrance hall was never without one of her beautiful flower arrangements. Visitors often remarked on the sense of well-being that they experienced upon entering the building. Flowergate, everyone agreed, was not just a school, it was a home.

I am convinced that the English-teaching world is mined and will be blown up by the new methods that are beginning to come in
Peter in a letter to Uncle Leonard

My father was passionate about teaching and learning, although his thinking could be chaotic and his interests overly diverse. In the early 1960s, he became enthralled by Professor Rand Morton at the University of Michigan, who claimed to have developed a system that could teach total beginners to speak fluent Spanish after only two hundred hours with a tape recorder: *This is doing to language teaching what Henry Ford did to automobile manufacture,* writes Peter to his uncle. He was excited too by the American psychologist B.F. Skinner's theory that all human activity was behaviour, and that all behaviours could be modified through reinforcement techniques.

One reason why the school survived in those early years was your mother's and grandfather's vigilance and involvement. Your father chose his spouse wisely, endowed with qualities that complemented his brilliant, occasionally saturnine idealism. He needed your mother's stable, dependable presence, anchored in concrete reality and affection. And he knew it. Amos Booth in a letter to me, 2006.

And whatsoever ye do in word or deed, do all in the name of the Lord Jesus
Colossians III:17. St Margaret's School motto

Shortly after we moved to Grimston Gardens, I started at St Margaret's School for Girls, conveniently situated next door to Flowergate. I hated going to school, and whenever there was a break in the timetable, I ran home. Day after day, my father carried me, kicking and screaming, back to Mrs Wicker's classroom. Most of the children were wary of me, and because I went home for lunch, I lost the opportunity to socialise outside the classroom. Every day, before my father took me back to school, I would lock myself in the bathroom, raise the frosted window a couple of inches and watch my fellow classmates in the dining hall across the road. I knew that the food was terrible, but I envied the games of touch-tag and hopscotch that the children played when lunch was over.

My father was keen for me to start school in order to *improve* my character but also to give me a jump start on learning. When I joined Mrs Wicker's Kindergarten group, I was four years old and the average age of the class was six. Thirty years later, I enrolled Polly at a progressive nursery school in Biel, having convinced the teacher that, although she was a little young for the class, she would be sure to benefit from the creative ideas of Maria Montessori. Unsurprisingly, Polly behaved in much the same way as I had at her age, and I decided to take her home and re-enrol her the following year, at which point she showed no signs of reluctance. Lucy begged me to allow her to go to school too, explaining that although she might be a little younger than the other children, Polly would take care of her.

I felt upset and confused that I was so often excluded from play dates and birthday parties. I watched the girls in my class go off to each other's houses, where I imagined them eating Viennese whirls, drinking squash, playing with Barbie dolls and watching television. I knew that a furious fiend lived inside me; indeed, my father often referred to me as 'a little hellion' and my mother called me a 'Tuefeli', a little devil. No matter how hard I sought to muffle my demonic outbursts, they seemed to detonate just as I was making some headway with children my own age. David Milne, the Vice Principal, remembers me wandering around Flowergate, muttering under my breath: 'I want to be good - I want to be good – I want to be good', but I didn't know how to be consistently kind and inviting. I was the 'Naughtiest Girl in Folkestone' a *self-willed, cussed, cross-grained little critter* and I couldn't seem to release the *affectionate, engaging, jolly little button.* On the few occasions when the 'Nicest Girl in Folkestone' did emerge, it was for the benefit of a small handful of trusted adults.

I sought my friends amongst the staff at SES, especially the cleaners. Mrs Clatworthy came to the school every weekday after the students had gone home, and together we would tidy the classrooms and empty the ashtrays of their Turkish cigarettes and Persian pistachio shells. Upstairs my parents drank Earl Grey tea from china cups; downstairs, Mrs Clatworthy and I drank sweet, milky PG Tips from big, heavy mugs. Her daughter had married a man called Hurlstone, and she always referred to Mavis as Mrs Chuckabrick because she knew it made me laugh. One day, Mrs Clatworthy told me that she was feeling a bit sad, because the Chuckabricks were leaving for a new life in Australia on the 'Ten Pound Pom' scheme. After the war, the Australian government, anxious to increase the country's population, offered Brits a one-way passage 'Down Under' for just ten pounds. I thought about Mum's frequent visits to see my grandmother in Switzerland, and I assured my friend, Mrs Clatworthy that Mavis would be back to visit her often, several times a year probably. She shook her head and told me that Australia was a long way away and that it cost a lot of money to get there. I struggled to imagine someone going so far away that they couldn't get back. Mrs Clatworthy was right though: it would be twenty years before she saw Mavis again.

My other special friend was Mrs Harrison, who came to Flowergate to polish the floors and shine the silver. Every Friday 'Hassie' would take me back to her bungalow in Cheriton for lunch. My mother took a dim view of what she called 'English convenience food' and there were a great many products she resolutely refused to buy. These included tomato ketchup, frozen peas, baked beans, peanut butter, sliced white bread and sugary cereals. Hassie knew that I loved fish fingers and butterscotch-flavoured Angel Delight, so, every Friday, that's what she would make. At Hassie's house, the kitchen table was right by the window, and we could watch the world go by as we chatted and laughed and dipped our fish sticks in great blobs of salad cream. At home in Flowergate, all you could see as you ate your lunch were the crowns of the chestnut trees and the wings of circling seagulls.

In March of 1963, when I was four years old, my father sat me in front of a microphone and told me to sing something. As I listen to the tape, fifty-five years later, I hear the anxiety in my voice as I struggle to remember the words of a song:

Suseli: (in an almost inaudible whisper) 'I don't know anymore, I'm sorry.

Daddy: I <u>told</u> you - It's no good trying to sing something if you don't know it. <u>Do</u> you know it?

Suseli: Yes... No - I think so.

Daddy: No, you <u>don't</u> know it, do you?

Suseli: I know 'Polly put the kettle on', that's easy -

Daddy: Where did you learn that?

Suseli: In my book, I've got a nice blue book.

Daddy: How did you learn the <u>tune</u>, or did you make it up yourself?

Suseli: (very proudly) I made it up myself.

Daddy: (laughing) Oh, I see - <u>that's </u>why it's so bad'.

Suseli: (upset) Hassie learnt me.

Daddy: Hassie <u>taught</u> me.

My father then leads me into a trap, as he encourages me to mispronounce certain words with which I was known to have trouble – 'cafedal' (cathedral), 'puvolo' (pullover) and 'hostipal' (hospital). 'Yes, that's right', he says brightly into the microphone, but, of course it wasn't right. And, I knew it wasn't right because he had often told me so. My strategy, if I couldn't remember lyrics or numbers was either to be robotically polite, or to speak extremely fast and roll the lyrics of one song into another. The deceit became easier, and my voice more confident, when I sang Swiss songs that I had learnt from my mother, because Daddy couldn't understand Swiss German and he didn't know whether the words were correct or not. On the tape, I sing 'O Tannenbaum', recite The Lord's Prayer without drawing breath, and regurgitate a string of random numbers.

To this day, I speak too fast, always conscious that my audience of one or many, might become irritated by my mistakes, or bored by my stories. At Ashford School, when I took my French and German oral exams at the age of sixteen, my rapid speech was interpreted as near-native fluency. In my spoken English exam, however, the examiners told me that I was close to incomprehensible. I knew that the speed of my speech corresponded directly to the level of my anxiety, but I had no way of explaining this to them. Years later, teachers and students alike would say to me: 'Suseli O'Connell - Aren't you the girl who was awarded A grades in spoken French and German and an Unclassified in spoken English?

In 2000 Tom McNealy, the young man from Chicago who had taken Peter under his wing at Groton, wrote to my father: *I can still recall that you had a sort of twitch or blinking of one eye – the fantastic forgiveness of each of us and the recognition that you made of your students' differences and our separateness. You are in my thoughts constantly. There must be some truth to the fact that we never forget important people in our life. You are so important to me in my order of things. I thank you for being in my life.* This gracious and generous portrait of Peter is now familiar to me. In 2019, Loring Conant, Class of '57 at Nobles, hosted a lunch at his home near Boston in my honour and in memory of Peter. Five of Dad's former students, all of whom were nudging eighty, spoke about him with affection and admiration. Bill Gallagher later wrote: *Imagine... at Nobles for just one year and there we were sharing happy memories of Peter over 60 years later.* I was touched, but I also struggled to separate my irritable and unforgiving father from the tolerant and kindly teacher who holds such a powerful place in the hearts of these elderly men.

Peter in the classroom, The School of English Studies, Folkestone

Once I had accepted my destiny in terms of a daily commitment to St Margaret's, Daddy's early efforts began to bear fruit. I won the School Prize for Reading Aloud and Mrs Wicker entered one of my essays for the Alice Green Memorial Cup. I was good at Bible Story, Percussion and Singing, although never quite up to scratch in Handiwork and Drawing. Once

I moved up to the Junior School, I continued to improve in all subjects bar Maths: *Suseli is reluctant to face up to difficulties or to work things out for herself,* wrote Miss Cousins in my end of term report.

St Margaret's advertised itself as: *a high class school for the daughters of gentlemen.* When I arrived, it was recovering from a scandal which ultimately proved to be its undoing. The sixty-two-year-old headmaster, Mr Hasson had married his head girl, causing widespread outrage amongst the parents, many of whom withdrew their daughters from the school. When Dudley Hasson died of a heart attack in 1966, St Margaret's limped on for another year before being declared bankrupt.

The list of unsecured creditors totalled over £30,000. Many shops and providers in the town, who had long operated a policy of trust and goodwill towards the school, never recovered their money. For The School of English Studies, however, the collapse of St Margaret's provided an opportunity. SES was fast outgrowing Flowergate, and Peter and Lea had been looking for new premises for some time. In 1967 they were able to buy 24 Grimston Gardens, and, when Grandpa died a year later, Peter named the building Henry House, in memory of his father.

I sometimes reflect on the course my life might have taken had Peter remained at St Paul's School, or had SES not proved to be such an unqualified success. Dad would probably have become a local secondary school teacher, and Mum would have remained a housewife. The challenges they faced in their marriage would almost certainly have been intensified in the spotlight of a much smaller stage, and their opportunities would have been more limited. As it was, Peter had the freedom to pursue his ideas, Lea could go to Switzerland as and when she chose, and my own life, growing up in the SES family, provided me with a much larger canvas than the one I would have experienced as an only child of older parents in a quiet seaside town.

Human beings, not bricks, make a school
Eliot Putnam Headmaster, 1943 – 1971

In 1960, Paul Longland decided to accept the still vacant position of English master at Nobles, and he and Helen made a permanent move from London to Dedham. In 1967, therefore, Peter was surprised to hear that the Longlands were returning to England. America in the late 1960s was a very different world from the one my father had known in the early 1950s. It was the era of Flower Power and the Vietnam War, and drugs were rife all over the country, including on the campuses of Nobles and Groton. The Longlands moved to Folkestone, and Paul accepted a position at The School of English Studies: *We were the third in a 'trilogy' – St Paul's, Nobles and SES – distinguished company,* wrote Peter to Paul when his friend retired in 1979.

Three years after Paul Longland left Nobles, the school said farewell to Eliot Putnam: *Noble and Greenough is a place that has been awfully good to me and I have never had the slightest inclination to leave.* However, the tide had turned, and Eliot was dismayed, not only by the drugs but also by the long hair and the floating shirt-tails. For many years he had actively resisted the idea of co-education, but by 1971, he recognised that it was coming, and that he was not the man to oversee it. He died in 1988, and his obituary in the Boston Globe included the following quote: *Being a schoolmaster requires patience, under-standing, respect for and absolute fairness with one's students. It is sometimes frustrating, but never dull; and far more often than the layman realises, it is downright thrilling.*

Sid Eaton left Nobles shortly after Eliot, exchanging *the cottage for the castle* as he spent his final teaching years at Groton. Mr Eaton was a doppelganger for General Eisenhower and I remember him as a jovial, whimsical man who lived with us one summer and taught on the English Vacation School. Sid had experienced a difficult few years with his wife, Jessie, who had become a Christian fundamentalist. In a letter to Peter, he writes:

Jessie has developed a heavy reliance on Bible, Prayer book and uplifting tracts – of which I am not scornful but unable to respond to with satisfactory conviction. These agencies, I find, lead to rather bleak plateaux of dissociated piety, a Calvinistic security in one's own salvation and a deep doubt of the salvageability of the unenlightened. Anyhow, we have nothing rational to grapple with, and since communica-tion with me simply stirs up the feelings of grievance, I'm incommunicado, mainly sitting out the storm. Meanwhile we wait and pray (quite literally, though my spiritual unwor-thiness is suspect). Jessie has spoken of going into a religious retreat institution.

Eventually, Jessie asked Sid for a divorce, and he agreed to move to Reno for six weeks; until 1970 'The Silver State' had the shortest residency requirement for putting asunder what God had joined together. I wonder whether Sid and Grandpa ever spoke to each other about their experiences of being married to women who had loved the Lord more passionately than they had loved their husbands.

Mummy and Daddy are in America. I am alone with Grandpa and Margaret and Blackie. I miss Mummy and Daddy.
St Margaret's School, Composition Book. Age six

In 1965, my father finally took my mother to visit his beloved Nobles and Groton. Mum sent us a postcard from New Haven, Connecticut: *Darling Suseli and Grandpa, Everything and everybody is wonderful. What an exciting, modern and beautiful country. How much I would love to share all this with you two.*

A little boy was going to London to buy a bag of gold and his mother was going too, but she went and hid from him and so he went without her. He got on the wrong train and his mother stayed at home.
Suseli, Composition Book. July 1965

Until 1965, Rosa lived with Frau Roth. I always thought that she was my grandmother's friend, a kindly woman who looked after her because Mum lived in England and Uncle Bobi didn't have a spare room. In fact, Frau Roth managed a small and friendly nursing home in Biel. When I was six years old, my mother explained that Rosa was beginning to behave a little strangely; she would, for example walk out of restaurants with her handbag full of linen napkins. This didn't strike me as a particularly serious offence; nevertheless, she was no longer able to remain with Frau Roth and she moved to Bern.

Her new home was in a much larger building, set in parkland. Children weren't allowed inside, so Aunty Heidi and I would walk around the grounds while Mum and Uncle Bobi visited their mother. Sometimes, we stood beneath Rosa's window and waved to her. On the way home in the car, Mum would cry inconsolably and there was nothing any of us could do to make her stop. It was not until 2016, when I found Aunt Bertha's will, that I discovered the truth about my grandmother's final years. At the bottom of the long list of beneficiaries I read: *Rosa Kummer-Gilomen, half-sister, born December 7th, 1887, currently a resident at the Waldau Psychiatric Clinic in Bern.* My first reaction was denial. Fifty years ago, I told myself, the Waldau had almost certainly been a state-run nursing home; conversion to an asylum would have come much later. But I knew that this wasn't true, because Godi had been sent to the Waldau when he was fifteen years old. As recently as August 2017, an article in a Bern newspaper described disturbing practices at the Waldau with regard to isolation and restraint procedures. A commission subsequently recommended that patients should not, in future, be handcuffed or placed in solitary confinement for longer than a prescribed period of time.

We had lived in the village of Magglingen near Biel for several years before I met Hanna. Her son and Polly were in the same class at school, and we got talking to each other one morning at the bus stop. I warmed to her immediately, and was both surprised and delighted when she invited me to lunch.

Everything about Hanna and the home she lived in with her family was beautiful, reassuring and inspiring. She was bright and funny, and we had many interests in common. As I had always experienced myself as balancing on a bit of a social precipice in Magglingen, I felt as though I'd turned a corner through this chance meeting with Hanna.

After our lunch together, I didn't hear from her for a while. Then, one morning, she arrived at our house, looking dishevelled and acting a little strangely. She had brought me a book which she insisted was important and that I should read immediately. A week later, the postman told me that Hanna was 'back in the Waldau'. It was several months before I saw her again. She had gained a lot of weight and she moved slowly and spoke rather deliberately. She told me that she had stopped taking her lithium medication because she didn't like the way it made her feel, and eventually, the men from the Waldau had returned, put her in a straightjacket and bundled her into a white van. I tried to imagine the scene, which struck me as both archaic and humiliating. Eventually, Hanna found a steady path. She moved to Biel, where she lived with a group of like-minded friends and remained in good contact with her children. She was never quite the same Hanna I had first met at the bus stop, but her soul had re-surfaced and, as far as I know, she hasn't been back to the Waldau. Lucy tells me that every year, Hanna messages her on her birthday.

I decided to visit the institution where my grandmother had spent the final years of her life. In 1491, the city of Bern established the site as a leprosy colony, and in 1749 the first *Irrenanstalt* (lunatic asylum) was built. The Waldau is proud of its heritage, and claims some of Switzerland's greatest artists and writers as former patients. The most internationally celebrated of these is Robert Walser, who was born in Biel and whose dead body was found in a frozen field on Christmas Day in 1956. His work was much admired by Hermann Hesse, and several characters in Franz Kafka's *The Castle* were reputedly influenced by the author's early reading of Walser. I recognised the mustard yellow brickwork and surrounding parkland immediately. The building reminded me of St Patrick's College in Cavan, where my grandfather had been sent in anticipation of his training for the priesthood, and I thought of the parallels that are often made between the monastery, the asylum and the prison. The inmates I passed as I walked through the grounds looked relatively young. They were slow of gait, cloudy of eye and many of them were sucking hungrily on cigarettes.

I went into the cafeteria where I ordered one of my mother's favourite desserts – chestnut vermicelli with crumbled meringue, whipped cream and a maraschino cherry. Why had my grandmother been institutionalised in this place? Perhaps pilfering from smart restaurants was considered to be a slippery slope that might lead to more serious breaches of the law? Maybe, like many of her generation, she had been diagnosed with religious mania? I think of the letter Rosa wrote to her daughter in 1954, encouraging her to place her trust in the good Lord, insisting that He would eventually crown her in glory. Perhaps that was how she survived the nine years she spent in the Waldau – praying and trusting in God's ultimate goodness and wisdom.

Rosa was a remarkable woman. She never doubted her purpose and never faltered in terms of the vision she had for her beloved 'Leneli'. Scandal, severe illness, the call, first of Massachusetts and later of Kent, not to mention ticking biological clocks, held no sway over my grandmother. She was generous and self-sacrificing and, like the mother in my story, Rosa recognised that in order for Lea to find her bag of gold, she needed to go forth, unencumbered by the burdens of her past. *The little boy got on the wrong train and his mother stayed at home.* Whether or not Lea got on the wrong train is arguable, but Rosa certainly stayed home, collapsing into insanity once her ambitions for Lea had seemingly been fulfilled beyond her wildest dreams.

My mother used to beg me never to put her in a nursing home, and I knew that whatever money she squirreled away was her insurance policy, a guarantee in case I failed her. I used to wonder why Mum never brought Rosa to live with us in Flowergate. We had plenty of room, after all, and plenty of carers too. Hassie, Mrs Clatworthy and the au pairs could all have pitched in and helped out, just as they did with me. However, if Grandpa was - *not the kind of elderly man who would fit in easily to the American scene*, then my grandmother was certainly not the kind of elderly woman who could have adapted well to a country where she didn't speak the language, and where her confusions would surely have been exacerbated. Rosa died on May 13th, 1975, at the age of eighty-seven. It was a quiet funeral, attended only by close family.

Uncle Bobi followed his mother to the grave the following year, dying of a massive heart attack shortly after returning from his daily run in the forests of Magglingen. My uncle had been a great athlete in his youth, winning trophies for swimming and medals for skiing. He also loved rich food and fine wine, and was dangerously overweight. I was seventeen when he died and I did not accompany my parents to the funeral, a decision they later regretted. From Biel, my mother writes:

Our dearest Little Girl,
How we missed you today – we needed you near us in our deep grief. You could barely see the coffin for all the floral tributes and yet I shuddered at the thought of my little brother lying beneath them. Oh Suseli, this is so hard for me – for you too, I know.

My uncle was much loved, and his funeral was well attended. The *Bieler Tagblatt* sent a reporter, which my mother considered to be a great honour. After the shame of her father's suicide, her mother's mental illness and Hans's untimely death, Lea was, at last, able to openly acknowledge her love and her grief: *Perhaps Bobi's death will bring us closer, you and me. This is what I wish for with all my heart. I love you, Mami xx.*

My father's letter is equally melancholic:

My darling Suseli,
It has been a sad but wonderful day – sad because a world without Onkel Bobi seems lonely and very incomplete. We are now very sorry we left you at home to grieve alone: we should have had you with us. 'Suseli has a good heart' Bobi used to say. It's the loss of this relationship that breaks me up more than anything else. He was so good for you in a difficult time in your life. I'll try to be more like Onkel Bobi, darling and a better father to you. Nothing means so much to me as being a good family man. Please help me to prove it to you and Mum. My warmest love to you, Papi. .

Somewhere within that man we know is the best of us, in fact or aspiration.
Judith Crist, film critic of the actor Gregory Peck

Peter was occasionally compared to James Stewart or Cary Grant but was generally considered to be a dead ringer for Gregory Peck. Eldred Peck was born in California in 1916. His father was Irish Catholic and his parents divorced when he was young. He described himself as a shy and lonely child and said that acting gave him a sense of family as well as the ability to communicate. Like Gregory Peck, Peter was in search of family and he had a deeply felt need for truthful communication. In a letter to his friend and colleague, Earl Stevick, he wrote: *Gimmicks and tricks, visuals and drama – all must be subservient to the prime purpose: communicating with our students and giving them real opportunities to communicate with us and each other. We would improve our performance immensely if we like actors had 'directors' who taught us the basic skills and helped us to become aware of our own deficiencies and showed us how to overcome them.*

In 2003 the American Film Institute named Gregory Peck as the greatest hero in the history of motion pictures. In 1962 his most famous performance as Atticus Finch, the Southern lawyer in *To Kill a Mockingbird* earned him an Academy Award. Peck later said that he put everything he had learned about family, fathers and children into the role. In spite of Dad's urgent plea, I couldn't help him become the good father and family man he so clearly wished to be. Peter had lacked the 'director' figure in his own life, the father who might have taught him basic skills and helped him overcome his own deficiencies.

Harry may well have been detached and emotionally unavailable, but he had some pretty radical ideas. In the mid 1960s, Edith, our au pair girl at the time, fell pregnant and told my parents that the father of her unborn child was an Arab student on the General Course. Edith was adamant that she intended to keep the baby, but a future life for the couple, either in Saudi Arabia or in Switzerland, was out of the question. My grandfather had a solution which he offered one morning at breakfast. He could marry Edith. This would offer her respectability and provide the child with a name. More importantly, as his wife, she would be entitled to his pension after he died. It made complete sense. Of course there would be no expectation that the two of them live together as man and wife. He offered it simply as a practical solution to a difficult problem.

My mother was horrified by her father-in-law's proposal. People would be scandalised. How could he suggest something so deranged and irresponsible? Dad was more circumspect, recognising that his father's suggestion was certainly very practical and generous spirited, although he agreed with Lea that others might not see the arrangement in quite the same way. Some might even believe that the baby was his! Once this idea was off the table, I came up with one of my own – we could adopt the baby ourselves. I badly wanted a little brother or a sister, and I knew that there were no plans in the pipeline to provide me with a sibling. In comparison to my grandfather's idea, adoption must have seemed quite a tame proposition, so it wasn't rejected out of hand. This encouraged me, and I continued to pester Mum and Dad with the idea for several weeks. Edith, however, remained resolute; she would return to Biel and have her baby there, and that is what she did.

I sometimes wonder what became of them. It seems likely that the road ahead for a dark-skinned baby born to a young, unmarried woman in 1960s Switzerland would have led either to the orphanage or to life on a farm as a Verdingkind.

Chapter Eight

Worms in the Woodwork

January 31st, 2018 was the night of the Super Blue Blood Moon Eclipse, a celestial phenomenon not seen since 1866. It was also the night that the breast surgeon removed my shrivelled tumour. I was relieved to be told that I wasn't going to die: at least not just yet, because of course we're all dying, just at different speeds. For six months, death had been with me like a piece of luggage I carried and couldn't put down. Gradually and almost imperceptibly, I came to realise that what I imagined in the afterlife wasn't a God in Heaven, but the possibility of reuniting with those I have loved and lost. I feel their support and guidance in my life every day, and yet there are times when I experience a pure longing for their physical presence. *Noli timere/Do not be afraid,* and I no longer am. Like a religious conversion, it doesn't seem possible that I could have reached this perspective via a process of reasoning and deduction. I experienced a reckoning, perhaps with God, but certainly with something that exists beyond time and place. There was a perforation, followed by a breach in my understanding of who I am and I now recognise, at a cellular level, that I am quite simply a human being who will die someday, just like all the other seven billion human beings with whom I currently share the planet. But, the time is not now.

Initially, I felt a bit stunned. My friend John, who has also survived cancer, perfectly described my feelings: *Maybe you would scream the house down if you won the lottery, but this is much, much bigger than that, and you need time to realise the magnitude of it. Of course, you are also battle-weary. Relief after such struggle often comes out more as a sigh than a scream of delight.* I thought, not for the first time during those long months, of my grandfather and I wondered how Harry had felt on the day the guns fell silent.

In 2017 following our meeting in Bern, I told Scharli Probst the story of my grandfather and of my inability to discover any information about the circumstances surrounding his death. Scharli mentioned that he had a contact in the State Chancellery who might be able to access Ernst Kummer's records. Three months later, I received a document from the Biel Police Department which revealed that: *On August 6th, 1943, Corporal Kummer, following the embezzlement of cashed market funds, took his own life. During interrogation he admitted to misappropriating funds and signed a document to that effect. His next of kin has repaid the amount in full.* The accompanying report was five pages long and titled: *The case of Corp. Kummer, former Market Sergeant.*

My grandfather had been in charge of collecting payments from stall holders – farmers and their wives who came to town twice a week to sell vegetables and flowers in the marketplace. Corp. Kummer had taken their money, issued false receipts and skimmed off funds for his private use. On September 1st, 1943 the Parish Council called a meeting which was attended by the Chief of Police and the Director of Public Relief. One of the issues raised was whether the five thousand francs they had received from Corporal Kummer's family was adequate recompense. It was felt that the amount could very well have been substantially higher, but Kummer had not been willing to testify to the period of time, nor to the scope of his embezzlement. As the store holders were unable to submit accounts, it was not possible to gather sufficient evidential proof. My mother was a pupil at the exclusive Pensionnat Saint-George in 1933, so it is entirely possible that the hypothesis was correct, and that my grandfather had been stealing money for at least a decade and possibly longer.

The tone of the report is surprisingly muted; it is factual, never angry or denunciatory, and is punctuated by a sense of disappointment in a man who was considered to be entirely trustworthy. As my grandfather had chosen to remove himself from further scrutiny, those standing in the dock were his supervisors, senior ranking officers who had failed to keep track of the weekly payments deposited in the cash register. It was suggested that had Corporal Kummer known his activities were being monitored, he would never have entertained the idea of stealing on such a routine basis. The court decided that no further investigations would be conducted, and Ernst Kummer's next of kin would not be required to pay more than the amount they had already paid.

This report defies any alternative explanations. The facts are indisputable. My grandfather had been a thief and a maverick, whose honourable reputation as a police officer had enabled him to continue his deceit over a prolonged period of time. He had stolen money from the city coffers, most of which he had spent on fashioning an illustrious future for his daughter. Lea in turn had carefully protected her father's reputation. She had lied about the cause of his death, and when I was thirty-four years old, she had looked me in the eye and told me that my grandfather was an innocent man. It is this particular lie that I struggle with the most. I was an adult, no longer a child, but perhaps my mother didn't trust me to fully comprehend the magnitude of the situation, the weight of her father's criminal and moral wrong doing. Even Peter and Heidi were excluded from knowing the full truth about their father-in-law.

I must accept, therefore, that Ernst Kummer was no Paul Grueninger. He was not a man with strong principles who died in the name of persecuted Jewish refugees. I suspect too that the year my mother spent at a private sanatorium in Davos was paid for, not by small contributions from Uncle Bobi's salary, but from the secret stash of cash which my grandmother had chosen to keep rather than return to the Police Department. Once public records declared that the stolen money had been repaid in full by his next of kin, Rosa was home free. The lie was tightly wrapped and carefully hidden at the very heart of the family. Had circumstances been a little different, had my own heart not been touched by the story of the Swiss Verdingkinder, had I never met Scharli, then the secret would have gone to the grave with my mother, the last of those who knew the truth about Corporal Ernst Kummer. I spent the following week trapped in a riptide of anger and judgement. I felt betrayed and ashamed of my grandparents, deceived and abandoned by my mother and, every morning, I would wake before dawn, my head flooded with disturbing images and memories.

In the summer of 1991, Stephan, Polly, Lucy and I were on the lakefront in Biel, watching a hot air balloon preparing for take-off. Its burner was breathing fire into an already swollen skin, and two men were in charge of releasing the anchor ropes. As the balloon rose slowly into the sky, they both grabbed the lip at the base of the basket, calling to each other and swinging their legs as they sought a stronger grip. One man let go quite promptly and dropped back on to the ground, but the other, perhaps trying to impress his friend and the small crowd gathered below, chose to hang on a little longer. Very soon it became obvious that he was too far off the ground, and that if he let go, he would almost certainly break a limb. Stephan was holding Polly's hand and I was carrying Lucy in a baby sling when the thought occurred to me that we should perhaps move away from the mesmerised crowd. In that moment, I heard the man say softly: 'I can't hold on any longer'. With that, he dropped out of the sky. As his body hit the ground, it made a dull thwacking sound, immediately followed by a noise that reminded me of wood being sliced in a log splitter. Everyone stood around in stunned silence. Eventually, Stephan put Polly's hand in mine and walked over to the man lying motionless on the ground. He was the first to do so, and he told me later, much later, that the man was still breathing, but there were bone splinters protruding from his body in all directions. On Monday morning, the *Bieler Tagblatt* reported, in a short paragraph on the front page, that a man had died at the weekend as a result of *falling out of a hot air balloon*.

My grandfather and the man on the balloon had both taken risks and pursued them to a point of no return. Ernst could, in those early days, have taken a decision to stop stealing from the Police Department and entrust his daughter to a future of her own making. Rosa could have encouraged him in this, and it's possible that she did, but I have no way of knowing. The police report suggests that Corp. Kummer stole money simply because it was possible for him to do so: he was unsupervised and it was there for the taking. There is no mention of right and wrong, of moral standards or personal principles; an assumption is made that this was something anyone might have done, given the opportunity. In both the case of the policeman and of the balloonist, the general public was given incomplete and therefore inaccurate information. The full truth was, for whatever reason, withheld.

When I was in my early teens, I stole a scarf from a London department store, and occasionally I would help myself to a Liquorice Allsort from the Pick and Mix buckets at Woolworth's but in general, I am fastidiously, scrupulously, even compulsively honest, a gene I must have inherited from my O'Connell and Arnold forefathers.

Two weeks after receiving the police report, Dan and I left for a holiday in Ireland. On our way to Sligo, we spent a couple of days in Virginia, where my cousins, Patrick and Eamonn still farm the land that belonged to our great-grandfather. The heifers were calving, the sheep were lambing and, as we walked the fields and stood in the barns, we talked about life gone by and about the brothers who left and the brothers who stayed. Our ancestors were a quiet bunch who worked hard and spoke little. The O'Connells are honest people who abide by the rules and pay what they owe. If Eamonn or Patrick find that they have been undercharged by a supplier, they don't hold their tongues in the hope that the oversight will be overlooked, and they teach their children that telling the truth is easier than remembering a lie. It helped me to be in the company of my Irish family. I was able to take a small step away from the Kummers and breathe a quiet sigh of relief. Thank God I'm an O'Connell: Just like my cousins, I am honest, fair and true, and these are the values Stephan and I communicated to our daughters as they were growing up. Only last Christmas, Lucy discovered that she had received her annual bonus twice. She could have waited for the error to be discovered in the new year, but she chose to return the money immediately because, as she said, it wasn't hers to keep. Then, in the early hours of an Irish morning, a memory knocked my self-righteousness straight into a cocked hat. How could I have forgotten? How, in God's name, could I have forgotten Alfa Romeo?

It was 1988 and Stephan and I were running a promotional watch company. As one of the first of its kind in England, we were doing rather well and had landed several contracts with big name clients, including Heinz, Alfa Romeo and Tate and Lyle. Alfa Romeo made a repeat order and then cancelled it the following week, omitting to inform their finance department, who subsequently sent us a cheque in the mail. Rather like the balloonist hanging onto the basket by his fingernails, we chose to hang on to the cheque, waiting for the error to be discovered, because we realised, of course, that it would be. But ... it wasn't. Even our accountant, when he came to do the annual audit, didn't seem to notice that there was an extra three thousand pounds in our account. Stephan and I never intended to keep the money. Fancying ourselves as modern-day Robin Hoods, we were of the opinion that if a luxury car company couldn't keep track of its pounds, shillings and pence, then we were quite justified in taking from the rich in order to give to the poor. The only trouble was we couldn't agree on how to spend the money: should we buy goats for a farming community in Uganda or hens for a village in Kenya? The money roosted in a savings account and over time we spoke about it less and less. We never forgot about it though, and once Polly and Lucy arrived, Stephan suggested we invite their opinion as to where and how the money should be used.

Ten years later I was co-facilitating a personal growth training in Biel and I suddenly recognised the folly of what we were trying to do. Our intentions, although honourable, were entirely misplaced. The three thousand pounds were not ours to give away. For better or for worse, the money belonged to Alfa Romeo, and the only solution was to return it to its rightful owner. Stephan, who had more experience of the business world than I did, suggested that this was a rather dangerous idea. We could be sued for fraud, possibly even sent to prison. No matter, I declared, it had to be done, and I sat down and wrote a letter to Mr Moncrieff. I was completely honest, telling him of our honourable intentions, acknowledging and apologising for our past mistakes and, most importantly, enclosing a cheque for three thousand pounds. A week later, the postman delivered a handwritten letter from Alfa Romeo. Mr Moncrieff had left the company and his successor expressed astonishment at the contents of our letter. He also admitted to a certain admiration at the courage we had shown in admitting our crime which, he pointed out, should not be underestimated. He continued with a paragraph about legal rights and consequences, but in the end, he let us off the hook. He returned the cheque and we spent the money on putting a Tanzanian boy through school. We were lucky. However, remembering the Alfa Romeo story made me realise that what I did was not so very different from what my grandfather had done forty-five years earlier. Like him, I had believed in my own justifiable cause. Like him, I had taken money that had not belonged to me.

Somewhat ironically, I have, during the course of the past twenty-five years, been involved in four separate incidents of fraud. In each case, the courts ruled unanimously in my favour. At SES I was confronted with an incident involving serious financial mismanagement, which threatened to bankrupt the school. We had won a number of government teaching contracts, the funding for which was provided in advance. However, an insufficient number of students enrolled, and several of the courses were subsequently cancelled. The Principal in situ failed, for whatever reason, to refund the money, and, rather like the Chief of Police, I was not informed of what had happened until shortly before the arrival of an investigating government inspector. Fortunately, I had heeded my father's advice and ring-fenced his 'SES in crisis' savings account. The school was, therefore, in a position to refund the six-figure sum before the deadline date, and as the inspector accepted that no individual had personally benefitted from the money, SES avoided criminal prosecution. Her Majesty's Revenue and Customs, however, declared that, for a period of ten years, they would be keeping a close eye on our activities, and we were warned to keep our financial noses clean. The Principal was fired. My father would have been utterly mortified by the entire episode.

Lea's early role at SES was somewhat ill-defined. She was neither a native speaker of English, nor a trained teacher, so she set about creating a beautiful home. Profits were, for the most part, re-invested in the school, and my mother learnt to be inventive in her interior design strategy. On one occasion, a student from the Middle East couldn't afford to pay his fees, and my mother enquired whether he had anything of value he could trade. The young man offered her a prayer mat, which she accepted and the following morning, three more students showed up, bearing rugs and offering to cut a deal with Mrs O'Connell. She declined, recognising that she was, after all, running an English language school and not a souk; she knew too that neither Dad nor HMRC would stand for the arrangement if conducted on a regular basis.

Lea was a talented artist, and if my father's fingers were often paging through books, my mother's were busy with needlepoint, knitting and upholstery. She was best known, however, for her porcelain painting which she took up when she was six years old and gave up when she married my father. She used only the best porcelain – Rosenthal, Dresden and Limoges – and 22 karat gold paint. She told me that in the nineteen thirties, a single drop cost twelve Swiss francs. The brushes were extremely fine, and the work required enormous patience and a steady hand. Sotheby's once expressed an interest in buying her collection, but she told the dealer that it wasn't for sale. The plates, bowls and dishes were used only on very special occasions, and we all knew never to put Mum's china in the dishwasher. I used to smile when I heard Polly and Lucy bossily tell their boyfriends to be very careful when drying up the dinner plates, because: 'Grandma painted them herself and we mustn't break them'. I have a friend who insists that the tiny daisies and butterflies are not hand-painted but appliqué, and I grow indignant with her for doubting both my mother's honesty and her creative credibility. Mum's porcelain was part of a large trousseau, lovingly collected by Rosa through the long years of her daughter's marital uncertainty. They included thick and creamy linen bakers' aprons, tablecloths, tea towels and sheets, all monogrammed in duck egg blue stitching. In 2012, when Dan and I got married, I carefully cut my mother's initials from a worn tea towel and sewed the linen fragment into the lining of my wedding dress. It subsequently passed to Polly, who wore it on her wedding day in 2019.

Flowergate, 26 Grimston Gardens

My father had led a peripatetic life, living in furnished rooms, hotels and school boarding houses and he very much wanted a home of his own. However, like his alter ego, James Tyrone in Eugene O'Neill's play *Long Day's Journey into Night*, Peter struggled to settle down. Mary Tyrone tells her husband that in a real home one is never lonely, and she reminds James that she gave up a real home in order to marry him. My mother, like Mary, had enjoyed a happy childhood, full of laughter, companionship and fine things, and it was this life she wished to re-create in Flowergate, with her husband and with me.

Consider my role to be that of loving shepherd rather than shoving leopard.
British Council Inspector on a visit to SES in 1964.

Peter's vision of the ideal community, and his interest in the relationship between student and teacher had their roots in his early childhood experiences. Harry and Grace, each in their own way, had consciously rejected the idea of the all-powerful priest as God's representative on earth. My grandfather's search for the divine was defined by God as a Loving Creator rather than a Punishing Deity, and my grandmother's faith lay in the daily study of scripture as part of an evangelical Christian community. Peter, like his parents, rejected the all-knowing teacher in favour of the loving shepherd, and recognised the importance of community as a way of supporting and nurturing individual growth. In 1971 The Reverend Edward Gleason succeeded Eliot Putnam as Headmaster of Nobles, and defined the school as: *a family in which each member cares and to which each member contributes, a family of interaction and respect, personal integrity and commitment to excellence, a family where one may develop the mind, the body and the spirit for a life of service.* This was my father's template for The School of English Studies, Folkestone.

At times I feel I am dim-witted: then assure myself that my intelligence is good, only blocked
Peter, journal entry, November 7th, 1950

After St Margaret's School collapsed, I was sent to Brampton Down for a few years, before it too began to teeter on the brink of bankruptcy. I was what was commonly described in the 1970s as 'a bit thick', and my reports ranged from *fair* to *slow* to *disappointing*. I struggled to stay focussed in class and couldn't remember facts: *Suseli never really gets down to work because she fusses too much,* declared one teacher. My understanding of English, Latin and French grammar was *weak,* and I was *out of my depth* in Arithmetic. Everyone on the faculty agreed that *thorough learning* was essential if I was to do well in the examinations. There were however, three exceptions to my dim-wittedness: I could keep whole poems in my head, I was *very good indeed* at dictation and spelling, and, my French accent was *delightful.* In spite of being such a poor student, I was recognised as having *very pleasant manners* and my teachers unanimously agreed that I was: *polite, courteous and cheerful.*

In the spring of 1971, when I was twelve years old, my parents decided to remove me from the ailing Brampton Down and send me to live with my aunt and uncle in Biel. I attended the Benedict School, where I flourished and achieved my first, and never to be repeated, high mark in Maths. Swiss schools do not go in for chatty reports: Parents and pupils are simply provided with a mark ranging from a low grade One to a high grade Six. Herr Koechli considered my Maths skills worthy of a 5.5.

My darling Suseli,
How is the apple of my eye, the Spring of my content, the pain in my neck? You'd better be well and happy because that's the only consolation we have for being deprived of all the noise and rhubarb and fun and nonsense and gaiety and screams of rage and laughter. It's all very quiet and dull without you.
1) 2+2 = 5
2) 2+2 = 4
3) 2+2 = 3.
Can you get that one right? Then you're improving your Maths and all praise to Herr Koechli. I must take lessons on teaching Rechnen from him. Please give him my warm thanks and Congratulations! Your always loving Daddy.
May 18th, 1971

I was happy in Biel. It was a quiet life compared to SES, but I enjoyed the gentle predictability of our daily routine. At weekends Uncle Bobi would take me to the Seeteufel, followed by ice cream at the Florida Tea Room, or we'd take a pedalo out on the lake. I adored my aunt and uncle, but I missed Mum and Dad dreadfully. Every day, after lunch, I would lock myself in the bathroom, stuff a flannel in my mouth and cry until the sadness subsided. Uncle Bobi and Aunty Heidi would have known about my homesickness, and I am grateful that they never embarrassed me with consoling words of comfort. We all recognised the situation for what it was, and we understood that there was nothing to be done. I would return to England in the summer and not before.

In the autumn of 1971, I started at Ashford School for Girls. My father, encouraged by my good grade under Herr Koechli, kept an eye open for signs that I had finally cracked Mathematics, but failed to see any. At the end of my first year, he wrote a letter to the Head of Maths, pointing out that the weaker vessels, such as myself, clearly needed more nuanced teaching: *The one lesson our daughter has learnt very thoroughly is that she will never understand Maths. For much of that wonderful discipline she is probably quite right: it is permanently out of her mental reach. But the basic concepts are, I am sure, not beyond her grasp.*

To Miss O'Halloran, he wrote: *My wife and I have been worried for some time at Suseli's continuing failure to understand mathetical concepts. I know she is gifted with very little ability in Maths and must be very difficult, not to say tiresome to teach. I do hope you will excuse a teacher of English giving views on Maths and I should be happy to meet you to discuss the problem, if you were willing?*

I am embarrassed by my father's letters. His writing style is condescending, although he manages to side-step being openly rude by tendering questionable olive branches. The word *mathetical* is his own and I feel a shiver of shame as I imagine Mr Hartley and Miss O'Halloran shaking their heads at the English teacher's ignorance. The *wonderful discipline* of Maths implies that my father is quite the expert, when, in fact, he left Dulwich College with only a School Certificate in Elementary Mathematics. No-one took up Mr O'Connell on his offer, and I wonder now whether Miss O'Halloran's seething anger towards me had as much to do with my father's presumptuous interference as with my own *mathetical* ineptitude.

At Ashford School, I thrived in a few subjects and failed miserably in all the rest. I was conscientious and interested in History, French and German, slow and confused in Biology, Art and Geography. Eventually, I suppose, I gave up on myself too, relieved that there were a few subjects I was good at and delighted that, after years of loneliness in the playground, I had finally discovered the secret to making friends.

My other nemesis at Ashford School for Girls was Miss Taylor, the Geography teacher. Our first misadventure occurred during a lesson on the physical geography of Switzerland. Following Miss Taylor's repeated mispronunciation of the word 'Thun', I raised my hand and helpfully explained that the correct way to pronounce the name of the town and its lake was 'Toone'. Just as my father had embarrassed Miss O'Halloran with his suggested improvements, I had humiliated Miss Taylor in front of an entire class and she never forgave me for it. In my end of term reports, she declared me to be *overly chatty and generally uncontrolled* in my behaviour. In the summer of 1973, I was suddenly inspired to study hard for my end of year Geography exam, and I came second in the class with seventy-six percent. I was excited as I sat at my desk, anticipating Miss Taylor's delight, but all she said was: 'Why can't you always work this hard?'. She then waved a warning finger at me and declared that unless I pulled my socks up, I would end up on an assembly line in a factory. I felt crushed and shamed and promptly took the decision to give up on Miss Taylor and her stupid Geography. I paid a high price but was secretly pleased when I achieved the lowest possible grade in my Geography O'Level exam. That summer, my father sent Miss Taylor a gift accompanied by a card: *Kindest regards and my thanks for your positive patience with my chatterbox.*

In 1975, the year I graduated from Ashford, Dad wrote his swan song letter to the Headmistress. He thanked Miss Thompson for teaching me to lay out my work well, to write with a reasonable degree of fluency, accuracy and felicity and to draw straight margins. He was satisfied with the As and Bs I achieved in my O Levels, but: *Her E in Geography could have been a B if Miss Taylor had encouraged her more. Suseli is no intellectual at any level but she's got common sense, a gift for languages and an interest in people. She's also rather a talkative flibbertigibbet but beneath that flippant manner is an earnest little girl terribly anxious to do well and to be liked by her teachers. Some of the shorter-sighted ones can only see the children's external behaviour and their repression and anger are often counterproductive. Miss O'Halloran is no doubt a good teacher for bright mathematicians, but with our little duffer, she created only frustration, confusion and despair. I intend to have her privately coached to restore her to the land of the simple numerates: the tutor will have to be as much psychologist as mathematician.*

I am grateful for Dad's insightful understanding of my struggles but hurt and humiliated by the harshness of his criticisms. He wished to engage with my education in a way that Harry had found impossible. Peter spent his life in pursuit of excellence and the expectations he handed me were no less severe than the ones he gave himself.

We must hope for a better future. I know that with a bit of good will, it will be possible.
Lea in a letter to Peter, May 1956

Seventeen years after my mother wrote those words, Peter and Lea were still hoping for a better future. By the time I was fourteen, I had come to accept their daily quarrelling as normal, and assumed that this was the way all parents behaved in the privacy of their own homes. Sometimes, when their arguments became too hot to touch, they wrote each other letters:

May 14th, 1973
My dear, dear Lea,
I want you to realise that I am very, very anxious to make you happy. I hate being an inadequate and unsatisfactory husband to you and should like nothing more than to love you as you deserve. Unfortunately at the moment this is impossible. I don't want to bore you with details of my early family life but, whenever I hear you talking about your free, happy childhood, I feel deeply nostalgic. When you relate your experiences in your latest visit to Biel – the people you've met, their family history and connexions, the associations with 50 years of your life, I am jealous of your roots, your free running memory, your identity with a small area of the earth. My own memories come with very little emotional colouring. My childhood scenes were set in places with which I now have no associations: I'd be a total stranger if I returned to any of them – except Groton and Dedham, which may account for some of my love for New England: I put down roots there. You mock me sometimes about my age. It's true I fear the waning of my powers before they have been given true expression. I simply must find out what manner of man I am. I don't think you realise how difficult it is for me to keep going from day to day. It hurts me to see how much I have hurt you. But I still feel the way ahead lies through a period of retraining for me.

Peter's retraining plan involved what he referred to as: a *tough regime of Meditation, Encounter groups and Gestalt therapy. Encounter work is painful and demanding, though finally exhilarating. You didn't approve its effects because I never had enough time to develop them. Give me that time and I promise results. Doing nothing will drive me crazy or to a breakdown or to desperation. I am not exaggerating, Lea. Take what I say very seriously.*

I've got to get rid of much of the rubbish inside me – what Pa never got rid of because he never had the chance, perhaps. Things can be done today that were unknown or impossible to do in his time. My so-called 'modesty' stems to some extent from frustration: so many people praise me and my achievements and I am aware of how little my real strength was applied to these achievements. Most of it is wasted fighting myself. The frustration that stems from knowing one has unused powers is a terrible thing. To my mind it is the cause of much of the world's woes. It is one of the main incentives to me to invite someone to start an Institute of Excellence. It is one of the main reasons why I must go away to find myself.

My mother's letters speak of her own struggles:

Peter, Peter! I have been unkind to you sometimes, not very understanding, irritable – loving too. I don't know what to do. I think I just want to put an end to it all. We have someone for supper so I can't cry – and I want to so much. Suseli is home soon, an even more important reason not to. Without her you would be rid of me for good.
My experience 25 years ago taught me to be very careful in trusting people again. My heart feels like a shattered

windscreen, burst by the pressure, with a hole in the middle, except that it is still alive and can feel the pain burning. I have this inside tremble which seldom leaves me now and makes me sick at night. It feels as if a black cloud is hanging over me, ready to come down to crush me or what's left of me. It took years to gain confidence in myself again, and it improved when you came along and rescued me with your loving, understanding heart. But it had left a scar. Last night was another desperate night of loneliness and black thoughts. I felt I just couldn't go on, when suddenly I heard Suseli calling: 'Mami!' I went over to her, but she was asleep and called out in her dream. She is worth living for and I want to remember that deep in my heart.

I am sorry that I have caused pain too. I know that we don't see eye to eye on your problem. It is such a complicated one. You have tried all the things you wanted to. I did not always agree, but since you wanted to try out these strange ways – so they seem to me – you did them. Well, Peter you must do what you want to do, otherwise I shall always be blamed. You are basically an honest person but I am very bitter, so forgive me when it comes out at times. I have been hurt so much but as long as I can fight back, I am still alive, and not all is lost. I would leave you, if I knew where to go, to whom to talk. I don't want my family to change their high opinion of you. I am lonely and desperate, but we have Suseli to think of, she is at a very vulnerable age, and is as sensitive as I am.

I pray for you, for us, Peter and our daughter. May the sun shine on this desperate situation and may happiness mend our broken hearts in time.

God bless you, Lea

Chapter Nine

The Absent Prince

It is really noticeable how patient, understanding and downright sensible your mother is with people when her own feelings and personal identity are not involved.
Peter, March 4th, 1983

One of Lea's roles at SES was to interview students to ensure that they were happy at the school and in their host families. Her intuitive abilities and fluency in several European languages meant that she soon became the school's unofficial counsellor. She was discreet, but I would sometimes hear soft whisperings and muted sobs behind closed doors. One drama, however, that did see the light of day involved Heinz, the son of Lea's school friend from Biel. Heinz fell in love with Beatrice, a Swiss girl on the General Course who had come to SES with Rolf, her fiancé and sponsor. Rolf was naturally angry and upset at losing not only his girlfriend but also his money. Mum decided to speak to each of them individually, and quickly recognised that Beatrice was an opportunist. She advised Heinz to walk away, and suggested to Rolf that he'd had a narrow escape. At the end of term, Heinz and Beatrice left for Biel, where she refused to pull her weight in the family business and soon grew bored of small-town life. Three months later, she packed her bags and moved home to Zurich.

My mother once read an article in a Swiss magazine about how to tell fortunes with a pack of playing cards. To her it was all a bit of harmless fun, but many people were amazed by her detailed insights into their lives and word soon got out that Lea was quite possibly psychic. Like my father, I never really took her gift seriously, but some of her observations were uncannily accurate, and the au pairs, struggling with affairs of the heart, often relied on my mother and her cards for guidance. One summer the school hosted a fundraising fete and Mrs O'Connell, swathed in a headscarf of jingling coins, became 'Gypsy Rose Lee'. Customers queued all day outside her tent to have their fortunes told, and Lea made a tidy sum for the new Sports Centre.

Mr O'Connell does a lot for the town. I don't think people realise how much.
Shopkeeper in Folkestone

Mr O'Connell did indeed do a lot for the town. He was on numerous committees and gave financial support to the Adult Education Centre, the Folklore Festival and Folkestone Family Care. This last project was very dear to his heart. He believed in what he described as: *the old ideal of service and the obligation to carry out some of the principles of the Welfare State in our own small circle.* My father was forever lamenting poverty in Africa, in part I suspect to get me to finish the food on my plate. One Christmas he took an executive decision: there would be no tree, gifts or goose that year and the money would be spent on poor people living in our local community. My mother resolutely refused to cancel Christmas, but agreed to help a struggling family in Folkestone. Peter was given the name of a suitable family by Social Services, and I had to choose gifts for the children whilst Mum and Dad bought presents for the adults. It was quite a project, and we all felt flushed with self-congratulation as we rolled up at the house on Christmas Eve with our carefully wrapped packages. A woman and a trail of children opened the door and we followed them into the living room where a man was watching television. He looked away from the screen for just a moment and then waved his arm to a corner of the room and said: 'Just leave them over there,' and with that we were dismissed. I felt awful and Dad subsequently recognised that we must have appeared as bountiful benefactors rather than kindly Father Christmases. We had caused the family, and especially the head of the family, considerable embarrassment and humiliation. It was an important lesson for us all.

I ordained thee a prophet unto the nations - to root out, and to pull down, and to destroy, and to throw down, to build, and to plant
Jeremiah 1:4-10

I don't know whether Peter ever saw himself as a modern-day John the Baptist, but he was certainly messianic in his pursuit of new and unorthodox ideas in language teaching: *Language is central to a person's sense of individual and cultural identity; learning a new language must interact powerfully with these fundamental feelings. How then can the process be cool and detached like digging a trench or shelling peas?* He sought to escape the constraints of inductive learning and compulsive correcting in favour of what he referred to as: *a gradual fading of concern with the teacher and a growing interest in each other and the language.* Unfortunately, my father was burdened by low self-esteem and was reluctant to put his ideas into practice: *I would achieve only a pastiche, a faded garland of other men's flowers. I need more experience, more training, more time to reflect'.* What Peter was less transparent about admitting was that his professional search was inextricably linked to his psychological struggles and a quest for healing.

Dad decided he needed to move to London for a few months, but this plan was vetoed by my mother. She also refused to be dispatched to Switzerland, which saved me from being withdrawn from Ashford School when I was fourteen and re-enrolled at the Benedict Schule in Biel. This period, however, marked the beginning of my father's ever more frequent trips away from home.

In an undated letter, my mother writes:

Dear Peter,
I knew before we married that it would not be easy but was convinced, because I loved you dearly, I could heal your wounds.
Once we were married your way of talking to me about your problems always sounded like an accusation and a reproach. At the beginning you blamed your father for it all – your unhappiness in your childhood. I had long talks with him about your problems with him. It brought you two closer and your father even thanked me for it. But then suddenly I

became the one who is responsible for your pain. I am paying for what happened in your youth. Now you want to leave me to run after your lost youth.

I never thought that without being loved one could be so desperately lonely in a foreign country. If you leave me for weeks, don't think you will bring happiness for me and Suseli.

I can't say things correctly like you and nicely but I tried, Lea

In March of 1975 my father attended a ten day 'Arica' training. He lived in a serviced flat in Kensington Church Street and kept a detailed diary:

I feel a great need to escape the pains of an intolerable domestic situation – or rather to find a solution to the problems and conflicts that cause the pain; I have a wild hope of releasing the great surging energies within me for vigorous creative work. I feel an equally strong desire to make sense of the mad world in which we live and to find a workable solution to which I can commit myself. Ichazo claims no-one takes life's challenges seriously until faced with death.

Arica, founded by the Chilean, Oscar Ichazo, was a strain of scientific mysticism that appealed to a mainly young, wealthy and cosmopolitan crowd: *Anna comes in a patched boiler suit under an expensive mink. She is divorced, living with another man and in love with a third who is black. Pretty, but moody. Robin also has a child and no husband. Linda is an attractive black girl with an easy character who dances well.* The group sessions laid great emphasis on breathing, meditation and psycho-calisthenics, all of which Peter found helpful for getting in touch with his body. He professed surprise by how fit and strong he felt at the age of fifty-seven and hoped to get rid of his belly as a result of the prescribed diet – *protein and very little carbohydrate.* The group practised African drumming, sang Hindi songs, and each night participants were required to take a cold sponge bath followed by ritual wipings, referred to as 'woosoos'.

Peter soon found himself irritated by what he called: *the undigested gobbets of philosophical junk, so like a Christian Scientist church. There is a kind of cosmic pecking order. The lower depths are labelled 6144 and this embraces 99% of humanity, and it's hell! At the top is 3 (why not 1?) and these aristocrats are at the level of the spirit. I suppose this élite are in heaven.*

There were truth meditations and karma burning, which, compared to his experiences with psychodrama and Gestalt, my father found *naive and poorly handled.* Peter experienced his desperation differently from the other participants: *I have felt suicidal but because of frustration. I suffer from feeling overfull, not empty – a pressure cooker ready to burst.* He found some relief in Karma Clearing at the Ego level but did not shine at the Philosopher Charlatan stage.

Half-way through the training, my father had a dream: *Suseli and I were driving and there was a long unguarded drop to the left. Then I somehow swung the wheel and there was a cry from Suseli 'Mind Papi' and we were over. The strange thing was that there was no terrible panic but a feeling of lightness and release.*

Six years later, this dream almost became reality on a stretch of road near Giverny in France. I was asleep in the passenger seat and awoke with a start to discover that Dad had drifted to the wrong side of the road and was seconds away from a head-on collision with a truck. I screamed and he swerved, fortunately back into his own lane. I certainly had no sense of lightness and release, just terror and panic as I recognised that the three of us had been moments away from death or life-changing injuries.

During Peter's ten days with the Arica movement, Lea and Aunty Heidi travelled up to London to see The Danny La Rue Show. I think of my mother and my aunt howling at the tomfoolery of the cross-dressing Irishman while Dad sat in his Kensington flat, performing his nightly woosoos. In the end he decided that Arica was not for him: *I find it a self-regarding philosophy, the idea that man is alone and must accept responsibility for his own evolution.*

Over the course of his life, Peter was described as: *Christ-like; the finest character I have ever met; a benevolent despot and a cruel and selfish tyrant.* Some saw my father as a genius; others as charmingly eccentric, and a few thought he was quite mad. He could be vain and self-obsessed, even cruel, but his intentions were always for the higher good and for greater happiness in his own *intolerable domestic situation.* He desperately wanted to be a loving husband and a guiding father, settled in his life with me and my mother and creative in his work. The irony is that many of my friends, especially my male friends, idolised my father. One once said to me, rather wistfully: 'Mr O'Connell is more of a father to me than my own father'.

I decided to ask some of my Folkestone friends how they had experienced Peter as we were growing up. Ric's response was: 'Talking to your father was slightly nearer the confessional than any of us were used to. He would ask finely-tuned questions that made you think. He had a rigorous academic mind and he wanted serious conversation'. Andre described Peter as: 'an inspirational leader but not a manager', adding that the most important thing he learnt from my father was never to tell people they were going to fail. Lea was equally popular, for different reasons, and following her death in 1996, Andre wrote: *Your mother was a kind person. She had a good heart. Not keen on hippies or communists was Mrs O'Connell – I had long hair and left-wing pretensions and she saw to it that I was nonetheless never short of ice cream nor dispatched to India without money 'for a steak'. Your Mum and teenagers made a good team – she took as much selfless pleasure in giving as they did in taking.*

In May of 1975 my father left for America in hot pursuit of three new methods of language teaching. In Washington, he studied Lozanov's 'Suggestopedia', a gentle, fun-filled approach to learning which included listening to Chopin and playing games in class. In New York he learnt Hindi using 'The Silent Way' before travelling to Ann Arbor, Michigan to learn about 'Community Language Learning'. CLL was the inspiration of Charles Curran, a former Catholic priest and professor of psychology who noticed similarities between the anxieties of a beginner in a language course and the emotional difficulties of a patient in therapy. Peter was attracted by the idea of therapy in the community as it dovetailed with his own ideas regarding the importance of psychology in the classroom. Professor Curran's course drew people from all over the United States and participants included the Head of the CIA language division and his counterpart in the Mormon Church. In his diary Peter writes: *Both CLL and SP have an obsessive concern with what is happening inside the learner – not only, or even mainly, in his head, but also in his heart and in his whole personality.* He likened these new methods to sphinxes along the traditional path of direct method teaching, challenging followers to read their riddles.

It was during this time in America that Peter met Earl Stevick. Earl had a degree from Harvard, a Masters in the Teaching of English as a Foreign Language and he worked for the US State Department. Stevick was also a practising Christian and his approach to education was very much influenced by his faith. I recall him as an elegant, soft-spoken man whose delivery was free from the quirks of personality that sometimes hobbled the message of men like Curran and Lozanov. Earl had a profound interest in the role of memory and emotions in the learning process and offered his conviction that: *success depends less on materials, techniques, and linguistic analysis, and more on what goes on inside and between people.*

Peter saw Earl Stevick as the St Paul of the humanistic methods: *Your book is quite a bible to me - Scarcely a day goes by without my quoting your name/book/principles and never a day goes by without my thinking of you and wishing that you could be made Minister of Education somewhere (preferably the UK!). I'd be haunting your corridors of power.*

Earl's response was measured: *I will write frankly, because to write in any other way would be to waste our relationship. Let me tell you Peter how I see myself and it may not come across with as much modesty or humility as you have ascribed to me. I see no virtue in modesty or humility per se. What is desperately important to me is to be realistic. And, realistically, I see that I have considerable influence over a growing number of people. When one person tells me that ideas that have come through me have been instrumental in restoring his zest for work, or when another says that contact with me and my writings has been part of what brought him back after a suicide attempt, I'd have to be blind to miss it. I am influential and I know I am. Make no mistake. But precisely because I am influential and because I know I am influential, it becomes terrifyingly important to me that the ideas I put into circulation should be sound - It is, as a corollary, also essential that I should make every effort to see to it that what I myself do is consistent with those ideas. I want to sharpen a sense of the 'miracle' of being alive, and of the 'mystery' that each of us is, ultimately to all the rest.* Stevick recognised the seductive and corrupting influence of naked adulation and he wished, above all, to be grounded in service to the community: *I am trying to live according to Philippians 1:27: – whatever happens, conduct yourselves in a manner worthy of the gospel of Christ.*

Stevick's intention, as he described it to Peter in his letters, was to draw attention to a style of teaching that he called *sacramental*. My father's suggestion that *some kind of love* might be at the heart of what his friend was trying to access, resonated with Earl: love that transcended mimicry and memorisation, cognition and communication; love that helped teachers see more clearly how what they did and who they were affected classroom learning. Earl writes: *Suseli, as you describe her, is very much the 'incarnate' teacher, and from your remark about her need to learn to protect herself, I would guess that she may be 'incarnate' as the Peter Sellers character was.*

Ultimately, it was Suggestopedia that was to grip Peter's attention for the ensuing decade. Its founder, Dr Georgi Lozanov, was a Bulgarian doctor of psychiatry and parapsychology. He had also been a student of yoga in India. Lozanov claimed he could cure a fear of learning and replace low expectations with a powerful self-belief. When Peter arrived in Sofia in 1978, there were more than five thousand children in Bulgarian schools learning subjects through the Suggestopedic method. Dr Lozanov had also introduced experimental classes for what he described as 'neurotic' university students, claiming he could cure them of their mental disorders. In 1981 during my third year at Reading, Dad sent me on a Suggestopedia course for Spanish beginners in Lichtenstein. Perhaps he hoped that a dose of the good doctor's methods might cure his own neurotic university student.

On the current www.Lozanov.org website is an illustration of a little girl riding a bicycle, accompanied and supported by her mother. The caption reads: *The bicycle principle is the underlying concept of the motherly care and support shown by the teacher to the students in Suggestopedia.* The picture reminds me that it was neither my mother nor my father who taught me how to ride a bicycle, but an instructor at the local Cycling Proficiency Centre. Peter believed that in all things practical and educational, it was best to learn from the best, hence his desire to help establish an 'Institute of Excellence'. Too much time and money, he declared, was being spent on the failures in our society, the break-downs, the drop-outs and the inadequates. He did not begrudge these people help, but suggested that society would be better served if more of its resources were spent on synthesising rather than analysing.

Stephan taught Polly and Lucy how to swim, dive, ride a bicycle, tie their shoelaces, read an ordinance survey map, ski and skate. I was taught to ski by Koebi Vollmeier, the brother-in-law of Anneroesli Zryd, the 1970 Swiss World champion skier in the Downhill. If one wished to achieve excellence, my father said, then one must seek out experts. In spite of my high-profile coach, Polly and Lucy are far better skiers than I will ever be. I put this down to the fact that they have always loved skiing with their Dad, so they get a lot of practice. To be fair, my father did try to coach me in Maths, but I was hopeless and made him so cross that the lessons had to be abandoned. In 1974 when I needed help with French grammar, I was sent to Dr Radu Florescu, a refugee who had escaped the Russians and settled in Folkestone. Once a week, in the year leading up to my O'Levels, I would climb the stairs to Dr Florescu's tiny flat where he kindly and patiently untangled the mysteries of French grammar for me. Radu Florescu was in his seventies and had a jowly, deeply lined face, flecked with cigarette ash. His fingers were stained amber from smoking, and he would often stop mid-sentence and release a phlegmy cough from his smoky throat. In the final letter Peter wrote to the Headmistress at Ashford School, he declared, a little testily, that: *it was the valuable consolation given to Suseli by an old Rumanian High Court judge that gave her heart to face the written examination so successfully.* This was undeniably true, and my sessions with Dr Florescu were an important steppingstone on my journey to a degree in French from the University of Reading.

The entire species WOMAN has been so conditioned – through hint and innuendo – by the idea that it is less powerful, less creative than MAN, that it has grown to half believe it. The Hanover experiment is intended to give its female participants an opportunity to develop both as people

and as communicators. The English language is an almost
incidental vehicle for this.
Peter on the 'Anglo Club' School, Hanover.

In 1976, my father and a colleague, decided to open a school
in Germany, intended as a meeting place, *more sitting room*
than classroom, for the wives of professional men who wished
to improve their English in order to become better at entertaining their husbands' clients. His Royal Highness the Prince
of Hanover agreed to preside over the opening ceremony, and
later invited my parents to join him and the Princess for lunch
at their castle. After the meal the Prince gave Peter and Lea
a tour of his country home, through state rooms and along
corridors lined with oil paintings of his ancestors. One picture
was of a baby. Beside the cot stood a military man with a
handlebar moustache and a spiked helmet. Peter, unable to
restrain himself, blurted out: 'Good Heavens - that's Kaiser
Bill!' to which the Prince replied: 'Yes, that is Kaiser Wilhelm
and that is me in the cot. He was my godfather'. Peter later
admitted to having felt a powerful combination of astonishment and embarrassment. I wonder what Harry would have
made of Peter's friendship with the godson of the last Emperor
of Germany and King of Prussia. I suspect he would have felt
pride in his son's association with a man who, in spite of his
belligerent relatives, proved to be a generous supporter of Peter's
Hanover experiment.

The German project forced my father to decline an invitation to spend six weeks teaching university lecturers in
Peking. He decided, therefore, to make himself available to
the British Council for future overseas postings and offered, as

his speciality, *The Humanistic Movement in Language Teaching.*
Two months later, he was invited to China for a seven-week
teaching assignment at the Language Institute in Peking.

Friendship Hotel, Peking, July 1976
My dear, sweet, poor deserted wife,
I have been thinking of you. I hope you are all well and
sighing with relief to get that cross-patched old Papi out of
the way for a few weeks! Now you can have a bit of peace.
It's midnight and I am sitting in my suite at the Friendship
Hotel wearing nothing but my underpants, and feeling as if
I were in Chicago (weather-wise only). I am listening to 'My
Fair Lady' to keep in touch a little with the Western world.
In Canton we watched 10,000 people swimming down
the Pearl River in squads of 50. This was to commemorate
Chairman Mao's famous swim in the Yangtse on 16th July
eleven years ago. It was an impressive festival with thousands
of red flags blowing in the breeze.
The Friendship Hotel is like a small town, and can accom-
modate 4000 residents. It is enclosed by high railings with
access for inmates through one gateway guarded by a PLA
sentry with a revolver in a holster.
Don't worry my little love, all will be well – for you and for
me. I love you sweetheart, Your wide ranging husband, Peter.

Peter and his two colleagues, Robert and Anne, arrived in
Peking during a turn-of-the-tide period in Chinese history:
Mao's death, just nine months earlier, had brought an end to
the Cultural Revolution and the vicious power struggles of
the previous ten years. The day the English visitors arrived,

they were informed, by the Minister for Education, that the government had successfully 'smashed the Gang of Four'.

The food, Peter tells Lea in his letters, is good, but there are no newspapers, televisions, biscuits or cocktails: *I find I miss little except you, Suseli and the dogs, your lovely roses and the bright green of the lawns. There is little grass here. I think about you often and pray for your peace and happiness.*

The Institute applied strict censorship rules and the teachers were asked to black out the sections of their Advanced Learner's Dictionaries that listed Tibet and Taiwan as independent countries. One textbook, containing a picture of a young woman in a bikini, was banned, as was a tape of folk songs, declared to be too sentimental and insufficiently concerned with farming and tractors. Robert's group was especially fascinated by the contents of his wallet, which included his driving license (there were no privately-owned cars in China in 1977), a British Rail timetable and his airline ticket – all items his students had never seen before.

Wednesday afternoons were dedicated to compulsory Political Studies classes: *Each week we see the teachers and hotel workers through the windows, studying books and listening to a secular sermon. The ambience is of an evangelical prayer meeting or Bible study group* writes Peter in his journal.

July 29th, 1977
My darling Swiss wife,
I'm rather sad – no letter again today. The Chinese are having a big celebration – it's the 50th anniversary of the People's Liberation Army, so they'll be letting off a few firecrackers. We went round a printing works yesterday – the staff had

293

many lurid tales to tell of the horrendous Jiang Qing, and our
students were like children listening to stories from Grimm
on the wicked witch.
Write soon and get that daughter of ours to move her writ-
ing hand!.

Telephone communication with my father during his time
in China was complicated and expensive. A call had to be
booked in advance and a Chinese official would demand to
know who we were, why we were calling and what we were
going to talk about. In August, I received my A Level results,
and was desperate to tell my father the good news. The wait
was interminable, and the slow, dull questioning of the Peking
telephone operator immensely frustrating. Finally I was put
through to Dad's apartment on an extremely crackly connection. We could barely understand each other. I told him that I
had been awarded an A in French and a B in German. He heard
the A but he misunderstood the B. The conversation continued:

'D?'

'No, Dad, 'B'

'I can't hear you. Did you say D?

'No', I screamed down the line. 'I said B. I got a B in German'.

'You got a D in German?'.

I remember my face streaming with tears: I was distressed
that my father assumed I had done so poorly. Neither of us
thought to use the Phonetic Alphabet Tables: 'No Dad, B for
Bravo, not D for Dunce'. Eventually my mother took the
receiver and after a few more tries, the correct message was
passed down the line. He was pleased. Of course he was.

August 1st, 1977
Dear Lea,
I must send you a quick greeting for Swiss National Day. I told my dear Chinese of the brave Swiss peasants who threw off the yoke of imperial Austria in 1291 and created the first European republic. They seemed a bit puzzled by this early example of bolshiness in Europe. I must tell them about Wilhelm Tell.
The Chinese have faith in their system, in their country and, as far as one can judge, in their leaders. Such a faith may be naïve, but it's a lot healthier than Western cynicism and vulgarity. At the same time one can't feel easy at the large number of people one meets who are separated from spouses and children. There must be a reasonable compromise between the claims of the individual and his family and of the State. I've only had 3 letters from you since I left nearly 3 weeks ago. I'm feeling a bit neglected. Apart from small excitements we lead cloistered lives, eating together and then returning to our rather lonely apartments to work, read and write letters, but it's a great experience and I am very happy to be having it. I hope it's not at too high a price for you. Keep smiling my love, better days are dawning.
All my love and kisses, Peter.

At the end of July, Peter and his colleagues visited a boarding school for young children whose parents had been sent to work in distant parts of the country. A group of heavily rouged infants sang and danced for the Western visitors. My father thought they looked anxious and unnatural and the performance was unapologetically political: *I think it's wrong to use children for propaganda purposes and it's counterproductive for the image of China, this splendid country full of such warm and generous people. Politics is everywhere but love of the Chinese Motherland seems to me to be the real dynamic. And in this Chairman Mao fits very well for he was the quintessential Chinese. I admire and love these people very much and can see so much good in their society. I pray they may always get the leaders they deserve. All I can say is that I hope the 21st century will be Chinese and not Russian.*

The teachers also visited The Shin Wa Printing Press, where they were subjected to a ninety-minute harangue against Mrs Mao: *The speaker seemed to me to be self-exculpatory, self-indulgent and hypocritical. Why had he and his mates been so feeble as to accept Jiang Qing's demands and not seen her off? Madame Mao is a scapegoat – a horrid woman, I'm sure, but no evil Empress.*

It is possible that, in 1977, the collective madness that had taken over the country in 1966 and sunk it into a particular kind of horror had not yet been fully recognised in the West. Even so, my father's rhapsodic idealism seems wide-eyed and overly trusting; he sounds a little like a Communist himself as he rushes to defend the late Chairman Mao and his wife. A year after my father's visit to Peking, a young mechanic plastered a poster on Democracy Wall in Changan Avenue. It shook the country to its core because it was the first public criticism of Mao Zedong.

Peter and his students, Peking, 1977

A revolution is not a dinner party, or writing an essay, or painting a picture, or doing embroidery; it cannot be so refined, so leisurely and gentle. A revolution is an insurrection, an act of violence.
Mao Zedong from *The Little Red Book*

In his book *Behind the Wall*, written in 1986, Colin Thubron describes how in those early years following the death of Mao Zedong, China lay physically and psychologically frozen by the brutality of the Cultural Revolution. Many who survived were still living and working alongside those who had persecuted them, and the whole country lived in a limbo of remembering and distrust. Mao legitimised a decade of savagery and persecution. He authorised his Red Guards to direct their rage and frustration against academics and capitalists. Schools and universities were closed, and teachers were forced to wear dunce caps, before being insulted, beaten and publicly shamed by former students. Had my father been born in China, this could well have been his fate. His intellectual, bourgeois lifestyle would have made him a prime target for the Red Guards as they rode roughshod over two thousand years of Imperial rule. Seventeen million young men, later referred to as China's Lost Generation, were exiled to the country to work on communes. Some were stranded there forever; others became factory workers.

During their time in Peking, Peter, Robert and Anne visited a commune. In his diary, my father writes: *I was very shocked to see girls little older than Suseli lifting great blocks of cement in a yoke device.* On an audio tape recorded that day, an interpreter explained that the policies introduced by the infamous Gang of Four had been reversed, and all communes across the country were flourishing and producing bumper harvests. When Robert asked whether young people were permitted to enrol in colleges and universities, the man's answer was evasive: 'Young people are very much needed in agriculture, but they all study Marxism and Agricultural Science here at the commune'.

A month after his return from China, Peter wrote to his former student, Lu Bong Hong: *I would be very happy if my daughter decided to study Chinese at the university. Meanwhile she is doing well in the domestic science course – learning how to scrub floors thoroughly and scientifically and to cook and clean and mend and sew and cultivate the garden and do all the practical things that our youth who go to university often learn nothing about. It may not be such a thorough experience as going to a commune for two years but it is better than nothing!*

*I think of the foreign language learner as comparable to
a participant in an Outward Bound school. These people
suffer quite a lot of anxiety but because they are part of a
group they rise to the occasion and perform way above their
normal capabilities.*
Peter in a letter to Earl Stevick, January 1976

My father never went so far as to post me off to a kibbutz,
and working on a Chinese commune for two years was, thankfully, not an option, but he did trick me into a four-week
Outward Bound course when I was seventeen. He casually
asked me one day whether I'd like to go on holiday with my
friend Sarah Lythgoe. It would, he explained, be a month of
rock climbing, canoeing, hiking and camping. I wasn't especially athletic, but the idea of a parentally unsupervised holiday
with Sarah sounded like fun.

In his letter of application to the Outward Bound Trust,
my father writes: *Although my daughter would probably choose
to go on the co-ed course, I think it will be more difficult to keep
her mercurial temperament from changing if she can only go to a
segregated one. She is a good girl, but at the awful adolescent stage
when she is totally wrapped up in herself and pop music and dates
and cosmetics. She does very little sport and my wife is worried
that she will not be strong enough to endure it, but I have assured
her that it is not a commando course – her brother went on one
in the Swiss Army and she confuses the two experiences.*

Sarah and I arrived in Wales, only to discover that we had
been put in different dormitories. This, we soon realised,
was intentional – even twins, we were told, were separated.
Our timetables ran parallel and, in the end, we saw each

other only once in the twenty-six days we were there. I was in a dormitory of twenty girls, many of whom were sponsored by local education authorities and came directly from youth detention centres and police cadet training colleges. Very few were like me, that is to say, middle class and privately educated.

Our section leader was a New Zealander whose parents had taken her to Everest Base Camp when she was still a teenager. She was unforgiving and took the catchphrase: 'Take the 't' out of Can't' very seriously. Outward Bound is the brainchild of Kurt Hahn, who founded Gordonstoun where both Prince Charles and the Duke of Edinburgh were educated, and its ethos is to build character, encourage teamwork and develop leadership skills.

Every morning at seven there would be an inspection of the dormitories, toilets and showers. At nine o'clock, half the course participants would leave to go rock climbing, abseiling, canoeing, hill walking and exploring mines, while the other half remained on site and did rope work, estate work, community work, cleaning and orienteering. I had a fear of heights, but was nevertheless forced to cross the 'Burma Bridge', a wobbly weave of ropes, strung between two trees, high off the ground. In the evenings there was effective speaking, drama, First Aid, initiative tests and talks by the Warden. On Sundays we could sleep in until 8.00. After breakfast there was church, and after lunch we cleaned out the transit vans.

At first I was under the impression that my father hadn't fully understood the extent of the physical and psychological terror to which I was being subjected. My holiday with Sarah was a misnomer and I insisted on coming home. I soon realised that this wasn't going to happen, that no-one was going home – not unless you dropped out of a tree and injured your spine, which one girl did. My father sent me letters offering encouragement: *You are going on a voyage of self-discovery and learning about yourself which is always profitable, though sometimes a little painful. You can find out how much stronger and cleverer and more capable you are than you believed possible. Stick it out. We're really proud to have a daughter like you. Your loving father.*

I got through it, made friends and together we challenged authority and fought adversity. My final report declared that I was easy-going and had a good sense of humour, but lacked confidence in my own abilities and sometimes got confused due to not listening to instructions carefully enough. My month at boot camp was nothing compared to commune life in China, but I learnt a lot and when Polly and Lucy were seventeen, I briefly flirted with the idea of hoodwinking them into a jolly holiday in Snowdonia.

O'Connell in Chinese means 'Your Health is Within You'
Peter in a letter to Lea.

The lack of letters coming from England was only in part due to the erratic Chinese postal service. My mother was busy in her new role as the crowned queen of SES:

My darling Fraueli,
Suseli's letter makes it sound as though you are having a pretty good time socially. Perhaps the social life also keeps you from writing to me. I know you are very busy with the house, the

school, the dogs etc but a <u>few</u> lines take 10 mins and that would make me feel more at ease when I am cut off from home by such a great distance and culture gap.

I hear you are a 'marvellous Prime Minister'. I'm not surprised – you needed a chance to prove yourself to yourself and to others. I'm sure you're being a strong Captain of Flowergate and SES.

It's a tremendous thing for me to have taken the bull by the horns and started teaching again – painful and worrying at first but now I am feeling my confidence.

You need not fear a rabid left winger or freak returning to Flowergate, but don't expect me to be completely unchanged either. Only 5 weeks more as of today. All my love, Peter

At the end of August, my father was diagnosed with hepatitis, which prevented him from joining Robert and Anne on a tour of Southern China. He wrote to them in Guilin:

My dear Gang of Two,

I hope you are having a very jolly time in the Deep South drinking mint juleps. How was Chairman Mao's birthplace? Mao was no ordinary peasant and I shall be interested to know how it struck you, though for a man of Chairman Mao's genius such details are not very important.

On September 7th, Peter left China, and on the plane home, he composed a list of twenty-eight goals for himself which included: *garden with Lea, learn Swiss German, engage in practical charitable work and prepare Suseli's Gap Year.*

To thine own self be true
Hamlet Act 1, Scene 3

In 1979 my father wrote an article which was a distillation of his core beliefs on teaching and learning. He titled it *The Absent Prince* and it became known as Peter O'Connell's signature piece. The subject under discussion at the Association of Recognised English Language Schools' annual conference that year was teacher training, and Peter returned to Folkestone feeling distinctly uneasy:

The ARELS conference at Stratford-upon-Avon was in many ways a triumph of organisation, discussion and decision. One could be proud of being a member of an association so full of intelligent, energetic and dedicated people. And yet throughout I felt a certain unease, a sense of unreality. There in Shakespeare's birthplace it seemed to me we were trying to play Hamlet without the Prince of Denmark. The Prince in our world is the student, the learner and without him there would be no teachers. The human qualities of a teacher are almost universally agreed to be paramount; but there seems also to be an almost universal agreement not to get drawn into discussing what these qualities are and how they can be fostered. As teachers we are more ready to admit a gap in our knowledge than a deficiency in our character, for the former can be filled much more easily than the latter can be corrected. The teacher is the main moral support in the early days and the bond established when the student is most vulnerable is of very great importance. A good teacher is one who is intensely aware of student sensibilities and who can read

*posture, gesture, silence, the pleading look, who empathises
and sympathises and who can offer a freedom to experiment
and make mistakes without fear of social punishment.*

The Absent Prince is a deeply personal piece of writing,
describing Peter's ideal teacher but also his unconscious desire
to engage his ideal parent. The Prince had been absent from
his own life and my father wished to avoid replicating the situation with me. Privately, he told people that the driving force
behind *The Absent Prince* was his own daughter's experiences at
school: *Suseli is still suffering severe psychological wounds inflicted
in the awful academy for young ladies where she was taught by
frustrated spinsters.*

*Well, I've made it at last: not quite like a Moslem reaching
Mecca, for Suggestopedia has never been a religion for me
– just the most promising of the humanistic movements in
learning and teaching that are so badly needed, not only in
our little world of EFL but in the whole urgent and bedev-
illed universe of education.*
Peter in a letter to Earl Stevick, 11 Feb 1978

Three months after he returned from China, my father left
for Bulgaria to learn more about *Suggestopedia*. Peter was the
first Westerner to penetrate the Iron Curtain and study with
Dr Lozanov. He felt very honoured to be distinguished in this
way, but harboured considerable guilt at leaving home again so
soon after his return from Peking. In a letter to me he writes:
I'm out here – not because of your immediate future (except perhaps

in Maths) but in a general way. I ask myself every day if I am being self-indulgent, and so far I have been able to answer no. Our country needs Dr Lozanov's message.

To my mother he wrote: *I am not going to play Moses, coming back to Folkestone with the tablets of the law, but I beg you, dear Lea, to do all you can to survive the two months. Get anyone you want to live in Flowergate, spend money freely, see the doctor for drugs or treatment, but please try and survive without me - remember that Penelope waited ten years for Odysseus to return from the Trojan Wars. I'm no Odysseus but I may bring back more important news than he did – and in two months, not ten years!* Penelope, in fact, waited twenty years for Odysseus to return, and when their only son, Telemachus, reached manhood, he left Ithaca in search of his wandering father.

Lieber, liebster Peterli,
You really write very interestingly, and I can picture your surroundings so well. It seems to be a friendlier place than China and Suseli and I are very happy about it. I do hope Suggestopedia will succeed here – it won't be easy, but you believe so much in it that it must be good and after all, you are a very good judge of this.
You are so far away and we miss you so much. It's starting to get me down again. During the day I am very busy, but the evenings and weekends are depressing. It's so hard to take, but I see your point, and try to survive. Well, God bless you my darling. I love you with all your funny ways.

During his time in Sofia, Peter travelled north to Pleven where he visited a third grade Maths class. He writes:

I was getting the sums wrong in the back row because my methods were so inferior. I told the kids this at the end and I asked their teacher if she would accept me as one of her pupils. The kids laughed. I'm going to say loud and clear that I think this man Lozanov has got his teeth into something extraordinary. Why should our kids be deprived of this opportunity? How splendid human beings are! And how terrible! And how confused and one-sided and ignorant! What chance have we? And yet with men like Lozanov perhaps a little. What can justify the continuation of the wicked, stupid, greedy human race except those few 'just men' who seem to be signalling to God for a little more time to prove his experiment hasn't been a total failure. Lozanov isn't in the same category as St Francis of Assisi or Thomas More; but he has in his outstretched hand a gift that might save our children. Say a little prayer for me and for anyone I may help by a little evangelising at home.

> *Jack Sprat could eat no fat*
> *His wife could eat no lean;*
> *And so betwixt them both,*
> *They lick'd the platter clean'.*

English nursery rhyme

My parents had very dissimilar interests. In fact, they had little in common, save playing Scrabble and visiting stately homes. They had me of course, and The School of English Studies, and, in these two areas, they shared a passionate interest. They had created us both from scratch, and were powerfully invested in making us perfect. They struggled to understand each other, and thus struggled to understand those aspects of me that they were unable to recognise in themselves. Dad would tell his friends that: 'Suseli is practical, like her mother,' and Mum would explain to her Swiss family that: 'Suseli is an intellectual, like her father'. I grew up, acutely aware of the split inside me. I was *neither fish, nor fowl, nor good red herring.*

My mother liked coffee and honey for breakfast. My father preferred tea and marmalade. He read the Times and she read The Daily Mail. She was a Conservative voter, he was always a Liberal. Dad enjoyed reading and listening to classical music. Mum liked watching television and talking on the telephone. Peter pursued a mainly vegetarian/macrobiotic diet, whilst Lea favoured dairy and pork products. Holidays were a challenge, as my mother liked cruises and Mediterranean hotels whereas Peter preferred boating on the river with friends or visiting his cousins. We never took summer holidays, because July and August were the busiest months of the year at SES. I was generally dispatched to Switzerland, either to stay with the Kummers or the families of former au pairs. One year I went to Scotland to visit my godfather, David Metcalfe and his family. I flew as an unaccompanied minor, but was put on the wrong plane and narrowly missed spending my holiday in Montreal. The following Easter, perhaps because they still harboured some guilt over my misadventure, Mum and Dad took me on a farmhouse holiday to Wiltshire. It wasn't the kind of vacation that either of them would have enjoyed, but I loved it! Before breakfast and after supper, I would help the farmer with his animals, and during the day, my parents took me, not to boring National Trust properties, but to gorges and caves, castles and beaches.

You're a very bad man!
Oh, no my dear. I'm a very good man. I'm just a very
bad Wizard.
L. Frank Baum, *The Wonderful Wizard of Oz*

In September of 1978 I left for university, and within two weeks, I was summoned home: my father was leaving my mother, albeit, as usual, only temporarily.

The three of us sat around the dining table, and I was invited to listen to both sides of the argument and then declare a winner. Dad was calm and eloquent; my mother was bitter and emotional. When I chose my father, Mum, her eyes streaming with tears got up from the table and locked herself in her bedroom. I felt terrible – torn and troubled by the awareness that my decision had almost certainly been based on an incomplete rule book, which offered me only a partial version of the truth. Dad was relieved that I favoured his point of view, because it provided him with an ally who, if the time ever came, might sanction his escape and ease his guilt. When I got back to Reading, I wrote my mother a letter. It offered no apology, but I was clearly trying to extricate myself from my new role as in-house psychotherapist. Perhaps I feared too that if my father left, I would be expected to fill his shoes. I end with the rather empty and helpless words: *Take care and don't be sad, it's going to be OK. Kisses, your ever-loving daughter.*

Peter never did leave Lea, because abandoning her would have broken the promise he had made to himself all those years ago. Deserting his wife would have categorised him as a no-good scoundrel, a fugitive from responsibility and a man no better than his own father; a man no better than Hans Balmer.

Peter confided in very few people, preferring to engage the world with his hail-fellow-well-met persona. One friend with whom he did share his difficulties was Peter Davidson, and in 1981 the two men exchanged ideas on several audio tapes. Peter D responds to my father's earlier message:

You talk about being happy and relaxed, but in fact what you're saying is: 'if you play my game, my way, according to my rules, we'll all be happy and relaxed'. You tell me that Lea is a despot and that she is the cause of most of your troubles. What you're telling me is that she refuses to see things your way. I have no doubt whatsoever that Lea is a despot. She must be an extraordinarily difficult woman to live with, but it's not surprising she feels insecure, since you yourself have made no real commitment in relation to the future for her. You either have to find a formula for putting up with her difficulty and thriving under it, or you have to leave her. It is the vacillation that is so self-destructive. You have a need to believe that what Lea says is true. It could be argued that by so doing you are able to remind yourself how unfair she is, and if she's unfair, you have a right to reject her. You cannot go on saying: 'This is something I must solve'. You are reaching the stage when you must solve it.

I never felt comfortable around Peter Davidson; he was reasoned and articulate but there was often poison in his tail. In February 1983, Dad wrote to me in America: *Peter Davidson says you have all the important qualities to be a 'facilitator' – listening and respecting other people's opinions. He said in other roles he could think of, you would be hopeless – as a nun in a silent order or as a militant feminist! He also said your appearance was very important in communication — you were 'appetising and inviting'. His careful choice of non-sexist epithets would have gained your approval.*

Chapter Ten

Gurus and Mentors

On Tuesday I'm going to a lecture by a Swami on 'Yoga Nidra'– an intellectual version. I feel wonderfully free and energetic these days but am still a long way from achieving 'sartori' – necessary before your mother and I can live comfortably together.
Tuesday perhaps -?!
February 5th, 1983

In August 1981, my father and I were driving through Suffolk when he announced a detour via the village of Herringswell. We pulled up outside a mock Tudor mansion, and a man, dressed in shades of salmon and peach, welcomed us inside. His gait was floaty, his manner intense and I soon realised that this visit had nothing at all to do with English Language teaching. As we sat drinking our tea, I noticed the mala beads around his neck, framing a medallion portrait of Bhagwan Shree Rajneesh and I shivered with the realisation that we had come calling on 'The Orange People'. I sat in stunned silence while my father told the man about his great interest in the work they were doing and the commune they had established there at Medina Rajneesh. Later, I asked Dad what previous experience he had had with the Rajneeshees, and to my astonishment he told me that he had attended one of their weekend encounter groups.

I had had my own encounter with a group of sannyasins at a party in North London. A man, dressed in orange, had stared at me intently from across the room, before walking over and telling me that he wanted to sleep with me. I wish I could say that I slapped his face and turned on my heel, but that wasn't the way we did things at SES, so I mumbled something about a boyfriend and then locked myself in the loo. I remember feeling frightened and violated. I tentatively, and a little awkwardly, mentioned to my father that I'd heard that the Orange People had a reputation for uninhibited sexual behaviour. He smiled, a little bashfully I thought, and told me that he had been gracious in appreciating their advances, but had explained that he was a married man with a family: *They left me alone after a while. I think they thought I was rather quaint*, he added.

Bhagwan was well educated, extremely charismatic and he attracted not only hippies but successful professionals. Bernard Levin, a well-known British journalist, visited the Poona ashram in 1980 and wrote in the Times: *They all feel they have come home, and I have to say, I am not in the least surprised.* Levin compared Rajneesh's discourses to the parables of Christ, and said that those who recoiled from his ideas had clearly missed the point. *There is nothing either good or bad, but thinking makes it so* says Hamlet and Bhagwan agreed, declaring that guilt and shame were constructs of the mind and religion and truth lay within.

In *Bhagwan – the God that Failed*, Hugh Milne, his bodyguard for many years, says that Rajneesh offered his followers a family and a sense of righteous purpose. Milne's father had been a night bomber pilot in WWII and, like my grandfather, had lost many of his friends. Hugh describes him as a rather gloomy father, reluctant to open up his heart. Like Harry, however, he never criticised his son's ideas and envied him his ability to go to India and be free.

Rajneesh's psychotherapy turned out to be a series of uncontrolled experiments, and broken bones at encounter groups were interpreted as a release of negative energy. The marathon sessions, where anything short of murder was acceptable, could be very frightening, as they often attracted unstable and volatile individuals. As the movement caught fire around the world, meditation grew less important and sannyasins were made to work long hours on huge building projects, crushing rocks and planting fields. The ashrams remind me of the communes in the People's Republic of China and I wonder how my father would have reacted had I told him I was going into Orange. Would he have supported me, joined me or, got on a plane to Oregon to rescue me? Ultimately, the movement became about power, greed and corruption. Bhagwan was arrested as he attempted to flee the United States in 1985, having abandoned his sannyasins at the Muddy Ranch ashram. Many of his disciples had burned their bridges and, with nothing and no-one to return to, some took their own lives. Others, like Michael Barnett, who had made a name for himself as a leader of intensives at Poona, moved to Switzerland, where he bought himself a Ferrari and opened up his own stall of spiritual offerings.

Many people, myself included, were unaware of the fact that in 1988 Bhagwan changed his name to Osho. In 1993 when I was co-facilitating personal growth trainings in Biel, we often used Osho meditations. My colleague, Katja, was a great admirer of Michael Barnett and had attended several of his workshops. For the 'Body Flow' meditation, we wore blindfolds, and after ten minutes of rapid breathing, we unshackled ourselves from all constraints. There were no restrictions in terms of noise levels, although we were forbidden from invading anyone else's personal space – a lesson learnt from the days of broken bones in Oregon. I can only imagine what the well-mannered burghers of Biel made of it all. The dynamic meditation was followed by stillness as we lay *'ausgeblisst'* on our yoga mats, listening to bells and birdsong. Had I known I was channelling the spirit of Bhagwan, I might have been a little more cautious in my participation. I reflect on my father's lifelong difficulty in making wholehearted commitments. Coupled with a concern that others might view him as fanatical, this almost certainly protected him from falling in with the Rajneeshees, a movement that ultimately proved to be psychologically damaging for so many of its followers.

I'm delighted you are taking up Yoga. I hope you'll take a course in TM one day too. We all talk too much which is one of the reasons I aspire (so far unsuccessfully) to the joys of meditation. But don't disappear into an ashram in India! I am struggling along, occasionally seeing some light, at other times feeling the gloom is all encompassing.
Peter in a letter, March 1981

Transcendental Meditation was the brainchild of Maharishi Mahesh Yogi who, like Bhagwan, attracted celebrity followers the highest profile of which were The Beatles. TM was straightforward and, for only a few pounds, you could buy a personalised mantra which you were told never, under any circumstances, to share with anyone. Twice a day you sat in a quiet corner and repeated your Word of Wisdom for twenty minutes and that was your individual contribution to World Peace. In 1977 Maharishi declared 'The Year of the Ideal Society' and moved his headquarters to Switzerland. He also pinpointed Kent as an ideal community and encouraged teachers to practice TM with their students as a way of neutralising negative tendencies. The idea was to get the whole world meditating, thereby creating Heaven on Earth. I received my mantra from a centre in London and practised every day for several weeks. You were discouraged from writing down your magic word because, rather like a bank card pin code, somebody might steal it. I haven't practised Transcendental Meditation for more than thirty-five years and yet I can still remember my Word of Wisdom. I remain reluctant to share it though, for fear of throwing a wrench in the World Peace process.

I am tired of orthodox trends – dominated by the universities and the applied linguists. My impatience has grown stronger after Suseli's first term at Reading. Too much direction comes from the 'university wits' who daunt lesser mortals with their learning and disguise with 'scholarships' their poverty in teaching. It's the Emperor's New Clothes situation.
Letter to Earl Stevick, January 1979

During my final year at the University of Reading, my father wrote to me regularly, offering his support and encouragement: *My dear angelic stinker, Congratulations on the 2:1 – a 1st next time, please, and better punctuation!* In May 1982, he sent me a five-page letter with advice for my French oral exam:

Practice sitting in a relaxed and at the same time courteous posture. Don't rush into an answer. A short pause is restful and doesn't need covering up with ums and ers. You have a tendency when nervous of making rather odd gestures with your hands – the fingers pointing all different ways. Use gestures but make each one count as if you were on stage. And avoid flapping or tapping your feet.

You're an attractive girl. Don't be shy of giving an occasional smile. Obviously this is not a suggestion that you vamp the examiners but a reminder to remove the exchange as far as possible from the ambience of the Inquisitor to the drawing room. Don't a) guess b) get confused and - Do remember to relax physically and to breathe deeply (but unobtrusively).

Dad's suggestions were thoughtful and well-intentioned but they highlighted problems I hadn't even considered, thereby amplifying rather than reducing my already high levels of anxiety.

You have to go and be where your own star leads you. We want you to go across the Atlantic without hang-ups about yourself or about us.
Letter from my father, September 1982

After I graduated from Reading, I left England for a one-year internship in New York. I had missed my Groton opportunity, but I wasn't going to let this one get away and, just like my parents before me, my plan was to emigrate to America. I had been invited to live in Greens Farms, Connecticut with Alan and Erica Pifer, from where I would commute into Manhattan. Alan picked me up at JFK Airport, and as we drove north on I-95 I caught my first sight of the Twin Towers, silhouetted against a crimson skyline. In a scene straight out of *The Waltons*, Erica was standing on the porch when we pulled into the drive of their beautiful eighteenth century home. Later, as I sat by the fire in the Library, a bourbon on the rocks in my hand and two border terriers at my feet, I knew that this was what I wanted for myself, a life just like this one.

In the summer of 1975, I spent a month with my mother's family in Wisconsin, where I learnt to waterski, play baseball, drink gin martinis and date a different boy every week. *I'm all for going unsteady. Nothing like variety when you're 16*, wrote my father in one of his letters. The boy I liked best was Ethan, a handsome sun-kissed, blue-eyed seventeen year old who was less rowdy and more sensitive than the other boys. By 1982, Ethan was working for Morgan Stanley in Texas and the night I arrived in Greens Farms he called and invited me down to Dallas. In my diary I wrote: *The situation will need careful handling. As long as I make my case clear and stick to it, things should be OK.* Three weeks later, my plane landed at Love Field where I discovered that the beautiful Ethan had become a chain-smoking, beer-drinking stockbroker. He was still kindly, although he talked a lot about shares and investments, about which I knew nothing. My father was my role model that weekend: I remained impeccably charming and polite and successfully convinced myself that I had mended Ethan's broken heart with my leaky reasoning. He took me to The White Elephant Saloon near the Fort Worth Stockyards, where I kicked up my cowboy boots to the Texas two-step, drank jugs of ice-cold beer and taught the locals how to speak the Queen's English. We also visited Southfork Ranch, made famous by the long-running television series *Dallas*. Near the privately-owned house stood a telephone box, strategically positioned so that visiting fans could call their loved ones and say: 'Hey - guess where I am?!' I called my mother and she couldn't guess but was beyond delighted when I told her that I was in sight of the Ewing family home. Lea was a big fan of JR and Miss Ellie. My father despised the drivel of *Dallas*: *I hope the human landscape of JR country is better than the one portrayed on the box each week to Mummy's delight. It's odd how people who react to adultery in real life as if it were worse than murder revel in multiple revelations on the screen.*

My mother's favourite programme was *The Waltons* which was on British television throughout the 1970s. It tells the story of a three-generation Baptist family living in rural Virginia during the Depression. Critics considered the show naive and sentimental, but its dedicated followers found it charming and sensitively written. I liked it because there were so many Walton children and I desperately wanted siblings, especially a thoughtful older brother like John Boy, who would take an interest in me and help me feel safe in the world. My mother liked company when she watched television, so when I reached an age where I was at risk of drifting away from *The Waltons*, she hit on a plan: She suggested I sew a patchwork quilt, just like the one Mary Ellen had made in the quilting bee episode. She told me that she had a pillowcase full of material, including pieces of her wedding dress and scraps of linen and silk that had belonged to my grandmother. So in the evenings, I began to sew my quilt, joining my mother not only for *The*

Waltons, but occasionally for *The Galloping Gourmet* and *The Val Doonican Show*. With Mum as my ally, my father's strict television schedule was all but abandoned.

In 2010 I was on a road trip through Virginia, and decided to make a detour to Schuyler, where the real Walton family had lived during the Great Depression. I was completely enchanted by the small town with its general store and one-time school-house, converted into a museum of memorabilia. I wished with all my heart that I could phone my mother and get her to guess where I was, but Mum had been dead for fourteen years. I thought of calling Polly and Lucy, but they would have been battling fractions in the classrooms of St Christopher, Letchworth. As I stood in line waiting to pay for my 'Goodnight John Boy' fridge magnet, I suddenly saw the Waltons not as idealistic clichés, but as a supportive and loving family. John Walton was a man of integrity, a kind and responsible husband and father who protected his wife and guided his children, helping them reach considered and principled decisions. I touched my own sadness too as I recognised the longing I had had as a child to belong to parents like John and Olivia Walton.

Alan Pifer and Peter O'Connell were men with progressive, highly-developed social consciences and were forceful advocates of educational initiatives. As President of the Carnegie Foundation for seventeen years, Alan led a new generation of philanthropies that aspired to revolutionise what he saw as a deeply-flawed American society. He was in his late twenties when he first got into trouble with the then Secretary of State, Dean Acheson. As head of the Fulbright Commission in London, Alan had given security clearance for a left wing, African American, female academic to spend a year at Ruskin College, Oxford. Acheson took the view that young Pifer should be fired for this misdemeanour and immediately appointed a senior man to replace him. When his successor arrived in London, Alan barred him from entering the Fulbright offices, claiming, correctly, that the State Department did not employ him and could not, therefore, dismiss him. Acheson backed down and Alan remained as director of the programme for a further six years.

Andrew Carnegie, an early pioneer in the steel industry, believed that a man who died rich died disgraced, and that it was his moral duty to devote himself and his great wealth to *the advancement and diffusion of knowledge and understanding.* Alan's legacy at the Carnegie Foundation was rich in its diversity, but children were his number one priority: *What worries me is the failure to understand that investing in children is the smartest thing we can do for the country's future.* Under his leadership, a commission study helped influence President Lyndon Johnson's Public Broadcasting Act of 1967, which heralded the development of educational television and radio. The New York Times referred to Alan Pifer as *a one-man early-warning system,* and *the conscience of the foundation field.* His endeavours to provide greater educational opportunities for women, blacks and hispanics prompted Gloria Steinem, the founder of Ms. Magazine to name Alan their Man of the Year in 1982. Erica wryly remarked that Ms. Steinem should try living with him for a while.

Alan Pifer was not universally popular and drew sharp criticism from people across America who did not share his liberal, progressive views. Unlike Peter, however, Alan was a pragmatist as well as a visionary, a man with a thicker hide and a less fragile ego than my father. Peter's idealistic views on America prompted a long letter from English-born Erica in 1958:

The 'drive to Utopia or bust' which stimulates you, depresses me; not because I am afraid of the busting, but of the Utopia. I wouldn't mind risking all for something I believed in. Unfortunately I cannot, after a mere two and a half years in this country, sense any aura of the promised land. Though McCarthys may fall amidst the sounding of wise trumpets, the Dulleses go on, and the Nixons.

Did you see the January 'Country Life' with its leading article about photographing otters under water? Alan's comment on this was: 'This magazine is absolutely remote from reality. Wherever else would you find a leading article on such a subject?'

What is the purpose of living? Americans give so much attention to improving the technique of it that I often fear they have not yet come to the question. The first ones they ask are: 'What is its function? Does it work? And so it is with otters under water. But national character is being formed all the time, and when the task of building is complete, and Utopia prepared for the grand unveiling, mightn't it be too late to change? No-one in England would think the otters under water were remote from real life, but a necessary part of it for those who like otters. You say, Peter, that the thoughts in your letter were 'obvious'. To me, they were not.

I was always a little in awe of Alan. Peter would vent his fury at Mrs Thatcher's educational policies, but when Alan exploded at Reagan's decision to shift to state control many of the federal welfare services, I knew that he had been at the White House and his rage, therefore, was based not on a Times newspaper article, but on a day spent with the President's advisers.

Grown-ups say to kids, 'You need to work harder'. What kids really need to do is work smarter, but they can only do that if they know what their problems are.
Herman Hall

Herman Hall was a consultant psychologist to education and industry. Amos Booth, who had left Groton in 1979 to become headmaster of St Bernard's School in New York, was so impressed by the man and his skills, that he hired him to spend three days a week at the elite, all-male, elementary school on Manhattan's Upper East Side. For several years, Amos had been writing to Peter, applauding Herman's breathtakingly accurate psychological assessments of the most troubled boys at St Bernard's. He worked mainly with test scores, although he could also draw information from an extended piece of writing or resume. In 1981 my father sent Amos an essay I had written on the novels of Henri Stendhal and requested that Herman evaluate my personality:

Dear Amos, your letter and its astonishing enclosure arrived today. At first reading of Herman Hall's interpretation, Lea and I gave him only Cs, but Suseli seemed very impressed by the analysis, though the compliments to her ability strained her belief, though not her wishes. As she read she kept saying 'amazing' but would not make extensive comments. The most interesting reaction was her 6-page diary entry – I wish I could read that!

I'm not sure about her 'idealism' – I think she's got a strong streak of Swiss practicality. But there, parents lack insight into their children's deepest aspirations. The lack of discipline and the need for it – that rings true. The 'rich fantasy life' surprised me. Her romantic life <u>has</u> been colourful and extensive and she's had problems, but my feeling is that she handles her love life very sensibly and fairly. <u>But</u> the 'pain in the neck' accusation hit home and was, I'm sure, accepted by Lea and me too! Suseli gets on amazingly well with everyone – old and young, men and women, all nationalities. It's a danger to her and one I've warned her of. The 'amazing possibilities' and 'unrealised potential' – I can't see these – but then I've consistently undervalued Suseli's academic potential.

I am totally confused on HH's principles. The really important question is: has he got a transferable skill? If he can train people of normal intelligence and sensitivity to equal successes, then he's a very valuable man. March 31st, 1981

I remember feeling unspeakably grateful to Mr Hall for his nuanced understanding of my private struggles. He hadn't categorised me with broad brushstrokes but had delicately lifted my soul out of the mud and held it up to a mirror. In all the years I knew Herman, I never felt judged or criticised.

I first met Herman Hall in 1981 when Amos brought him to Europe to consult with several schools and colleges. He had a gravelly voice and a warm chuckle and the two of us formed an immediate connection. Herman thought I could learn to do what he did and told my father that, if I was interested, he would be willing to take me on as an intern after I graduated from Reading. Peter found Herman Hall's methods compelling but baffling: *You speak with real authority, not as one of the scribes and Pharisees and you get immediate attention from the congregation grown tired of the formalities of the orthodox. I am not suggesting that the provenance of your inspired interpretations goes quite as high as our Father who art in Heaven, but you stick your neck out.* The prospect of my going to New York for eight months to learn alongside this unusual man was an offer my father couldn't refuse. And, for once, I was delighted to serve as a *cavia porcellus* to Peter's latest passion.

People use tests to deny access, to hold others back. The idea is to look at a test and see what you can do to help someone.
Herman Hall

Herman Hall humanised test scores by unravelling the relationship between numbers and an individual's learning and behaviour patterns. In the United States scholastic aptitude is measured through a battery of verbal and quantitative tests, commonly referred to as the WPPSI and the WISC. Verbal evaluations, which include Information, Vocabulary and Spelling can reveal a student's inter-personal sensitivity, emotions and even levels of idealism. Non-verbal tests, such as Maths, Mechanical Reasoning and Geometric Design describe a student's logical abilities and his capacity to analyse and conceptualise. A high verbal and a low non-verbal score characterise affective rather than effective learners. These students are often good readers and spellers but have trouble organising their thoughts. They have a mastery of detail but a weak sense of comprehension, so they'll be able to tell you *what* happened in a story but will struggle to tell you *why* it happened.

An understanding of reality is vital in order to develop a strong sense of self. Herman's definition of reality was: *How many chairs are there in the room?* Numbers have an objective and absolute quality and only when linked to nouns - thirty thieves - do they acquire emotional characteristics. Students who score highly in mechanical and abstract reasoning show an ability to find points of congruence and synthesis, and are often self-directed individuals. In Maths, there is only one right answer, and there is only one way to operate a piece of machinery and so a high score in this area can also indicate stubbornness and a desire for predictability. Vocabulary, on the other hand, is the core of the interpersonal but it doesn't necessarily offer direction. High scoring verbal children lack structure and often need to have their thinking formulated for them. I recalled the many months I spent in a Paris library, prowling round the camp of my dissertation without ever quite being able to find the centre of what I wanted to say. I felt as though I was holding all the jigsaw pieces in my hand, but was forever wondering how they fit together. Students like myself, I discovered, are idealistic, with a poor grounding in reality and common sense, characteristics which are generally provided by the father. A question I often heard Herman ask while review-ing the test scores of a St Bernard's boy was: 'where's this kid's father?' Sometimes the mother would compensate for her husband's severity, or indeed his absence, by over-indulging their son.

Herman Hall was funny, passionate and tender, but there was a steeliness about him as well. His approach was unpretentious and simple though never simplistic. I experienced him as unfailingly kind and curious, with a deep respect for children and an ardent desire to help those most at risk of being marginalised, either academically or socially. He believed that every child had unique talents and that none were without promise. James Shapiro, who wrote a book about Herman, described him as *a global father looking to make sure everyone got a fair shake.*

As the in-house educational psychologist at St Bernard's, absent fathers and father-hungry boys featured frequently in Herman's working day:

This guy needs a model, and I don't think there's one in his mind. His thought process is piecemeal, and a rising anxiety is interfering with his basic value system. I think he comes from a rather disorganised home where he never got to feel like someone. There is no 'I am' in this boy. His parents haven't ignored him intellectually, but they have neglected his emotional growth and failed to nurture a sense of self-belief. They may well have had some intellectual discussions in front of him, and probably spoke to each other about their important days, but the problems this little kid had in his day were just as important as the grown-up problems they had in theirs. He can't tune into the social system, the things we hold in common and share, and so he remains an outsider.

Herman believed that students needed to be part of their own salvation. He never lectured them, preferring to ask open-ended questions that made them think or provided an opportunity for deeper conversation: 'So, your Mom and Dad aren't getting along too well at the moment?' or 'Your Dad's a busy man and is away a lot?'. I don't think I ever saw him make a mistake, but he always allowed the child to confirm or refute his observations by adding: 'Is that right?'. There was something about naming the underlying suffering, as opposed to talking about a poorly written essay or a low Maths score, that generated a rush of gratitude and a release of gagged emotions. These kids suddenly felt recognised and understood: Being listened to is sometimes indistinguishable from being loved.

Herman pointed out that praise was best offered intermittently. If you applaud children for everything they do, they feel they have to be the best and the brightest, and each time they fall short, their anxiety levels increase. Herman was very proud of his two adult sons, Rick and Doug, but he neither overly praised nor excessively criticised them, choosing instead to recognise their individual strengths and weaknesses, and his own contribution to the development of their personalities. He had the greatest admiration for his wife Ruth and whenever he spoke about her, his face would light up. In faculty presentations and workshops, he invariably managed to slip her name in somewhere. It was as if he simply couldn't believe his good fortune at having met and married her all those years ago.

Long before I began to appreciate the importance of seeing families in a systemic context, Herman taught me the importance of not judging parents, no matter how calamitous their parenting style might appear to be. The following is taken from an audio tape, recorded at a faculty meeting:

'I recently met with a man in his early thirties, who was crying as he told me about his father, a successful entrepreneur. When he was sixteen, he said to his father: 'You don't love me,' to which his father replied: 'Of course, I love you. I buy you shoes. I feed you - '. I told the young man that he would have to come to terms with his father just the way he was, because that was <u>his</u> way of loving his son. It was the only way he knew how. He started something important, and I'm not saying he's a great man because of that but he's a good man as far as the organisation is concerned. He isn't a good father as far as you're concerned, but if you go through life thinking what a terrible man your father is, it isn't going to do you any good'

I knew the young man in Herman's story because our fathers were friends. In a taped letter to Peter, recorded at around the same time, the father speaks of his worries and fears for his son:

'- is acting, modelling and doing some PR for night clubs, which is just about where his mind and spirit is at the moment. It's not the field I would have had him plough, and I can't imagine his poor ancestors giving their approval to this kind of work. I am being incredibly broad minded and giving him, to some extent, my blessing and as much money as I can afford, but it is a problem. I would have loved to see him doing what so many young people do, washing dishes etc, to get himself started, instead of relying on his own soft backbone and the soft backbone of his father. His cousin is a stonemason, and he's high up on cathedrals or down on the ground carving archangels and gargoyles, and he's tremendously skilled and loves the job. He's going to be someone – he's an artist as well as an artisan. God bless them – they turn the flesh into spirit, matter into objects of pride and beauty. I think that's one of the things we're put here on earth for and I give them full credit for what they do. I sometimes think of my grandfather and my father and my brother, who worked the land and were somehow doing the same kind of thing. They were dealing with living organisms and trying to make them grow, keeping order in the chaos of nature and producing something useful. It's the same kind of simplistic idealism, a commune spirit I suppose, because you're all working together for something which you feel is somehow right.'

Many years later and shortly before he died in 2010, my father's friend wrote to me: *Ages are golden when children are small. The alchemy of the heart? What remains of my mainly absent mind is not easy to live with, so I tend to wander into the past and I tremble for all my goofs and inadequacies that will be inherited by my children. Good intentions are never sufficient.* The irony is that I knew this man as the kindest of all my father's friends, the one who was most understanding and supportive of my own inadequacies. I loved and respected him.

Herman Hall and Suseli, New York, 1983

Herman is like another father to Suseli
Peter in a letter to Bill Polk, Headmaster of Groton,
28th March 1987

I loved living with the Pifers in Greens Farms, but it was a long commute into Manhattan. I was spending Tuesday nights with Gina Murray, who had separated from Jack, the art teacher at Groton, and was living in the Bronx. Herman was encouraging me to make a permanent move from 'Greenland' as he called it to Manhattan, which would allow me to be in school for 8am, the time of day when teachers and parents most often came to him for consultations.

It was through Gina that I met Anna Hill Johnstone, her neighbour in Riverdale. 'Johnnie' was a costume designer in the film industry, had been nominated for several Academy Awards and knew a lot of people in the city. She put me in touch with Karen, a former dancer on Broadway, who offered me the sub-let of a railroad apartment. The owner had gone to California to make a movie, and wouldn't be back for several months. The rent was a steal, the apartment quirky and charming and, having convinced Mum and Dad that the move was in everybody's best interests, I packed up my life in leafy Connecticut and moved to 'Hell's Kitchen'.

My father suggested I contact Lola, who had worked at SES in the late 1960s and subsequently moved to New York. I remembered Lola well. She had cascading auburn hair and wore miniskirts which showcased her long legs. Aldous, her boyfriend, was an art student, and they were the most glamorous couple I had ever met.

Without Johnnie, Karen and Lola, the fabric of my social

life in Manhattan would have been very different. I had left the gentility of the suburbs for a dodgy neighbourhood in New York. Today, Hell's Kitchen has been re-zoned and gentrified, but when I lived there it was full of red brick, low-rise apartment buildings, popular with actors and musicians. In the 1850s it had been home to Irish immigrants, escaping the Famine, and the area quickly gained a reputation for violence, organised crime and street gangs.

Lola lived in the East Village and had some high-profile friends, including John Belushi and Dan Ackroyd. John had recently died of a drug overdose at Chateau Marmont in Los Angeles and New York was still buzzing from the shock of his loss. Belushi was one of the founding members of *Saturday Night Live*, a show which has produced some of the greatest American comedians of their generation, including Bill Murray, Eddie Murphy, Kristen Wiig and Will Forte, the son of my 'first love', Reb, the Nobles boy who visited us in England in 1959.

My friendship with Lola has lasted for more than thirty-five years. She is not only beautiful but gracious and generous, and as I wrote in my diary in 1983: *there is nothing phony or artificial about her*. Lola introduced me to a whole new world, and I learnt as much through the contact I had with models and actors as I did from studying the test scores of the super-rich in Carnegie Hill.

Herman worked in several schools on the Upper East Side, including Chapin, Brearley and Nightingale Bamford, the alma mater of Cecily von Ziegesar who used Nightingale as the inspiration for her *Gossip Girl* novels. He also worked in a large insurance company on Fifth Avenue, and it was at Anistics that I learnt how to analyse resumes and extended pieces of writing:

Dear Herman, I grow a little anxious at the thought that I am giving such a large sample of myself to the Arch Evaluator! Suseli tells me that you give a negative score to parentheses, or too many of them. I use them a lot but believe I use them effectively – certainly consciously for specific rhetorical effect combined with brevity. Looking back over this letter I can see I have inhibited myself, probably because of my knowledge of your 'evaluation'. I then glanced through another long letter I had just written and it has 17 in 4 pages! - I think I can justify them all. Your affectionate and admiring disciple, Peter

The most important skill I learnt from watching Herman was to state facts rather than voice opinions, and to recognise that the other person has a point of view and a set of skills that can complement and contribute towards a good solution. Herman approached everyone with the understanding that they were being the best possible version of themselves they knew how to be, and that setting himself up as an adversary was unhelpful. In schools, he recognised the need to win the trust of parents and teachers, so they could all work together to improve the life of the child. By accentuating the positive, by listening and asking questions, Herman Hall subtly managed to lead both the child and the parents to the bigger picture.

Our schools are richer for what he taught us, and he blessed us in all he helped us to be
Joan McMenamin. Head of The Nightingale Bamford School 1971 – 1992.

In spite of the many accolades Herman received from heads of private schools and those in charge of admissions at Princeton and Amherst, he never made it to the top. He was not a self-promoter, and had little interest in being a lion amongst men. He did believe, however, that he had something to offer that could help schools treat each child as a unique and distinctive, never-to-be-repeated kind of learner. In a taped letter to Peter, Amos says:

There is a great deal of distrust and open hostility to what Herman does, largely because he is doing something which others resent, either because they never thought of it themselves or because it has tremendous implications which undermine sacred cows. They resent the idea that someone who hasn't gone to Harvard can come up with anything so fundamentally revolutionary in the area of psychology and so they deny that it is possible. Last time Herman was at Groton, the girl who had come in to do what Betsy Peabody used to do – remedial reading – was in absolute fits. She said to me next day that she had learnt nothing new, nothing the dormitory people couldn't have told us. She didn't trust it and what good could it do. What had he published, where had he been to school? Others were disturbed because they felt it was too revealing.

Herman Hall was born in 1917 in Springfield, Massachusetts and when his parents died he was sent to the New England Home for Little Wanderers, a Boston orphanage. Forced to drop out of Clark University when he could no longer pay the fees, he went to work as a moulder in a foundry. He joined the Navy in WWII, later became a travelling salesman and subsequently studied for a Masters in Education. I see Herman as a counterpart to Scharli, Godi and the semi-fictitious, John Walton. None of these men benefited from a traditional education, but all of them attended to the complex rhythms of life, acquiring skills and plumbing depths that others failed to fathom. Herman's social circumstances had not allowed him to follow the path of the St Bernard's/Groton/Harvard boy; he did not have a PhD and he had not published any books. It was perhaps for these reasons that the Carnegie Foundation turned down an application to fund more research into his work. The rejections never made him angry, just a bit grumpy and disappointed for the children.

In the eight months I spent as Herman's intern, I travelled with him across America. Occasionally he would leave me behind in New York with a project to manage or complete. I found these periods utterly terrifying. After a while, however, assumptions were made that I had some understanding of what Herman did. Because people had faith in me, I started firing a few bulls' eyes, which created ever-increasing circles of self-confidence and raised my success rate.

Socially I was having a ball, going to plays, taking courses in American history, skiing in Vermont at weekends and generally living a 1982 version of my father's 1952 life at Groton. I wasn't acquainted with Henry Ford's son-in-law or Edie Sedgwick's sister, but Lola introduced me to a world of rock stars and TV personalities. When the band Duran Duran came to New York to perform on *Saturday Night Live*, I had a backstage pass and, in Tim Kazurinsky's dressing room, I was introduced to Eddie Murphy and Simon Le Bon.

One night I attended a birthday dinner for sixty people, hosted by the mistress of Adnan Khashoggi, the Saudi billionaire, some-time arms dealer and uncle to Dodi Fayed. I had nothing suitable to wear, so borrowed a gown from one of Lola's friends and then made the mistake of visiting a tanning parlour. My skin turned an angry, spotty red and as I was not as well-endowed as the owner of the slinky dress I had been given to wear, my carefully sculpted persona of 'Surfer-Girl-cum-Sloane Ranger' fell hopelessly flat. I didn't enjoy the party much, but I made an important discovery about myself: perhaps, for the first time in my adult life, I was unable to cruise along on my listening technique. I asked a lot of questions but most people, I found, had no interest in talking to me because I was physically and financially unremarkable. The women at the party were young and beautiful and the men were middle-aged and wealthy. I spent some time with Celeste, an aspiring model from California who had met her date, a short Iranian gentleman, at a party the previous evening. He was, she told me in a confidential whisper, the owner of an island in the Caribbean and he had Leonardo da Vincis hanging in his apartment.

This shallowness was never true of Lola's closest friends. When Tim Kazurinsky discovered it was my birthday, he invited me and Lola to dinner at Elaine's. He was funny, but also interesting and interested, and when *Saturday Night Live* fans approached our table Tim was gracious and friendly. At the end of the evening, he accompanied me home in a taxi, concerned perhaps to hear that I lived in Hell's Kitchen. Tim moved to Chicago in the mid 1980s, and in 2012 Dan and I were at Second City to see our niece Devin in a comedy sketch night. Second City launched the careers of many SNLers, including Kazurinsky and I knew from Lola that he was still active at the venue and often attended performances. Thirty years later and Tim still remembered our evening at Elaine's and his cab ride to the dark side of town.

In April 1983 I returned, somewhat reluctantly, to England. My father had encouraged me to go to America and follow my own star: *although we are naturally very keen to see you come back soon to England.* My bed was made, and I always knew that, sooner or later, I would be called home to sleep in it.

It was the worst of times - it was the season of darkness - it was the winter of despair.
A Tale of Two Cities by Charles Dickens

In September of 2001 Herman made his last trip to Europe. He was eighty-four years old, his health was poor and upon his return to New York he was admitted to hospital. When the planes hit the Twin Towers on September 11th, every effort was made to delay telling Herman the news that his son Rick, who worked in the South Tower as a senior Vice President at the Aon Corporation, had perished in the attack. It was impossible, however, to hide the news for long. One hundred and seventy-five Aon employees died alongside Rick that morning, and Herman died just eight days later, on September 19th.

In January of 2002 Ruth, Herman's widow wrote to tell me that Rick's remains had been found, identified by his dental records: *The medical examiner told us that death was instant before the fall, so we're grateful.* On the day Rick's body was laid to rest, there was snowfall mixed with rain, *and I had the thought* writes Ruth, *that our compassionate God was crying too. It was closure for us, and Rick's wife will have a place to talk with Rick which she needed and wanted.* Ruth was mourning not only the loss of her son but also of her husband: *Herman's great wish was to leave something meaningful to his family and future believers in the help and guidance of young people. Keep him in your heart, Suseli, and remember that he had a truly happy life with his family and friends and chosen profession, which he loved. He was very fond of you and had faith in you as you carry on your work.*

The Herman and Richard Hall Scholarship Fund for graduates of White Plains High School was set up in 2002. In the same year, Aon established an education fund to provide post-secondary school financial assistance to the dependent children of Aon employees killed in the attacks on the World Trade Centre. Herman would have been pleased to know that his grandson's college education was secure, and that Christopher would never have to work nights or drop out of college because he couldn't afford to pay his fees.

I spent a year in London after I returned from America. I partied hard and drifted in and out of yet another relationship. My father, worried about my lifestyle, wrote to me: *You have developed ways, techniques of listening and showing flattering approval that people find irresistible. There is now a danger that you are being taken over by your own technique. You are more consciously using your power. I am in no position to offer concrete advice as I am still searching myself. There's only one thing in life*

I want more than your happiness, and that's your serenity. Love yourself as well as other people.

In May of 1984 I left my job as a consultant at International Secretaries and bought a one-way ticket to New York. I travelled North to Maine and South to Virginia, using Riverdale as my base camp. I was offered a position teaching French at Rye Country Day School in upstate New York, but I needed a visa, and having consulted an immigration lawyer, I was told that the chances of being granted one were slim. Eventually, my time ran out and Dad suggested I return home and teach at SES.

Suseli is so sweet and pretty. She told me what she was going to do with her life. I hope she will be happy and I do wish her all the luck in the world.
Violet, cleaner at SES, in a letter to Peter, 1977.

I taught at SES for a year before moving to Switzerland in 1985 to live with, and later marry, Stephan. I wish I could say that I became an exemplary wife and mother, correcting all the mistakes my own parents had made, but I stumbled through those early years, experiencing confusion about my own 'I am' and the exact location of my personal star. I didn't want to disappoint my father by wasting my education, but when I accepted a part-time teaching position at the Rudolf Steiner School in Biel, I sensed my mother's disapproval. Like Mum, I was homesick and returned to England as often as I could. Like Dad, I was on a path to enlightenment, although my spiritual practices, which included fire walks and sweat lodges, were not ones with which he was familiar. I was relieved to have exceeded his expertise as I advanced under my own banner of heaven, conscious too that in Biel no-one ever asked me that all-too familiar question: 'O'Connell? Are you any relation to Peter O'Connell?'

Lea and Peter with Polly and Lucy, Switzerland, 1994

In 1996 following several months of ill-health, Mum booked her and Dad a holiday in Sicily to co-incide with our family vacation to the American Southwest. Her doctor, however, decided that she wasn't well enough to travel, and insisted she cancel the trip. A week later, I telephoned her from Flagstaff, Arizona. She sounded incoherent, barely conscious and it turned out that she had stopped taking her heart medication. I asked the doctor whether he thought I should return home but he assured me that all would be well: 'Your mother is a jack-in-the-box and will be right as rain in no time. Stop worrying and enjoy your holiday' he said. A few days later, I called her from Las Vegas. She sounded quite normal and then, in a clear, calm voice, she said: 'Suseli, I'd like you to come home'. I was confused and spent the rest of the day sitting on a rock in the Mojave Desert, wrestling my angels and questioning whether this was another of my mother's cry-wolf strategies. I realised, however, that Lea's decision to stop taking her medication had been a calculated one, a conscious choice intended to accelerate the process of her dying. She had done it once, and she could do it again. I decided to fly home.

Mum died five days later, on what would have been Hans Balmer's 79th birthday: October 12th. She had chosen the verse for her obituary notice, and left it where I could find it: *Do not be sad at my passing, for I have gone to those I loved in order to wait for those I love.* As the Swiss do not issue death certificates, I do not know the cause of my mother's death.

Your sweet Mama was a heroine.
Peter in a letter to me, 1996

Dad struggled after Mum died and his dementia grew more pronounced. His behaviour was strange, his conversation woolly and often nonsensical, but his diaries remained fluent and lucid. In February, 1997 he wrote:

It has been an interesting and varied life, and I am grateful to whatever Powers There Be for this and for generally good health and a good career in a fascinating field. My nearest and dearest have been splendid people, but I have been denied the opportunity of knowing the joy of close intimacy at all levels.

His memories of my mother were romantic and idealised, but quite clear and candid too: *If only I had my Lea still living, life would be comfortable and cosy. We had very different tastes and interests, but we complemented each other in many ways. And every day we had Scrabble after breakfast!. Oh Leneli, how can Flowergate be a real home without you? Should I continue to exist? Should I commit suicide? - Aye, there's the rub.*

A month before he died Dad became very agitated and spent an afternoon anxiously searching for his passport: *I won't be allowed in without it*, he kept saying. He was frustrated too by his failure to recall a verse from *Hamlet*. All he could remember was the first line: *Now cracks a noble heart ...* He told me it was important and that I should write it down. I was convinced he was going to die that day, but he didn't, choosing to wait until I was three thousand miles away, on a sailing boat in Narragansett Bay.

Amos Booth, Peter's oldest and closest friend, wrote to me the day after my father died:

Aix-en-Provence, September 6th, 1998
Dear Suseli, I feel a deep sense of tragedy that a mind so able and a heart so entire should be afflicted with fear, suffering, and the inevitable loneliness that accompanies the periods of lucidity. Peter knew that he was alone only because his loneliness was a precious part of him, his Daemon, and a spark to his wonderful mind and heart.
'Now cracks a noble heart. Good night sweet Prince,
And flights of angels sing thee to thy rest'

THE END

Acknowledgments

My thanks to family members, friends and those who generously shared their time and memories.

Jim Amory, David Arnold, John Barnett, Clare Beels-Metcalfe, Gottlieb Brunner, Tessa Campbell-Metcalfe, Loring and Louise Conant, Erastus Corning, Brigitte Curtins, John Damon, Jo Devlin-O'Connell, Chris Doherty, Nicola Dunn, Andre Evans, Newell Flather, Anne-Isabelle Fleming, Reb Forte, Bill Gallagher, Edward Gammons, Richard Haynes, Jean-Pierre Jacquet, Patty Key, Maggie Lee, Maxine Linnell, Dominic Lynch, Temba Maqubela, Bob McElwain, Michael Metcalfe, Nigel Metcalfe, Lola Michael-Russell, David Milne, Eamonn and Martina O'Connell, Patrick O'Connell, Jeremy Page, Matthew Pifer, Peter Pitt-Brown, William Polk, Charles 'Scharli' Probst, Peter Raetz, Stephan Raetz, Ruth Rosa, the Sinnott-Giobbi family, Gloria Stanford, Eileen 'Judy' Stone, Rosy Strub, John Valentine, Christabel Waters-McDowall, Karen Whittaker, David Woods, Walter Zwahlen.

Special thanks to Doug Brown and Isa Schaff, who patiently answered all my questions about Groton and Nobles and never tired of cross-referencing facts. I am grateful to Tappan Wilder for his permission to quote from *Our Town* and to Barbara Hogenson and Lori Styler at the Barbara Hogenson Agency in New York for their time and patience. Thank you to Eliot and Jesse Putnam for allowing me to step into their family history as I investigated my own and to Lisa Iversen for her input and ongoing support. Thank you to James Essinger at The Conrad Press for his encouragement, enthusiasm and inspired suggestions.

Finally, thank you to my husband, Dan, for supporting me during the four years it took me to write *The Absent Prince* and for helping me process the discoveries I made along the way. I am especially grateful to him for suggesting that I not destroy my parents' diaries until such time as I had accessed my grief and soothed my anger.

Motivating my interest and guiding my perspective in researching and writing my family story have been the insights I received from Systemic Family Constellations and its founder Bert Hellinger.

www.unaoconnell.co.uk
www.nicoladunnconstellations.com
www.ancestralblueprints.com

Sources and References

CHAPTER ONE

Merlin and the Gleam by Alfred, Lord Tennyson.

Goodbye To All That by Robert Graves. Penguin Modern Classics, 1980 edition. Page 157 – 159

From a letter to Lorna Linnane-Boyd, February 11th, 1990

The Battle of the Somme (1916) – Geoffrey Malins and John McDowell. Digitally restored by The Imperial War Museum, 2008.

Gitanjali, XCVI, Collected Poems and Plays of Rabindranath Tagore, Macmillan & Co Ltd 1962

The Last Fighting Tommy: The Life of Harry Patch, The Only Surviving Veteran Of The Trenches by Harry Patch and Richard Van Emden. Bloomsbury Publishing Plc, 2007. Page 203

The Last Man On The Moon by Eugene Cernan with Don Davis, St. Martin's Press, New York, NY, 1999. Page 347

For All Mankind - a film by Al Reinert, 1989.

To Reach The Clouds: My High Wire Walk Between the Twin Towers by Philippe Petit, published in 2002 by North Point Press, New York, NY

The Irish Republic by Dorothy Macardle, first published in 1937

CHAPTER TWO

Bone of Space: Poems by Zen Master Seung Sahn, published by The Kwan Um School of Zen, 1993

Cinquieme Promenade from Les Reveries du Promeneur Solitaire by Jean-Jacques Rousseau, 1782

Human Misery. Life in A Death Camp by Hans Kopp: donauschwaben-usa.org

The Vanishing by Frances Stonor Saunders, The Guardian, April 15th, 2000

Versorgt und Vergessen – Ehemalige Verdinkinder erzaehlen, by Marco Leuenberger and Loretta Seglias, Rotpunktverlag, Zurich, 2008

Switzerland's Shame: The children used as cheap farm labour by Kavita Puri, BBC News Magazine, October 2014

Swiss minister apologizes to victims of forced welfare. https://www.reuters.com

Huguenot Heritage by Robin Gwynn, Sussex Academic Press, 2011 edition.

Huguenot Museum, Rochester, Kent.

Soldiers can keep guns at home but not ammunition. https://www.swissinfo.ch. September, 2007

Das Boot ist Voll: Die Schweiz und die Fluechtlinge 1933 - 1945 by Alfred A. Haesler, Diogenes Verlag, Zurich, 2008

Grueningers Fall: Geschichten von Flucht und Hilfe by Stefan Keller, Rotpunktverlag Zurich, 1993.

The Jewish Foundation for the Righteous: https://jfr.org > rescuer-stories > gruninger-paul

Swiss in Wisconsin by Frederick Hale, The State Historical Society of Wisconsin, 2007

They Came to Wisconsin by Julia Pferdehirt, published by the Wisconsin Historical Society Press, 2003

Southwestern Wisconsin: A History of Old Crawford County. Carl B. Fritz Volume IV, S.J. Publishing Company, Chicago, 1932

The Other Side of the Mountain directed by Larry Peerce, 1975

Jill Kinmont Boothe, obituary New York Times, February 10th, 2012

Davos, eine Geschichte fuer sich: Historischer Stadtbegleiter 13 – 21. Jahrhundert by Yvonne Schmid, Verlag Desertina, 2012

Davos von 1860 – 1950. Zeit des Krankseins – Zeit des Gesundens by Klaus Bergamin, January 2013

Living in the Shadow of Death – Tuberculosis and the Social Experiment of Illness in American History by Sheila M. Rothman, The John Hopkins University Press, 1995

Spaete Ehrung auf dem Zauberberg by Thomas Sprecher, Neue Zuercher Zeitung, August 29th, 2006

Der Zauberberg/The Magic Mountain by Thomas Mann, published by S Fischer Verlag, Berlin, 1924

CHAPTER THREE

La Traviata, Opera by Giuseppe Verdi, 1853

Reality Profession or Possession – Which? by M.D. Metcalfe, published by Marshall, Morgan and Scott, Ltd.

Timebends by Arthur Miller, published by Methuen London Ltd. 1987. Page 114.

The Kon-tiki Expedition by Thor Heyerdahl, published by Gyldendal Norsk Forlag, 1948

Scott's Last Expedition by Captain Robert Falcon Scott, first published, 1913

The Stolen Prince by Dan Totheroh, published by Samuel French, London 1931

Ungeduld des Herzens/Beware of Pity by Stefan Zweig, published by S. Fischer Verlag, 1939

The Desert of Love by Francois Mauriac, published by Eyre and Spottiswoode, 1949

Brief Encounter, directed by David Lean, 1945 and based on the play *Still Life* by Noel Coward, 1936

The Snow Goose by Paul Gallico, published by Knopf, 1941

Perfume from America, interview with Peggy O'Connell, Radio Eireann, 1999

CHAPTER FOUR

Views from the Circle - Seventy-five years of Groton School, published by the Trustees, 1960: *My First Year at Groton* - Henry Howe Richards. Page 59

History of Groton www.groton.org/about/history

A Memoir of Jack Crocker by Robert A. Moss 1995, published by Douglas Brown for Groton School. Excerpt from a Talk to the Faculty, late 1940s. Page 89

Timebends by Arthur Miller, Page 372

... *sicklied o'er with the pale cast of thought* ... Hamlet, Act 3, Scene 1

A Portrait of the Artist as a Young Man by James Joyce, Penguin Books,

1992, Chapter 3, Page 142

Betsy Peabody, A Tribute, March 1977, Paul Wright

Memorial Service for Margery Peabody, February 1993, William M. Polk

The Jungle by Upton Sinclair, published by T Werner Laurie Ltd, 1946

Alistair Cooke, 1908 – 2004. *Letter from America*, 1946 – 2004

Lost City of the Incas – The Story of Machu Picchu and its Builders by Hiram Bingham, published by Atheneum, NY, 1979

Hiram, A. (Tony) Bingham, New York Times, Deaths, April 4th, 2008

Saving the Jews of Nazi France by Peter Eisner, published in The Smithsonian Magazine, March 2009. https://www.smithsonianmag.com>history>saving-the-jews-of-nazi-franc

In My Blood - Six generations of Madness and Desire in an American Family by John Sedgwick, published by Harper Perennial, 2008

Brown v. Board of Education of Topeka, 1954

The Irony of American History by Reinhold Niebuhr, published by Charles Scribner's Sons, New York, 1952

The Reinhold Niebuhr Story a film by Martin Doblmeier, Journey Films, 2017

The Cruel Sea by Nicholas Monsarrat, published by Alfred A. Knopf, New York, 1951

What Cares the Sea (or in later versions, published as *Man on Raft*) by Kenneth Cooke, McGraw-Hill Book Company, Inc. New York, 1960

Kenneth Cooke Interview, from the files of David Arnold.

'No missiles wanted here' sang marchers. Dave Whitfield, *Morning Star*, October 26th, 1981

The French Line directed by Lloyd Bacon, 1953

Jane Russell https://www.biography.com

https://cometoverhollywood.com

CHAPTER FIVE

Forty Years More: A History of Groton School 1934 – 1974 by Acosta Nichols, 1976.

America's Secret Aristocracy by Stephen Birmingham, published in 1987.

The Roosevelts: An Intimate History documentary by Ken Burns, 2014.

Excerpt from 2013 Harper Perennial – Modern Classics edition of *Our Town* by Thornton Wilder. Copyright 1938 by The Wilder Family LLC. Reprinted by arrangement with The Wilder Family, LLC and The Barbara Hogenson Agency, Inc. All rights reserved.

To learn more about Thornton Wilder, go to www.ThorntonWilder. com

Letter from the Head: Sesquicentennial Reflections, Nobles Magazine, Winter 2016

In Their Voices – The Sesquicentennial History of Noble and Greenough School by Joyce Leffler Eldridge, published in 2016.

Arthur and Betsy by Jesse Putnam, performed at Noble and Greenough School, December 19th, 2015

https://betsyandarthur.wordpress.com

https://www.cdc.gov>polio>us

Huis Clos/No Exit by Jean-Paul Sartre, first performed in May 1944

The Story of Noble and Greenough School 1866 – 1966 by Richard T. Flood

Spalding Gray, New York Times, March 4th, 2004

CHAPTER SIX

From the field of battle, an early strike at cancer. https://medicine. Yale. edu>news>yale-medicine-magazine, 2005

The Nazis and Thalidomide: The Worst Drug Scandal Of All Time, Newsweek, September 2012

The fault, dear Brutus, is not in our stars,

But in ourselves, that we are underlings. Shakespeare, Julius Caesar, Act 1, Scene II.

Interview with Leonard Arnold: tape recording conducted by a family member in 1966. From the archives of David Arnold

CHAPTER SEVEN

Folkestone, Sandgate, Hythe, Canterbury, Dymchurch. Illustrated Guide Books. Ward Lock and Companies. 1923.

Folkestone during the War (1914 – 1919), a record of the town's life and work by John Charles Carlile. The War College Series.

Folkestone in the Great War by Stephen Wynn, Pen and Sword Military, 2017

Folkestone and the Belgian Refugees during World War 1 by Eamonn D. Rooney,

In Search of Paddy Finucane RTE Radio 1 2004

Paddy Finucane Fighter Ace by Doug Stokes, published by William Kimber and Co. 1983

The Dover Historian, Kearsney Abbey, http://doverhistorian.com

'Kritik an der Waldau' by Marius Aschwanden, *Berner Zeitung*, August 2017

Universitaere Psychiatrische Dienste, Bern

Still Small Voice – the Fiction of Robert Walser by Benjamin Kunkel, The New Yorker, July 2007

To Kill a Mockingbird, 1962, directed by Robert Mulligan, based on the book by Harper Lee, 1960.

CHAPTER EIGHT

Long Day's Journey into Night by Eugene O'Neill, 1956

Edward Gleason from *In Their Voices*, Page 30.

CHAPTER NINE

Walling up democracy, November 2013, The Economist

Quotations from Chairman Mao Tse-Tung, Foreign Languages Press, Peking, 1967

Behind the Wall, A journey through China, by Colin Thubron, 1987

www.outwardbound.org.uk

The Absent Prince by Peter O'Connell, The Association of Recognised English Language Schools (ARELS) Journal, Spring 1979

CHAPTER TEN

Bhagwan The God that Failed by Hugh Milne, Caliban Books 1986

'President of Carnegie Corp to Resign' *The New York Times,* February 17th, 1982

Capturing the Essence. How Herman Hall interpreted standardized test scores by James Shapiro, New York 2004

https://www.aon.com aon-memorial-education-fund

Eulogy at the Memorial Service for Herman Hall at St. Bernard's School, November 2001 - Joan McMenamin

About the Author

Una Suseli O'Connell was a teacher in traditional and alternative schools for twenty years before training in Systemic Family Constellations at the Hellinger Institute of New York in 2001. She worked in inner city schools, supporting children with emotional and behavioural difficulties and managing issues around belonging, inclusion, family and culture. Una now works independently, providing workshops for educators, school therapists and social workers. She has two adult daughters and lives with her husband in North Hertfordshire.

www.unaoconnell.co.uk